ROUTLEDGE LIBRARY EDITIONS:
ECONOMICS AND SOCIETY

Volume 16

THE HISTORY OF TRADE UNION ORGANISATION IN THE NORTH STAFFORDSHIRE POTTERIES

THE HISTORY OF TRADE UNION ORGANISATION IN THE NORTH STAFFORDSHIRE POTTERIES

W. H. WARBURTON

With and Introduction by
R. H. TAWNEY

Routledge
Taylor & Francis Group
LONDON AND NEW YORK

First published in 1931 by George Allen & Unwin Ltd.

This edition first published in 2026
by Routledge
4 Park Square, Milton Park, Abingdon, Oxon OX14 4RN

and by Routledge
605 Third Avenue, New York, NY 10158

Routledge is an imprint of the Taylor & Francis Group, an informa business

British Library Cataloguing in Publication Data
A catalogue record for this book is available from the British Library

ISBN: 978-1-032-97576-4 (Set)
ISBN: 978-1-041-13164-9 (Volume 16) (hbk)
ISBN: 978-1-041-13165-6 (Volume 16) (pbk)
ISBN: 978-1-003-66839-8 (Volume 16) (ebk)

DOI: 10.4324/9781003668398

THE HISTORY OF TRADE UNION ORGANISATION IN THE NORTH STAFFORDSHIRE POTTERIES

by

W. H. WARBURTON, B.LITT.

WITH AN INTRODUCTION BY

R. H. TAWNEY.

LONDON
GEORGE ALLEN & UNWIN LTD
MUSEUM STREET

FIRST PUBLISHED IN 1931

PRINTED IN GREAT BRITAIN BY
UNWIN BROTHERS LTD., WOKING

TO

K. E. W.

PREFACE

Owing to the kindness of Mr. R. H. Tawney in writing an introduction to this book it is unnecessary for me to state its scope and contents, but I take this opportunity of expressing my thanks to the many friends who have kindly assisted me.

Mr. Arthur Hollins, M.P., of the National Pottery Workers' Society, has been unfailingly courteous and helpful. He has not only given me access to documents in his possession, but has as freely given me the advantage of his special knowledge and experience of Pottery Union affairs. My thanks are also due to Mr. F. Hand, of the National Council of Pottery Workers, for books and information, and also to Mr. W. Oliver, of the London branch, and Mr. G. Gould and Mr. A. Mellor, of the Bristol branches of the National Society of Pottery Workers, for information regarding the "out-potteries". I am greatly indebted to Professor D. H. Macgregor, Mr. G. D. H. Cole, Mr. E. Lipson, and Professor H. Clay for friendly criticism and advice.

Above all, I am grateful to Mr. R. H. Tawney, who has given me help and encouragement throughout the writing of this book.

CONTENTS

CHAPTER		PAGE
	PREFACE	7
	INTRODUCTION	11
I.	IN EARLY DAYS	17
II.	THE FIRST POTTERS' UNIONS	27
III.	THE NATIONAL ASSOCIATION AND THE POTTERS	34
IV.	THE NATIONAL UNION OF OPERATIVE POTTERS	59
V.	THE STRIKES OF 1834 AND 1836	80
VI.	THE UNITED BRANCHES	102
VII.	CONFLICTING IDEAS	123
VIII.	ARBITRATION	140
IX.	THE CHANGE	168
X.	THE PROBLEMS OF THE LAST GENERATION	179
XI.	HOW THE PROBLEMS WERE MET	200
XII.	TO-DAY	222
	APPENDIX	
	A. WAGES	242
	B. PROCESSES OF MANUFACTURE	252
	C. LETTERS FROM POTTERS TO ROBERT OWEN	256
	D. EXTRACTS FROM "THE TIMES" AND THE "STAFFORDSHIRE ADVERTISER"	261
	E. THE STRIKE OF 1836–37	263
	SELECT BIBLIOGRAPHY	283
	INDEX	287

INTRODUCTION

Mr. Warburton's book contains a history of Trade Unionism in the potting industry of North Staffordshire by a potter and trade unionist. It describes the efforts of a century to create a stable organisation capable of negotiating on equal terms with the employers from the first spasmodic struggles of 1825 down to the establishment of the powerful National Society of Pottery Workers in 1919. And since the structure and methods of a trade union are unintelligible apart from the economic background against which it develops, it is also a study of the growth and organisation of the potting industry. All who have worked, on however humble a scale, in the same field as Mr. Warburton, know the difficulties caused by the scarcity of reliable monographs. They will find in his pages an indispensable contribution to an important chapter in the general economic history of the nineteenth century, and of the Labour Movement in particular.

The Potteries were once described by a resident in them as separated from civilisation by the North Staffordshire Railway till communications were established by Mr. Arnold Bennett. Since three-fourths of the pottery workers of the country live within five miles of Stoke Town Hall, they are the most self-contained of the great industrial areas, and their isolation, combined with the peculiar characteristics of the potting industry, has given a peculiar stamp to their economic development. Unlike those in textiles and engineering, the changes which turned potting from the peasant industry of the seventeenth century into the great manufacture of the early nineteenth were improvements in the quality of the ware—better bodies, colours and glazes—and the widening of markets, not mechanical inventions, and long after potting had passed into the factory it continued to be a handicraft or an art. There was an increasing specialisation of different trades, but no minute subdivision of different processes within them. If the industrial revolution is to be identified with the introduction of machinery, it was not till after 1870 that it took place in potting.

The technical conservatism of the industry was reflected in the relations between wage-earners and employers. The system of annual hiring, with its corollary that a workman leaving his job before the end of twelve months could be summoned for breach of contract, lasted down till 1866. The curious practice by which the potter paid his employer for the use of gas, preparation of the clay, and sweeping of the shop, because he had once been responsible for these things himself, and the allied custom of "good from oven", which meant that he was paid only for ware that stood firing successfully, lingered on till 1919. The typical undertaking continued to be a small family business, the heads of which had themselves not infrequently been manual workers. Prices paid by employers for the same class of work varied widely from firm to firm, and there was periodically an orgy of reckless underselling which was ruinous to the workers without benefiting the masters. There was on a pot-bank little of the mass organisation and regimentation of the factory in which the operative must keep pace with the machine. Discipline, if it existed, was lax, habits casual, and hours irregular. To an observer accustomed to the atmosphere of the Lancashire cotton industry it seemed, even so recently as fifteen years ago, that pottery workers started work and stopped work much as they pleased.

Such an environment gave men pottery workers, though not the women and young persons, of whom they were often themselves the employers, a sense of personal freedom unknown in most factory industries. But it increased the obstacles in the way of the development of an effective trade unionism. Like the technique of their industry, the organisation of the potters, after a first brief outburst of energy in the thirties, seems down to the beginning of the present century to be a generation behind that of the more advanced sections of the Trade Union Movement. It can hardly be said, indeed, to attain maturity till the establishment of the National Society of Pottery Workers, with a membership of 48,000, in 1919. Its history falls into three well-defined periods, which are distinguished from each other by different policies and different forms of organisation.

The first phase, which runs from 1825 to 1850, is in potting, as in other industries, the heroic age of the Trade Union Movement. It has as its central episode the establishment in 1831 of the National Union of Operative Potters, which was said in 1833 to have a membership of 8,000, probably a larger percentage of the workers eligible than any subsequent union before 1914. It is marked by persistent, and, for a time, successful, efforts to draw all pottery workers into a single society; by enthusiasm, at any rate among its leaders, for large schemes of social reconstruction; and, after a brief interval in which relations between workers and employers were surprisingly friendly, by an attempt on the part of the latter to stamp out trade unionism by refusing to "recognise" the union and by the legal persecution of trade unionists.

In the second phase, which runs from 1850 down to the end of the century, the characteristic features of the movement are different. The idea of a single society, embracing all the wage-earners in the industry, had been abandoned in despair, and an attempt to revive it in 1883 by the foundation of a new organisation called the National Order of Potters was an ignominious fiasco. Combination takes the form of a multitude of small craft unions, each catering for a different section of workers. The emphasis for the generation down to 1880 is all on the need of creating machinery for the peaceful settlement of disputes. In 1867 a Board of Conciliation and Arbitration is established, which survives, with certain alterations, down to 1892, and which is succeeded by a Committee of Conciliation, which lasts till 1897.

The third phase of the movement begins when organisation is at its lowest ebb, with the coalescence of three craft unions into the National Amalgamated Society of Male and Female Pottery Workers in 1906. Though weak in membership, it had by 1914 absorbed the majority of craft unions. Then came the war, and a rush into organisations among both workers and employers, with the result that 1919 saw the establishment of the National Society of Pottery Workers and of the British Pottery Manufacturers' Association. A Joint Industrial Council had already been formed eighteen months before. It was the pioneer of the institutions which afterwards were associated with the name of Mr. Whitley, in the days when it was fashionable to talk of social reconstruction.

A trade union is an organisation with two distinct aspects. It is at once a professional association and an organ for giving practical expression to the aspirations of a class. From the first angle its history is the record of the struggles of a particular body of workers to grapple with the specialised problems of their craft or industry: from the second it is the story of the changing intellectual influences and social ideals which have determined the outlook of the working classes during the last hundred years. Mr. Warburton's book does equal justice to both sides of the movement among his fellow-workers. He shows them agitating for the right of combination at a time when the active members of a union could still be sent to gaol, insisting on the necessity of uniform price-lists and urging, in the very infancy of their organisation, the importance of the employers themselves combining, clinging to craft unionism long after it is out of date, bankrupt of ideas in the face of the menace of machinery, and intensifying their own difficulties by their suicidal refusal to organise the women who worked with them. But he gives due place to the influence upon them of the larger movements into which the pottery operatives, in common with other bodies of workers, have from time to time been drawn, and by contact with which their horizon has been widened, from the Owenite and Chartist crusades of the thirties and forties to the wave of trade unionism which swelled between 1910 and 1914.

It is easier, perhaps, for the student than for those engaged in the practical work of the movement to hold the balance even between these two sides of it. But the history of trade unionism, with its alternating periods of large ideals, which collapse for want of a firm foundation in practical organisation, and of a prosaic and uninspired routine which ignores the new problems presented by changes in economic organisation, suggests that its success depends on an ability to maintain a firm hold on both. Its objectives and methods are determined by the character of the economic environment in which it works, and the coming decade is likely, it may be suggested, to see a change in both. A conception of its functions which regarded them as confined to negotiating with regard to wages, hours and working conditions was natural in an age of economic expansion, when improvements could be secured by organised pressure, without raising fundamental issues of economic policy. But the limits within which progress can be achieved by such methods have become, if not rigid, less elastic than in the past, and the change in economic conditions will involve a corresponding change in trade union technique. The collective bargaining of the future will be increasingly concerned, it is to be anticipated, not merely with wages and working conditions, but with questions of industrial organisation and policy, which have hitherto been excluded from its purview as the province of management, but on which, in the long run, wages and working conditions themselves depend. This change in policy will involve, in its turn, a change in trade union machinery, and unions will find themselves obliged to equip themselves more systematically than is always at present the case for dealing with the technical and commercial questions on which in the future it will be necessary for them to possess an informed opinion. From such developments the pottery workers, at any rate, have nothing to fear. The enlightened leadership of their union, and the encouragement which it has given to the education of its members, qualify it, indeed, in an unusual degree, for acting as a pioneer in the inevitable transition.

With the problems of the future the present volume is not concerned. But they are most likely to be faced with success by workers who are familiar with the past history of their industries, and who have studied the process of development by which the trade union movement has reached its present position. The Workers' Educational Association and the Tutorial Class Movement, in which Mr. Warburton was for long a student, have done much to aid members of working-class organisations both to widen their horizons and to equip themselves for the more effective service of the movements to which they belong. It is to be hoped that his book will be widely read, and that it will encourage other workers to make similar contributions to the history of Trade Unionism.

R. H. TAWNEY

THE HISTORY OF TRADE UNION ORGANISATION IN THE NORTH STAFFORDSHIRE POTTERIES

CHAPTER I

IN EARLY DAYS

It is the purpose of this work to give a history of trade unionism in the pottery industry in England. It is not intended to be a history of British pottery or a descriptive account of pottery production. Nevertheless, as the failures and successes of workmen in organising themselves are more easily understood when something is known concerning the nature of their occupation, matters outside the narrow field of trade unionism will here and there be touched upon.

Pottery making is one of the oldest arts of civilised man, but it is not until after the birth of modern industry that we get, in England at any rate, organisations of potters. Pottery of a crude nature was made in England in very early times. Under the Romans improvements in methods of manufacture were introduced and ware of a high standard followed. After the Saxon invasion the making of pottery, in common with all other arts, suffered a rapid decline. Contrary to what might have been expected, it experienced no revival under the Normans, and throughout the Middle Ages, right up to the seventeenth century, English-made pottery continued crude. Throughout this period pottery manufacture was a peasant industry, and was practised wherever clay and fuel were to be found.

Several factors contributed towards the change which

came to the industry at the end of the seventeenth century, two of the most important being the movement towards the localisation of the industry and that towards improvement in the quality of the product. Apart from general causes, such as the rise of a prosperous middle class, the end of constitutional disturbances, commercial expansion and the beginnings of improved roads, the fact that ware of a high quality was being imported from the Continent and the East greatly stimulated the trade, while it received invaluable help from the foreign potters settled in England. This last fact must not be overrated, however, for although the trade owed much to foreigners, the commercial drive and the artistic and technical initiative which built it up and made it one of the stable industries of the country, came from the native potters themselves.

In the seventeenth century pottery production was already tending to be localised in North Staffordshire. From that time onwards the number of potters in this area increased. Court rolls and other legal documents, which during the fourteenth, fifteenth, and sixteenth centuries had shown the names of few potters[1]—no more, in fact, than would probably be seen in the rolls of other districts—contain henceforward references to potters and the trade of pottery.

Writing in 1686 of a visit to North Staffordshire which he had made in 1677, Plot speaks at great length of the potteries of Burslem.[2] At the time of his visit Burslem had become a busy centre for the making of pottery, though neither the range of its products nor the extent of its market was very wide. The ware was sold to travelling packmen, who distributed it about the country. A market so supplied could obviously not be other than a narrow one.

[1] J. C. Wedgwood: *Staffordshire Pottery and its History* (N.D.), 5.
[2] R. Plot: *Natural History of Staffordshire* (1686).

A North Staffordshire pottery at this period consisted of several sheds, an oven about eight feet high and six feet wide, and a sunpan for the drying of the clay. Pottery was made on the wheel and decorated with liquid clays of various colours. The glazing process was primitive, consisting only of powdering the ware, before baking, with lead ore which had been beaten into dust.[1] Sometimes manganese was added to the beaten lead, the effect of which was to give a brown glaze. If not mixed with the lead, but applied separately in patches, the manganese gave a mottled effect.

Moulds for the making of pottery, the lathe for the smoothing of ware made on the wheel, and paints and enamels for decorative purposes were as yet unknown.

North Staffordshire had certain economic advantages for the manufacture of pottery. It possessed in an easily obtainable form all the raw materials for the manufacture of earthenware at that period. Large beds of good common clays lay near the surface, and coal, which owing to the growing scarcity of wood was becoming essential to pottery manufacture, was abundant. Lead-mines in the immediate vicinity supplied the only material for glaze, and no raw material of any kind had to be carried from a distance.[2] Another economic advantage was that in Burslem, the mother-town of the Potteries, the land was split up amongst a large number of enfranchised copyholders. These copyholds gave security of tenure to the owner, but were not large enough to enable him to become a prosperous farmer, and the making of pottery afforded an opening for his initiative.[3]

[1] R. Plot: *Natural History of Staffordshire* (1686), 123.
J. C. Wedgwood: *Staffordshire Pottery and its History* (N.D.), 18.

[2] J. C. Wedgwood: *Staffordshire Pottery and its History* (N.D), 9.
S. Shaw: *History of Staffordshire Potteries* (1829), 16, 124.

[3] J. C.Wedgwood: *Staffordshire Pottery and its History* (N.D.), 3–4.

The peasant character of medieval pottery manufacture still clung to the North Staffordshire industry. The potter usually dug his own clay, and often his own coal. As late as the end of the seventeenth century any manufacturer who was a freeholder in Burslem exercised his supposed right of taking clay or coals, or both, from any unenclosed "land in the liberty at any time".[1] In 1616 we read that one "Richard Middleton demised Thomas Danyell of Burslem, senior, potter, a pasture . . . containing three acres, with right to dig clay filling up the pits after him, for 21 years at a rent of 4/-".[2] Such a state of affairs is near to the Middle Ages and very far removed from the agents, companies, and clay-mines of a few years later.

The rapid growth of the pottery industry during the eighteenth century was most marked in North Staffordshire. It is true that as great strides in technical and artistic advance were made in London, Derby and Worcester, and that Fulham was actually producing stone ware, and Lambeth Delft ware, at the time when Staffordshire potters were selling the crude products described by Plot. Nevertheless, whereas the story of these towns is that of the strivings of single firms, that of North Staffordshire is of the building up of a metropolis of the trade.

The rise of the North Staffordshire industry began with the introduction of the manufacture of white ware and the use of moulds. White pottery, being more attractive to the purchaser, penetrated into a market which was closed to the brown, red, and yellow wares, while the introduction of moulds made it possible for the potter to make ware of any shape required. Previously he had been restricted to round shapes only. The first moulds were introduced about 1730 and were made of pitches, i.e. unglazed pottery, but

[1] S. Shaw: *History of Staffordshire Potteries* (1829), 124.

[2] J. C. Wedgwood: *Staffordshire Pottery and its History* (N.D.), 8.

in 1745 (approximately) Ralph Daniel, a North Staffordshire potter, introduced the French system of making moulds of plaster of Paris, a much more suitable material for the purpose.[1] A few years before this Astbury, another North Staffordshire potter, had commenced making white stone ware. This ware, made of the local coloured clays, was covered with a thin coating of white Devon clay. Astbury's next step was to make his ware white throughout. The second half of the century saw much experimenting, and many improvements were made in the clay bodies, i.e. the mixture of which ware is made. The clay body finally used by Astbury and his contemporaries was a mixture of light-coloured local clays, calcined flint and Dorsetshire ball clay.[2] The discovery of white ware, and the necessity, if its whiteness was to be seen to the best advantage, of the use of a pure transparent glaze, gave a great impetus to salt glazing.

The white salt-glazed pottery was a stone ware made very thin, approaching almost to the transparency of porcelain. The earthenware potters who made the commoner kinds of ware still practised the old method of glazing with lead. This was, indeed, a necessity, for their ware would not stand the strong heat in baking demanded by salt glaze.

About 1750 Booth, a Tunstall manufacturer, adopted an improved lead glaze, together with an improved method of glazing. Under the old method lead dust was applied to the unbaked ware, but under the new method a fluid glaze of clay, lead and flint was used. This was used only for baked ware. Thus the new method involved a double baking, the first to burn the clay and the second to fuse the glaze into the ware. After the adoption of this method

[1] J. Ward: *History Borough Stoke-on-Trent* (1846), 49.

[2] J. C. Wedgwood: *Staffordshire Pottery and its History* (N.D.), 46, 84.

lead glaze no longer militated against the production of white ware. Improvements in earthenware quickly followed, culminating in the production of the famous Queen's ware made by J. Wedgwood, the forerunner of all the fine earthenware of to-day.[1]

The salt-glazed ware could not compete with the new and improved lead-glazed ware. A salt-glazed ware manufactory was a risky undertaking. The ware was made very thin and subjected to a more intense heat in baking than earthenware, and was consequently expensive owing to the heavy losses sustained in its manufacture. Moreover, lead-glazed ware, having a smooth finish, was more suitable for table use than the salt-glazed ware, which had a rough pock-marked surface. By 1787 the manufacture of salt-glazed ware in North Staffordshire had come to an end, being superseded by lead-glazed ware.[2]

These improvements in clay bodies, glazes and methods of making were accompanied by changes and innovations in the decoration of ware. Printing over glaze in enamels came to England in the middle of the eighteenth century with the introduction of the manufacture of porcelain. The North Staffordshire salt-glaze potters, who were at their zenith at this time, were quick to realise the commercial value of this method of decoration. The art was introduced into the district by two Dutchmen, who settled in Burslem and started an enamelling business there.[3] They were followed by porcelain enamellers from Bow and Chelsea, and the enamelling of salt-glazed ware and, to a much less extent, lead-glazed ware soon became general.

Enamelling was at first a subsidiary industry, but pottery manufacturers gradually made it a part of their business.

[1] J. C. Wedgwood: *Staffordshire Pottery and its History* (N.D.), 67.
[2] J. C. Wedgwood: *Staffordshire Pottery and its History* (N.D.), 81.
[3] S. Shaw: *History of Staffordshire Potteries* (1829), 178–9.

It was too expensive a process to be used for any but the better-quality ware, but the invention of transfer printing for pottery in 1756, and the improvements therein made in 1780, enabled the common run of goods to be decorated.[1]

The activities of the English potter in the middle of the eighteenth century were not confined to white earthenware. Owing chiefly to the great genius of Josiah Wedgwood, ornamental wares, such as Basalt and Jasper, began to be made. But, most important of all, and owing rather to the influence of the age than to the work of one outstanding man, the manufacture of porcelain was introduced and firmly established.[2]

The beginning of the nineteenth century saw the pottery industry practically centralised in North Staffordshire and catering for a world market. Moreover, as the market had widened so had the area from which the potter drew his raw materials. From the end of the eighteenth century onwards, unless making the commonest of earthenware, the potter, wherever he practised his craft, was dependent on distant places for the supply of his raw materials. Master potters had become men of business and had adopted the commercial practices which had arisen in other industries. They sent out representatives and appointed agents; and the more successful of their number also set up show-rooms and warehouses in London. It says much for the state of affairs ushered in by the Industrial Revolution that Wedgwood, the greatest potter of that time and the most renowned England has produced, was one of the most successful business men of his day. He was as interested in obtaining new and better clay bodies and colours as were any

[1] J. C. Wedgwood: *Staffordshire Pottery and its History* (N.D.), 133 S. Mayer: *The Art of Pottery* (1871), 40.

[2] J. C. Wedgwood: *Staffordshire Pottery and its History* (N.D.), 99, 102, 135.

of the great potters before him, but whereas to a man like Palissy the business of the potter was the making of pottery, Wedgwood's chief concern was the selling of it. To him the business of a pottery manufacturer meant, in addition to the making of ware, the petitioning for turnpike roads, the financing of waterway undertakings, and the pressing of the interests of the pottery industry upon Parliament.[1] By the beginning of the nineteenth century, in short, the pottery industry was, in all essentials, a capitalist one. The working master potter had almost disappeared, and, although there were small employers, the trade was dominated by men in a fairly large way of business.

The changes in the methods of pottery production during the seventeenth and eighteenth centuries resulted in a great division of labour. Under the primitive conditions previously obtaining it was possible for the potter to be a skilful workman in every process of the trade, but by the end of the eighteenth century such a possibility no longer existed. The making of pottery, from being an occupation not beyond the capacity of any one man, now included in its scope a score or more of skilled trades. Men of two or more distinct occupations were engaged in the preparing of clay; the making of ware was the work of men of a dozen different trades; the processes of glazing, baking and decorating included another dozen trades; the packing of ware into crates for dispatch to the customer was a separate occupation, while, in addition, there were warehouse workers and clerks. Besides these there were the workers in those industries subsidiary to the pottery industry, such as crate-making, flint-grinding, etc. Of all these occupations very few were unskilled and an apprenticeship of seven years' duration was usual for the majority of the workers. It would appear from the numerous trades mentioned as if

[1] J. C. Wedgwood: *Staffordshire Pottery and its History* (N.D.), 88.

the division of labour had been carried almost to extremes, but this was not the case. From the point of view of modern industrial management it had not gone very far, and certainly it had not gone to the lengths existing in many industries in the early nineteenth century. It was carried little further, in fact, than was usual in certain industries in the Middle Ages.

The division of labour which the Industrial Revolution brought to the pottery industry was not of the kind mentioned by Adam Smith as obtaining in the pin trade, nor of that which exists now in shoe-making, box-making and similar industries. What it did was to separate the trade into a number of skilled branches, in almost the same way as the building industry is divided into the trades of bricklaying, carpentry and other crafts. The seventeenth- and the eighteenth-century changes in production increased to an extraordinary extent the scope of the industry, and, consequently, the division of pottery making into a number of distinct occupations was not so much a managerial device to increase output as a recognition of the fact that, with the vastly increased range of products and the higher standard of workmanship demanded, it was clearly impossible to expect any one man to be an expert in several branches of the trade.

The mechanical inventions, however, which were so characteristic a feature of the Industrial Revolution, left the pottery industry almost untouched. That the character of the pottery processes was not favourable to machinery, and that the potters of the eighteenth and early nineteenth centuries were opposed to the standardisation which is sometimes supposed to be its natural corollary, appear to be insufficient reasons for this. As was discovered later, many pottery processes were easily adapted to machinery. The probability is that there was not a sufficiently large number of articles manufactured to make the application of machinery profitable. Whatever the reason, the bare fact remains that at the beginning of the nineteenth century, and for many years afterwards, machinery had practically no place in the pottery industry. The absence of machinery, coupled with the comparatively low cost of raw materials, made labour costs relatively high. This fact clearly had great influence upon the relationship of the master potter to his employees. Where the price of labour relative to other factors is high, the incentive to the employer to reduce wages is much greater than where the labour charge is low. On the other hand, as the employees in the pottery industry were mostly skilled persons, it was impossible to reduce wages by engaging unskilled labour from outside.

The modern pottery industry was built up without any legacy from the Middle Ages. There were no gild regulations to influence the lines of its development, it was not obliged to live up to any artistic traditions, nor did the merchant get control of the trade. This last was owing to the fact that the nature of the industry was such as to make it almost impossible for work to be put out, as was done in the textile trades, and also that the potter, in the early days at any rate, worked only where he had easy access to raw materials.

The rise of the industry began at a time which, in many respects, was the most barbaric in our industrial history. How much was lost by this, and how much was gained, one cannot say. What is fairly certain, however, is that trade customs which later so largely affected the lives of the workmen, and to a great extent determined the lines along which their disputes with the masters ran, would have been very different had the pottery trade at its beginning been either hampered or guided by gild or municipal regulations, or if the first stages of its growth had been delayed to a later period.

CHAPTER II

THE FIRST POTTERS' UNIONS

There is no evidence that unions existed in the pottery trade before the year 1824, although industrial conditions had long been ripe for such organisations. For more than half a century before this date the pottery industry had lost whatever peasant craftsman character it had once possessed, and had become a capitalist industry in which ordinary journeymen had little chance of becoming anything other than employed workmen. The time had gone by when "all the persons employed (on a pottery) were the slip-maker, thrower, two turners, handler (stouker), fireman, warehouseman and a few children, and, to be really useful to the master, and secure sufficient employment, a good workman could throw, turn and stouk; and which he practised in each week at two or three different manufactories".[1]

By the end of the eighteenth century the trade had become largely concentrated in North Staffordshire, and it is in that district, therefore, if anywhere, that combinations of working potters were to be expected. There had often been trouble between potters and master potters in that area, but it does not appear that any combinations of men existed of a permanent enough character to be described as trade unions. In September 1772 Wedgwood's employees threatened to leave him to go to a rival firm.[2] They apparently did not do so, but in the following month they threatened to strike if their demand for an increase in wages was not granted. The men who headed the deputation of the operatives were immediately discharged, and in a

[1] S. Shaw: *History of the Staffordshire Potteries* (1829), 166.
[2] *Letters: Wedgwood to Bentley*, 1762–1780 (1903), 481.

letter written shortly afterwards, in which he related this occurrence, Wedgwood said that he expected that more men would leave.[1] Four years later Wedgwood met with an organised resistance from his men when he attempted to reduce working prices.[2]

Although these incidents go to show that the potters could upon occasion act together, they do not imply that any combination existed which could be described as a trade union.

The masters had their selling-price agreements, and once they combined for the purpose of resisting the demands of the master-crate makers,[3] but it was not, as far as one can discover, until 1825 that they found it necessary to meet to discuss what wages they would pay for their men.[4]

In evidence before the Select Committee on Children's Employment in 1816 J. Wedgwood, a son of the founder of the firm of that name, stated, as if it were a matter of course, that pottery manufacturers always reduced wages when work was scarce,[5] a practice which would not have been easy if there had been opposition from even the most feeble of unions. One may conclude, therefore, that before 1824 the only organisation approximating to a trade union was the temporary combination of workmen in one or more branches of the trade of one particular factory. It should be remembered that in North Staffordshire, where the trade was concentrated and dominated the district, there

[1] *Letters: Wedgwood to Bentley*, 1762–1780 (1903), 495.
[2] *Letters: Wedgwood to Bentley*, 1762–1780 (1903), 187.
[3] F. Falkner: *The Wood Family of Burslem* (1912), 64.
[4] J. Boyle: "An Account of Strikes in the Potteries in the years 1834 and 1836," *Journal of Statistical Society*, London, vol. i (1839), 37.
Pottery Mercury, April 27, August 3, 1825.
[5] *Report of Minutes of Evidence taken before the Select Committee on the State of Children employed in the Manufactures of the United Kingdom* (1816), 60.

would be the natural union which exists when men of one trade work and dwell together, their lives being largely unaffected by the ideas of men of other occupations, as is the case even to-day in mining villages.

Two potters' unions were formed in 1824.[1] The larger and more important was the union of clay potters, which included hollow-ware pressers, saucer- and plate-makers, turners, throwers and handlers.[2] The smaller union was one for the printers. The other potters—slip-makers, ovenmen, painters, etc.—were not combined unless they formed unions at the end of 1825, in which case such organisations were very short-lived. The sphere of operations of both these unions was confined to North Staffordshire.[3]

In March 1825 the clay potters struck for an increase in their piece-rates, the abolition of truck and the regulation of the sizes of ware. The importance of the last-named to the potter will be understood when it is explained that jugs, to give one example, were being made and paid for as half-pint sizes and yet were large enough to contain a "wine quart".[4] The masters agreed to abolish truck, to commence immediately the business of the regulation of sizes, and to consider piece-rates after July 8th.[5] With these concessions and promises the potters were contented. The standardisation of sizes was taken up seriously by the

[1] J. Boyle: "An Account of Strikes in the Potteries in the years 1834 and 1836," *Journal of Statistical Society*, London, vol. i (1839), 37.

[2] *Pottery Mercury*, March 30, 1825.

[3] *Pottery Mercury*, August 17, 1825. Although Boyle in his paper before the Statistical Society, 1838, speaks of *the* Potters' Union of 1825, the *Pottery Mercury* for 1825 leads one to suppose that Printers and Clay Potters were in separate organisations. Moreover, a letter of "Journeyman Potter", *Staffordshire Mercury*, 1830, states of 1825: "... had potters, printers, ovenmen ... formed one union, instead of ... distinct ones ..." Up to August 1825 ovenmen were not combined.

[4] *Staffordshire Advertiser*, April 2, 1825.

[5] *Pottery Mercury*, April 20, June 22, 1825.

employers, who issued a notice declaring their readiness to agree to any measure designed to forward that end.[1] They met in April, and decided that all hollow ware should be brought under standard sizes by July 1st, and table and dessert ware by November 11th, and that copies of these standard sizes should be sent to each manufacturer in the out-potteries as well as in North Staffordshire.[2]

Truck abolished, and sizes in process of being dealt with, there yet remained the matter of piece-rates, which was to be considered on July 8th. By that date the employers had made no preparation to deal with the question, and they did not meet to consider it until July 27th. All they did at this meeting was to appoint a committee to deal with piece-rates.[3] Such dilatoriness on their part did not meet with the approval of the workmen, and at several manufactories they struck for an immediate advance in wages.[4] At those factories where piece-rates were particularly low, immediate advances were secured, but the terms offered generally by the masters were not sufficiently good to satisfy the operatives, who wished to regain the rates current in 1815, a year when they were particularly high.[5]

The decision of the men to continue the strike until their full demands were satisfied was unfortunate, for the commercial crisis which occurred at that time ruined whatever chances they may have had of defeating the masters.[6] The demand for labour destroyed for the time being by the

1 *Pottery Mercury*, March 30, 1825.
2 *Pottery Mercury*, April 27, 1825.
3 *Pottery Mercury*, August 3, 1825.
4 *Pottery Mercury*, August 17, 1825.
5 *Pottery Mercury*, August 24, 1825.
Staffordshire Mercury, October 30, 1830.
6 J. Boyle: "An Account of Strikes in the Potteries, 1834 and 1836," *Journal of Statistical Society*, London, vol. i (1839), 37.

commercial panic, the men found their position changed from that of striking to that of being unemployed, and they were glad to procure situations upon terms worse, in many cases, than those which obtained before the dispute.[1] The unions, which had paid out £3,000 during the strike, were not heard of again after the submission of the men.[2] Curiously enough, the commercial crisis was not the reason given by the men in after years for the defeat in 1825. They contended that the reason lay in the fact that so many branches of the pottery trade were unorganised (ovenmen, packers, etc.), and also that in striking for the high prices of 1815 they were making demands which were unreasonable, being more than the trade could stand, and more than the men needed in view of the fact that the prices of provisions were so much lower in 1825.[3] There is this much to be said for the contention that the strike failed largely because many branches of the trade had no union. A strike of clay potters and printers necessarily loses much of its effectiveness if ovenmen and packers remain at work, for, with a large stock of clay ware on hand, the men of the two branches named could keep a factory running for a long time. During the strike the operatives seriously contemplated manufacturing for themselves, but there is no evidence to show that this plan matured.[4]

1 J. Boyle: "An Account of Strikes in the Potteries, 1834 and 1836," *Journal of Statistical Society*, London, vol. i (1839), 38.
2 J. Boyle: "An Account of Strikes in the Potteries, 1834 and 1836," *Journal of Statistical Society*, London, vol. i (1839), 38. *Staffordshire Mercury*, February 1, February 22, 1834.
3 *Staffordshire Mercury*, October 30, 1830.
4 J. Boyle: "An Account of Strikes in the Potteries in the years 1834 and 1836," *Journal of Statistical Society*, London, vol. i (1839), 38. The statement of Boyle's, that "one of the expedients of the Union at that time was to commence manufacturing . . .", could be taken as meaning that the union *did* manufacture, but the local newspaper contains no statement of such a scheme being put into practice, and,

The master potters continued with their arrangements for the standardisation of sizes. With this end in view, they formed themselves into a Chamber of Commerce in August 1825, and in the following January they pressed for an Act of Parliament to enforce such standardisation.[1] This attempt on the part of the manufacturers to obtain for a trade regulation the sanction and support of the law is in curious contrast to the attitude of the men at that time, who wished the State to give them only the freedom to combine.[2] It was the men who stood for *laissez-faire* and the manufacturers who sought to have fetters placed upon the industry.

One point, though touched upon more fully later, may be mentioned here in reference to the *laissez-faire* attitude of the potter in 1825. In the cotton industry the adult male operative sought to reduce by Act of Parliament the hours worked by women, young persons and children, knowing that by so doing he was incidentally reducing his own. This was not the case with the adult potter. Legislative interference with the hours worked by women, young persons and children engaged in the pottery industry was, so the potter thought, injurious to his interests as a wage-

moreover, J. Peake, the most prominent of the potters' leaders of 1825, wrote, *Staffordshire Mercury*, February 22, 1834, that the potters in 1825, instead of spending £3,000 on a turnout, ought to have invested such money in trade—a course which he had advocated at the time. One may conclude that the potters in 1825 *discussed* manufacturing but went no farther.

[1] *Pottery Mercury*, August 31, October 19, December 14, 1825; February 1, 1826. They were unsuccessful: in pressing for regulation of sizes the masters probably thought of themselves more than of workmen. A jug made and sold as ½ pint but yet holding 1½ pints was a grievance to the men who made them, and also to those firms whose ½-pint jugs only held ½ pint and whose 1½-pint jugs were described as such.

[2] *Pottery Mercury*, April 13, 1825; letter of Peake, potters' leader, quoting Adam Smith on combinations.

earner.[1] Many operative potters employed women and children and betrayed the worst attributes of an employer in wishing to exploit such labour unrestricted by the State.

After the failure of the 1825 strike the evils against which the men had fought returned. Sizes once more became unregulated, piece-rates dropped considerably, and truck was again largely practised.[2]

Before leaving this account of the potters' first unions, we may call attention to one of their demands which is significant in that it was many times repeated during the century. This was an appeal which they made to the masters in June 1825 that selling prices should be raised. The operatives were of the opinion that the evil of low wages was due to low selling prices caused by competition amongst the masters. This competition they hoped would be replaced by combination to keep up selling prices.[3]

1 "Trade Societies and Strikes", *Report of the National Association for the Promotion of Social Science* (1860), 282.
2 *Staffordshire Mercury*, October 30, November 13, November 30, 1833.
3 *Pottery Mercury*, June 22, 1825.

NOTE: There are hints as to the existence of trade unions in the Potteries before 1824. *The Staffordshire Gazette and Newcastle and Potteries Advertiser*, December 12, 1816, speaks of a "Union Benefit Society". Webb, *History of Trade Unionism* (ed. 1920), 114, gives an account of a General Trades Union, the "Philanthropic Hercules" which is heard of simultaneously in London, Manchester and the Potteries, but of its progress in the last two named places nothing is known.

CHAPTER III

THE NATIONAL ASSOCIATION AND THE POTTERS

The great wave of trade union enthusiasm—the mania, as it was sometimes described, of the thirties—which eventually lifted even the agricultural labourers out of their lethargy, carried, as would be expected, the potters along with it. From being a comparatively peaceful movement in 1830, it became by 1834, in the eyes of middle-class onlookers, a fierce storm. The metaphor may not be exact in all particulars, but, at any rate, the trade union movement had some of the characteristics of a storm in that at its height it caused commotion, brought fear and broke into what had hitherto been thought sheltered places. Like a storm, too, it subsided fairly quickly and left much wreckage behind.

Before a history of the potter through this exciting period is given, it is necessary that as much of his conditions of life and labour should be understood as is required, if the immediate and ultimate effects upon him of this wave of trade unionism are to be fully grasped. Like men of other trades at the time, the potter shared in the trade union enthusiasm and, like others, what he built out of it was largely determined by his life and work. In so far as the conditions of the potter were peculiar, that which he built was peculiar to him also.

The fact of the pottery industry being almost localised in one area has already been mentioned, and it is now only necessary that it should be remembered in conjunction with other conditions. That the potter was a factory worker, and earned his wages under a piece-work system, are particulars which need to be no more than mentioned, as such conditions of labour were far from being peculiar to him. Of the conditions which were peculiar to the pottery trade—and it is only those that need to be studied here—the most important and far-reaching in its consequences, though unfortunately the least understood, is that which resulted from the tradition of contracting which ran right through the pottery industry. The term "contracting" is loose, and apt to mislead, but it is nevertheless the best that can be used. "Contracting", while not a definite enough practice to be exactly described as a system, was yet a vital part of the working of the industry. The potter was a pieceworker, arranging with his employer to make certain articles at a certain price. The tools he required he bought himself, and if the nature of his work were such that he needed help, he engaged it without any necessary consultation with his employer. The clay, which in the state supplied to him was not ready for use, he either made usable himself or paid someone to make usable for him. What artificial light he required he provided himself, and the cleanliness of the shop in which he worked was entirely his responsibility.[1] This condition of affairs was neatly described by J. A. Redgrave, Inspector, in his report to the Department Committee on Truck.[2] His actual words are worth quoting: ". . . a man took his gang of boys and girls and his candle to the pot-bank . . . he took a lump sum and paid his boys and girls and paid for his candle and everything". It was as if, in the beginnings of the trade, the working potter had been an independent producer selling his ware to a dealer, and then later coming to work upon the factory of the dealer, but bringing with him the independent producers' traditions and customs. Such a picture is historically incorrect, but it is the best clue

[1] Old Potter: *When I was a Child* (1903), 185.
[2] *Department Committee on Truck Acts* (1908), vol. ii, 40; evidence of J. H. Redgrave, Inspector, May 23, 1906.

towards understanding the working conditions of the potter in the period now being taken.

In after years, when machinery did many things for the potter and the Factory Acts forbade him doing others, this tradition of contracting was still kept up. The Factory Act said that potters' shops must be swept by an adult some hours after the cessation of work, and instead of making the potter, who was an adult, come back at midnight to sweep his shop, the employer engaged a man specially to do it, but as the cleanliness of the shop was the potter's and not the master's business, the potter had to pay for the sweeping.[1] The same thing applied in other ways. Preparing clay was the affair of the man that used it; therefore, when manufacturers laid down machinery to do this work, the potters paid so much a week for the convenience. In the same way, when the pottery factories were fitted with gas, the potter, without question, permitted a few coppers each week to be deducted from his wages for the use of it. The potter never argued that it was not his business to pay for the sweeping of workshops, the use of gas and the preparing of clay, although he sometimes grumbled that he paid too much.[2] In those branches of the pottery business where the workman requires the assistance of women and young persons in his work, such assistance is still directly employed by him; but, with this exception, the custom of the potter either doing a thing himself or paying for it to be done out of the wages he received, persisted until 1908, when by mutual consent net making prices for work were fairly generally adopted.[3] It is along two distinct lines that the effects of

[1] *Department Committee on Truck Acts* (1908), vol. ii, 39; evidence of J. H. Redgrave, Inspector, May 23, 1906.

[2] *Department Committee on Truck Acts* (1908), vol. ii, 40; evidence of J. H. Redgrave, Inspector, May 23, 1906.

[3] *Department Committee on Truck Acts* (1908), vol. ii, 40; evidence of J. H. Redgrave, Inspector, May 23, 1906.

the conditions just described upon labour organisation can be traced.

The first and most easily understood is the effect upon the status of women in the trade. Practically all the boys, other than apprentices, and the large majority of the women and girls engaged in the industry, were the direct employees of working potters. The manufacturer never concerned himself with the amount of wages that these employees of the working potter received, and it was not until he was compelled to do so by Factory Acts that he troubled to interfere with the conditions under which they worked.[1] It was to the immediate interest of the working potter to pay his employees as little as possible and not to encourage them to organise. The potter was human and short-sighted, and followed his immediate interests, with the result that the labour of children, young persons and women was exploited. From the point of view of trade unionism the exploitation of boy labour had little serious consequences. At an early age boys either left the industry or became apprentices in some branch of it. The case of the women was vastly different. During the period under consideration, and for many years afterwards, a woman in most of the branches of the pottery business could not hope to be anything other than an employee of a working potter. When, in later years, owing to improved methods of manufacture, women were able to compete with men for the same job, they came with a long tradition of low wages behind them and with no experience of union organisation. By their behaviour men had shown that they did not believe that the interests of all workers in the trade, men and

[1] "Trade Societies and Strikes", *Report of the National Association for the Promotion of Social Science* (1860), 282.
Department Committee on Truck Acts (1908), vol. ii, 39.
Potteries Board of Arbitration. Award of Mr. Brassey, the Umpire, November 1880.

women alike, were ultimately identical, and consequently it was not to be expected that women would believe it either. By their selfish short-sighted policy, men made of women much more serious and unscrupulous competitors than they otherwise would have been. Later it will be seen how men with their double policy, viz. to keep women out of the trade except as assistants to men, and, on the other hand, to pursue the practical policy of keeping the wages of women low, met with disaster. It will also be seen how the men belonging to the branch which was the largest throughout the nineteenth century, by persistently refusing to allow women to enter their trade, even as assistants, almost abolished the trade[1] altogether. The question whether or not they were wise in letting the trade die, rather than keep it alive with the aid of women, cannot at this point be answered. Before that can be done many circumstances not yet dealt with will have to be considered. It is mentioned here in order to stress the fact that the women labour problem has been, and for that matter still is, a real, difficult and many-sided one in the pottery trade. The "problem" is the woman's revenge for her treatment in the early days of the industry.

The other way in which the contracting tradition was harmful, from the point of view of unionism, was that, so far as the male workers were concerned, it tended to make industrial discipline very easy, and that, as will be shown, increased the difficulties that lay in the way of labour organisation. Noticed and remarked upon by almost every observer of the trade, this fact of running an industry with undisciplined workers is patently obvious throughout the history of the pottery workers in the nineteenth century.

J. Wedgwood, in giving evidence before the 1816 Com-

[1] Hollow-ware Pressers. Letter of W. Warburton, Union Official and Hollow-ware Presser, July 29, 1926.

mittee on Employment of Children, mentioned quite casually, and without intending to blame anyone, that on an average his workmen lost a day a week. S. Scriven, writing in 1841, made the complaint that, no matter how much work there was on hand to accomplish, the men seldom or never worked after Saturday noon, and often not before the following Tuesday or Wednesday morning.[1] In the 1863 Report the same[2] complaint is made, and, in the evidence before the Factories and Workshops Act Commission of 1876, R. Baker, a Government Inspector, made the statement that in 1864, when he was in the pottery district, there was little work done on Mondays and Tuesdays. In his award before the 1880 Potteries Arbitration Board the umpire, T. Brassey, said much the same thing.[3] As late as 1880 the *Pottery Gazette* grumbled that it was useless to keep pot-works open during an election as the potters would be certain to play for a week, "and in these matters the masters are too much in the hands of their workpeople".[4] Apparently it was always the same, for in the winter of 1772 Josiah Wedgwood replied to the grumblings of the men, whom, owing to lack of orders, he had forced to lose time, by saying "they (the men) can keep wake after wake in the summer when it is their own good will and pleasure".[5] The best and most conclusive evidence, for it is only given incidentally and moreover from the side of the workers, is in *The Voice of the People*. It speaks of a trade union meeting that had been called for seven o'clock Thursday night, and "at half-past seven

[1] *Children's Employment (Trades and Manufactures) Commission*, 1843 (Report of S. Scriven, 1841), C.5.

[2] *Children's Employment Commission*, 1863, p. 1.

[3] Potteries Board of Arbitration. Award of Mr. Brassey, the Umpire, November 1880.

[4] *The Pottery Gazette*, April 1, 1880.

[5] *Letters: Wedgwood to Bentley*, 1762–1780 (1903), 12–14.

only three persons had arrived. The night itself was inopportune to the class of potter." A few months later, of a meeting called for a Monday it reports "soon after six the business of the meeting commenced, and the yard was speedily filled".[1]

Leaving for a moment a discussion of the question of whether or not lack of discipline in daily life reflected itself in trade union organisation, there is much on other grounds to commend an undisciplined industrial life. The appearance of independence that an undisciplined working life gives makes it very attractive to the ordinary human being. There is a sense of freedom in working, from choice, irregular hours that must have greatly sweetened industrial life. The potters were not, as were the textile workers, slaves to the factory bell. But lack of discipline in the working life of the potter had disastrous effects upon his trade union organisation. Among the chief objects of a trade union would be placed an improvement for all the members of the trade in all matters relating to hours and wages. As a step to this end, it tries to obtain a standard working week and equal remuneration for equal effort for all members of a particular branch of a trade in a particular district or area. A trade union, in short, tries to lessen the number of hours per week worked, increase the amount of pay, and make conditions of labour uniform throughout the trade. In the pottery industry in the first half of the nineteenth century trade union rules concerning the maximum number of hours to be worked per week were little more than pious wishes.[2] As branch by branch machinery came in, this became gradually less true. The union was never

[1] *The Voice of the People*, February 12, 1831; September 17, 1831.
[2] Old Potter: *When I was a Child* (1903), 54.
"Trade Societies and Strikes", *Report of the National Association for the Promotion of Social Science* (1860), 282.
Staffordshire Mercury, July 21, 1832.

able to prevent the man who had lost Monday and Tuesday from working late Thursday and Friday, but amongst the men working late on these two nights were certain to be some who had been at work all the previous days of the week. It must be remembered, also, that all time lost from work was not necessarily spent away from the factory. Drinking, playing and idling took place in the workshop itself.[1] It was, of course, possible for a trade union, if one so strong can be imagined, even under such circumstances, to have fixed an hour of day past which no potter should be allowed to work, but the point to be noticed is that in most other factory industries the times of starting and finishing work were known and fixed, and all workers had to conform to them. In such cases a trade union only had to fight to get the machinery stopped half an hour earlier. To obtain such a result, had the potters desired it, would have meant the institution by the union of a system of nightly inspection and the locking up of workshops in face of the persistent opposition of the workmen as individuals. Because of their inability to deal successfully with hours, potters' unions found themselves seriously handicapped in their efforts to standardise and raise wages. It has already been mentioned that a man who had lost time at the beginning of the week would, because of his desire to draw a full week's wages, work at a greater pace and more hours a day at the end of the week. In the same way a potter making articles, the price of which was too low to enable him to get good wages in normal hours of work, would gratify his desire for a good week's wages by working excessively long hours. Both he and his trade union official would protest that the articles were underpaid, but to the master the fact that the man was earning normal wages was proof enough that the protest was

[1] Old Potter: *When I was a Child* (1903), 73.

unfounded.[1] Impotent in its efforts to deal with hours, and handicapped in its attempts to raise and standardise wages, it is easily seen that a trade union would find it no easy matter to convince the mass of potters that it was of use.

There is one side of this subject of lack of discipline which yet needs to be touched upon. It is an ugly side, and was emphatically remarked upon not only by witnesses in evidence before the Government Committees on conditions in factories, but by other people also. It is that the irregular time-keeping of the potter resulted in irregular time being kept by his assistants. In practice this meant that women and children were compelled to work at a quicker pace than usual, and for excessively long hours, at the latter end of the week, in order to make up for the time that their employers and they, willy-nilly also, had lost at the beginning of the week. The 1876 Commission speaks of potters rabbit-racing Monday and Tuesday, and then working the whole of Friday night, they and their women assistants, to make up the work that had been lost.[2] In his reminiscences of the early 'forties an old potter speaks of the little work that was done Mondays and Tuesdays, "and yet it was rare for any of the men to get on Saturdays less than a full week's wages. From Wednesday to Saturday they worked themselves and worked others, boys and women, like galley-slaves. From four or five in the morning until nine and ten at night this fierce race for

[1] Potteries Board of Arbitration. Award of Mr. Brassey, the Umpire, November 1880: ". . . by their manly determination to seek compensation for reduction in rates by increased diligence, the workmen have been enabled to earn the same, and in many cases higher wages than before."

Potteries Board of Arbitration, inquiry before J. C. Davis, 1876–7. Evidence of Mr. Maddock.

[2] *Factories and Workshops Acts Commission*, 1876. Evidence of Mr. Baker, April 27, 1875, vol. ii, 45–6.

wages was run". He goes on further to say that no discipline ever interfered with the men, and any revelry might go on unchecked by the master as long as a full week's work was done.[1] There was thus none of the joys of an undisciplined life for women. The men worked irregularly, largely from choice, but the women worked easily or feverishly, for short hours or for long, according to the caprice of their employers, the potters.[2] From the point of view of the unionist, the evils which arose from this fact are fairly obvious. With such treatment the women could not be expected to realise that, for the good of all workers in the trade, their interests were ultimately the same as the men's, and certainly the men did not realise it either. In the second half of the century, as will be noticed later, machinery and the Factory Acts imposed a form of discipline over women and young persons, but during the 'thirties, which is the period here specially considered, there was nothing to encourage a man to work during certain hours of the week because it was difficult or impossible for him to work certain others. Although it would be an exaggeration to say that the potter at this time pleased himself at what hour and upon what day he went to work, and how long he stayed there, it helps to impress the facts much better than does the literal truth, that the potter from choice worked very irregularly.[3] To guard against

[1] Old Potter: *When I was a Child* (1903).

[2] *Children's Employment Commission*, 1863, p. 1.

[3] *Factories and Workshops Acts Commission*, 1876. *Evidence of Mr. Baker, April* 27, 1875, vol. ii, 45–46.

Potteries Board of Arbitration. Enquiry before J. C. Davis. Mr. Davis: "It is no doubt a lamentable thing with reference to Monday. It might perhaps be better termed unholy Monday. . . ." Mr. Powell: "We make a rule amongst ourselves to work only four days . . . it is impossible to do six days' work . . . either one or another of the men would be off. . . ."

Old Potter: *When I was a Child* (1903), 73.

error, it should be remembered that irregular work was not always the result of the action of the potter. The pottery industry is sensitive to trade depression, and often many factories would only work four days a week by order of the employer.

The two trade customs, now abolished, "Annual Hiring' and "Good from Oven" should be understood, for both in their time were sources of irritation and bad feeling between the masters and men in the trade, and upon a few occasions were the direct cause of fierce conflicts. Annual hiring may or may not have been "immemorial", as claimed by the manufacturers,[1] but it was certainly in existence in the very early days of the trade, long before the earliest period dealt with here. In practice, this system meant that a potter on November 11th (Martinmas) hired himself to a master for one year, at a rate of wages mutually agreed upon. This agreement could not be broken or altered unless with the consent of both parties concerned.[2] The case of the employer who could not find work for his men was partially met by the system of "helping". Helping, which has survived until the present day, meant, as it means now, that the employer during a slack time permitted an employee to work or "help" at some other firm until such time as he again required his services.[3] In an industry that

[1] J. Boyle: "An Account of Strikes in the Potteries, 1834 and 1836," *Journal of Statistical Society* (1839), 41.
Royal Commission on Trade Unions, 10th Report (1867–68), 87.

[2] *Report from the Select Committee on Master and Servant* (1866), 60. Evidence of W. Evans, July, 1866.
Report from Select Committee on Masters and Operatives (*Equitable Councils of Conciliation*). Evidence of Magill Daintree Hollands (a mistake in name, obviously Michael Daintry Hollins is meant) (1856), 203.
J. Boyle: "An Account of Strikes in the Potteries, 1834 and 1836," *Journal of Statistical Society* (1839), 41.

[3] *The Case of the Manufacturers of China and Earthenware in the Staffordshire Potteries with some account of the Late Turn Out, its*

was, and still is, almost completely piecework, it is easily seen that an annual hiring agreement would be conducive to disputes. It was not the simple case of the day worker hiring himself to his master for the year at so much per day. The clay worker agreed to make articles and the printers and painters to decorate them at certain prices for the year. Naturally, the introduction of new shapes or new patterns would often lead to wrangling or dispute. The agreement only covered the prices of articles which were in existence at the time of hiring; it could not be prospective. In most cases the working prices of new shapes and patterns would be amicably arranged by fixing them at the same as existing work of a similar character. Thus a new vegetable dish would be settled at the same making price as the dish most similar to it in shape and size. On this rough system of settling prices, results to masters and men averaged out fairly equitably, for new shapes would be as likely to be slightly easier than the old to make as otherwise, and from both masters' and workmen's point of view work that gave good wages made out for work that did not. Nevertheless, the introduction of a new shape would not always be followed by an easy price settlement, and disputes did occur.[1] Engaged for a year, a potter could easily find himself after a few weeks in the position of having nothing to make other than articles the prices of which were in dispute. Unable to leave until the expiration of his agreement, the man was obviously in a weak bargaining position, despite the fact that the penalties for the breaking of agreements were often defied and a dispute carried to the length of a strike. Apart from the introduction of new

Origin, Proceedings and Termination, 1836–37, published by authority of the Chamber of Commerce. Hanley, pamphlet (N.D.).

Pottery Mercury, April 1825.

[1] *Report from Select Committee on Masters and Operatives* (*Equitable Councils of Conciliation*) (1856), 49.

work, there were all sorts of ways by which disagreement between master and man could occur during the year.[1] The argument that the men brought against annual hiring was that under all and any circumstances it operated to their disfavour. It prevented them from benefiting when labour was scarce, but it did not prevent wage reductions when labour was plentiful. In times of bad trade a master would ask his workmen to agree to a reduction in the making price of a certain article so that he would be enabled to obtain an order. If the men agreed, they had work and he the order; but if they did not, the master lost the order and the men idled. In times of good trade a potter could not take advantage of the fact and go to the master that paid him the most, for he was tied by his agreement.[2]

The other custom, "good from oven", although it never applied to many branches of the trade, was, if measured by the irritation it caused, of perhaps greater importance than annual hiring. The alternative system to "good from oven", and the one that is now general, was "good from hand". Under the latter system a potter was paid for all the work he made that was good when it left his hands, or, strictly speaking, when it left his workshop. Under the former, he was only paid for the ware which

[1] *Royal Commission on Trade Unions* (1867–68), 86.

Report from the Select Committee on Masters and Operatives (*Equitable Councils of Conciliation*), (1856), 202.

Staffordshire Mercury, January 4, 1845. Four potters charged before the magistrates and sentenced to three months' imprisonment each. The four men had had a dispute with their employer and as a result had left their employ, thus breaking their agreement. The employer had refused to advance the prices of these men to those at which he was then engaging journeymen.

Staffordshire Mercury, July 12, 1845. Two men charged with breaking their agreement. They had left their employ as a result of a dispute concerning non-payment for ware.

[2] Letter from Hollow-ware Pressers' Executive, *Staffordshire Potteries Telegraph*, November 20, 1852.

successfully withstood the test of "firing" or baking; that is, ware which came out of the oven good.[1] The manufacturers claimed that it was only by means of this system that they were protected against the mistakes of the unskilful workman. The potter, they said, could have flaws in his work, which, before it had undergone the firing process, could not be detected by any person set to examine it, but which, after the ordeal of the oven, would be plainly visible; moreover, the amount of ware made by the skilful man which came out of the oven bad was almost negligible in quantity, the large losses being incurred by the careless or incompetent worker.[2] The contention of the manufacturers that no person, unless he had made that particular article, or watched it being made, could tell whether or not it was flawless until it came out of the oven, was denied by the men, who claimed that any competent person could discover the flaws in a piece of ware at any stage of its manufacture.[3] The points of view and claims of masters and men are understandable. The masters fought for the retention of the system, because under it they were protected against loss for another stage in the manufacturing process, after the work of the men, whom they were making responsible for that further stage, had ceased, which was precisely why the men opposed it.

[1] J. Boyle: "An Account of Strikes in the Potteries, 1834 and 1836," *Journal of Statistical Society* (vol. i, 1839), 42.

Tenth Report of Royal Commission on Trade Unions (1867–68), 87.

"Trade Societies and Strikes", *Report of the National Association for the Promotion of Social Science* (1860), 282.

Report from the Select Committee on Masters and Operatives (*Equitable Councils of Conciliation*), (1856), 202.

[2] *Report from the Select Committee on Masters and Operatives* (*Equitable Councils of Conciliation*) (1856), 206.

J. Boyle: "An Account of Strikes in the Potteries, 1834 and 1836", *Journal of Statistical Society*, vol. i (1839), 42.

[3] *Report from the Select Committee on Masters and Operatives* (*Equitable Councils of Conciliation*), (1856), 216.

Potters in some branches were paid "good from hand", and in others, with few exceptions, "good from oven". In the latter class came all the potters of those branches that made ware from moulds, while the former included all those that did not. It is not a mere accident that the same line which divides the two systems of payment also divides two methods of manufacture. The reason was not, as may be supposed, because the ware made under the one method was likely to be more, or less, liable to flaws than ware made under the other. It actually has a relationship to a point touched upon earlier, the tradition of contracting. Ware which is not made from moulds requires, before it is ready for the oven, the services of three workmen of three different trades: the thrower, the turner and the handler. The first shapes the ware, the second makes it thinner and polishes it, and the third puts on the handles required. It would be difficult to fix the responsibility upon any one of these three men for ware that came bad out of the oven. The attempt was consequently never made.[1] With the branches which worked with moulds the case was different. Here one speaks of the past, for what will be said is not true in all particulars of the present. In one branch, hollow-ware pressing, the hollow-ware presser himself went through all the processes which were necessary to make the ware ready for the oven. From the time that it was a piece of rough clay until it left the workshop no other person touched it. In the other main branch of the "good from oven" division, flat pressing, the ware was made by the flat-presser and finished by another person, but that other person was an employee of the flat-presser. It would seem that in those cases where the responsibility for the quality of the ware could be

[1] *Report from the Select Committee on Masters and Operatives* (*Equitable Councils of Conciliation*) (1856), 202.

fixed upon one person, that person was compelled to take the responsibility far past the point where one could reasonably expect that it should have ceased. In those cases where the men were paid "good from hand", there is no doubt that, had the circumstances been different, they would have been paid under the other system. If, for instance, the turner and the handler had been employees of the thrower, that person, being alone responsible, would have been paid for his ware after it had been fired, and not before. "Good from oven" is but a case of the tradition of contracting holding in a sphere other than those already mentioned. The potter was responsible for the preparing of his clay and the lighting and sweeping of his shop, matters which in other industries would have been the employers' concern, and to make him responsible for the safety and quality of his ware, long after it had passed out of his hands, was but carrying out the same idea along another line.

One further fact to complete the description. Because of the extreme unhealthiness of the trade, potters were almost all young men. Bevan quotes the Registrar-General as saying, "The earthenware manufacture is one of the unhealthiest in the country . . . it exceeds the mortality of the publicans.[1] This was in 1875, and the census figures show that in the 'thirties it must have been infinitely worse.[2] The fact that potters were young is not without significance. It means that in their collective action as trade unionists they would not have the staidness and worldly wisdom of middle and old age, but rather the enthusiasm and instability of youth. When, later, it will

[1] G. P. Bevan: *Industrial Classes and Industrial Statistics* (1876), 150, quoting "Supplement to Thirty-fifth Annual Report of Registrar-General", 1875.

[2] In proportion to number of all men in trade the number of potters aged fifty-five or over increases.

be necessary to review some of the fascinating, but rather harebrained, schemes of the potters, this should be remembered. All these influences and circumstances, high mortality, good from oven, annual hiring, lack of discipline, contracting and localisation, must have acted and reacted each upon the other, but which of them were causes and which were effects it is difficult to say. At best, it is but possible to present a picture for the better understanding of the potter in his struggles, defeats and triumphs as a trade unionist. One thing, at any rate, is fairly certain—the potter in his thoughtless treatment of women sowed for himself a harvest of mischief.

In addition to the trade customs, traditions and methods of payment mentioned above, and in a completely different category, for in no sense was it an essential feature or peculiarity of the trade, the beginning of 1830 saw the system of truck operating in the pottery districts. Agitation for the abolition of the system began in the first month of that year, with a request to the Chief Constable for permission to hold a public meeting to consider the necessity of petitioning Parliament to pass a law to stop the payment of wages in truck.[1] The meeting was held and was followed by several others, and the petition to Parliament was made. The agitation was started and at first run by the small shopkeepers, who, next to the direct victims of the system, were the most hard hit. After a few weeks, the reputable manufacturers, who had all along paid wages in money, became interested, and on February 20, 1830, the Chamber of Commerce, which represented them, sent a petition to Westminster praying for the abolition of truck.[2] The anti-truck campaign was greatly hindered by

[1] *Cases of Distress and Oppression in the Staffordshire Potteries by Labourers' Wages being Paid in Truck*, pamphlet, 1830.
Staffordshire Mercury, January 30, 1830.
[2] *Staffordshire Mercury*, February 20, 1830.

the fact that distress at the time in the pottery trade was very acute. In February, the local paper referring to the pottery towns reported that there was "more poverty . . . more actual starvation . . . than at any period for years past, not excepting the winter of 1826".[1] In the same month in one small pottery district upwards of 4,000 persons were relieved by public subscriptions.[2] This distress helped to keep truck alive. The truck payers were not wealthy manufacturers with a good position in the trade; on the contrary, they were the struggling members of the potting business. They were the inefficient manufacturers who got their orders by under-selling the reputable firms, and their profits by under-paying the workmen; masters who, had they been forced to pay wages in money, would not have survived a period of very bad trade. A pamphlet distributed at the time pointed this fact out, but from a different point of view, for it was pleading for the retention of truck, and tried to show that the anti-truck agitation was a campaign of the big against the little manufacturers. Apparently the idea was that the workmen, out of self-interest, ought to support the weak against the strong master.[3]

One fact which is too outstanding to be passed over arises out of the anti-truck agitation. No body of workmen, not even the wretched victims of the system, made any audible protest against truck. The agitation was engineered by tradespeople, and helped by the better-class manufacturers; the workpeople themselves displayed no initiative whatever. There is no doubt that journeymen potters hated and cursed the system, but in their grumbling they were powerless. This in itself is fairly conclusive proof

[1] *Staffordshire Mercury*, February 6, 1830.
[2] *Staffordshire Mercury*, February 27, 1830.
[3] *Staffordshire Mercury*, February 20, 1830.

that no labour organisation of any kind existed amongst the potters, but, as it happens, there is other and more positive evidence. It may, therefore, be taken as fact that in the beginning of the year 1830 no potters' union or unions existed.[1]

The coming of unionism may in part be ascribed to the anti-truck agitation. For the better prosecution of the war against truck committees had been formed and, with the idea of making them representative of all interests, a few workmen had been put upon them. One of the methods of the campaign was to hold large public meetings at which the iniquities of truck were explained and denounced. These meetings succeeded in getting what was an apparently apathetic and despondent people keenly interested in the removal of a grievance, and to think of one grievance is obviously a preparatory stage to reflecting upon others. Moreover, as has been stated, some of the journeymen potters, though not through any initiative on their part, were holding directing positions in the campaign—a fact guaranteed, as it was intended that it should, further to stimulate the interests of the workmen.[2] All this was an ideal preparation for the propagation of the doctrines of combination.

At this splendidly opportune time the National Association for the Protection of Labour sent missionaries to preach trade unionism to the potters. To say that the

[1] *Staffordshire Mercury*, October 30, 1830, letter: ". . . you will say, 'O we have had unions enough . . . and they have failed, . . . but you have never had an union . . . or it . . . would have continued to this day . . ." Journeyman Potter.

J. Boyle: "An Account of Strikes in the Potteries, 1834 and 1836," *Journal of Statistical Society*, vol. i (1837), 38.

Staffordshire Mercury, February 22, 1834; letter from Joseph Peake.

[2] *Staffordshire Mercury*, February 20, 1830.

National Association delegates began their propaganda work amongst the potters during an anti-truck campaign is to say what is literally, and not merely generally, true. Their first speeches to the potters were made under dramatic circumstances at the close of an anti-truck meeting, on October 18, 1830. All the anti-truck speeches had been made, and the proceedings of the meeting seemed about to terminate, when some confusion was caused by a stranger, who attempted to address the people. He was called on to the platform and given permission to speak, on the condition that he was brief. After announcing that he was a delegate of the National Association for the Protection of Labour, the stranger made a few remarks which, although palatable to the majority in the crowd, would not be relished overmuch by many on the platform. These remarks were to the effect that, although truck was a bad thing, it was no worse an evil than low wages. It transpired that the dramatic entrance of the National Association delegates was the result of a mistake, and had not been deliberately planned. They had a few days previously distributed bills announcing the date, time and place of a meeting which they intended to hold, and it was not until the hour of the meeting itself that they discovered that the Anti-truck Committee was holding one at the same time and in the same place.[1] With the commencement of the National Association Mission the interest of the journeyman potter in the anti-truck campaign was overshadowed by his interest in trade union propaganda. In the week following the meeting just mentioned, a working potter published a letter in the local newspaper reminding his fellows of the reductions in wages which had taken place every hiring for several years. He then tells his fellow-workmen that the masters "will continue to

[1] *Staffordshire Mercury*, October 30, 1830.

reduce your price for labour till you famish at your benches without you take the concern into your own hand. Government cannot put a stop to this if they can to the truck system."[1]

On Monday, November 15th, just one month after their theatrical entry, the delegates of the National Association held a big meeting just outside the Potteries.[2] This meeting was called for the purpose of forming a general union of potters which, when formed, was to coalesce with the National Association for the Protection of Labour. In the weeks between their coming and the holding of this meeting the delegates had not been idle. Each week letters from potters and others appeared in the local paper discussing the National Association, and walls were placarded with notices calling attention to its aims and objects and to the meeting which was to be held.[3] The chair at the meeting was taken by a journeyman potter, and other potters moved the resolutions, but the principal speeches were made by the "Manchester men", Doherty, Foster and Hodgkins. Doherty and Hodgkins made a pleasing impression even upon those who did not favour their views. In the newspaper report of the meeting they are described as being sincere men and moderate of speech. Foster, however, displeased some of the crowd by talking too wildly. The meeting caused much talk and discussion among the potters, and the local newspaper, although distinctly and admittedly hostile to the whole movement for which the meeting stood, devoted a leading article to it, on the ground that it caused excitement throughout the pottery districts.[4]

[1] *Staffordshire Mercury*, October 30, 1830.
[2] *Staffordshire Mercury*, November 20, 1830.
[3] *Staffordshire Mercury*, October 30, November 6, 13, 1830.
[4] *Staffordshire Mercury*, November 20, 1830.

Besides being favoured by the excitement produced by the anti-truck campaign, the mission of the delegates was fortunate in beginning just before the potters' hiring time. At hiring time the potter was most acutely conscious of his grievances, and most ready to discuss them. It was the time in the year when he would be most likely to listen sympathetically to schemes for his betterment. In later years a potters' union would sometimes double its membership during the few weeks before Martinmas hiring.[1] Just as at a general election hosts of people appear to be politically conscious who at other times are apathetic, so at Martinmas the potter became conscious of himself as a wage-earner faced with a wage-earner's problems.

The first-fruits of the missionary efforts of the National Association amongst the potters was the formation in November 1830 of the China and Earthenware Turners' Society.[2] This was an independent society, and it was not until several months later, and as a result of a different set of circumstances, that it joined the National Association, which fact makes it appear likely that it was not too conscious of the debt which it owed to the larger body for its birth.

About this time trade began to improve, and with the coming of the New Year the newspapers were able to report that "men generally speaking are now fully employed".[3] In January and February 1831 the National

[1] *Eleventh and final Report of Royal Commission on Trade Unions* (1868–69), vol. ii, Appendix D, 58.

Answers to questions to secretaries:

"Name of Society? United Hollow-ware Pressers, etc."

"Proportion of unionists to non-unionists? 1 to 2; towards hiring time, 3 to 1."

[2] *The Voice of the People*, March 5, 1831.

[3] *Staffordshire Mercury*, January 29, 1831.

Association delegates were again in the Potteries, this time seeking support for the Ashton spinners, who were on strike. Several public meetings called for this purpose were made the occasion of Association propaganda.[1] The China and Earthenware Turners' Society, being the only organised body of potters then in existence, gave its support to the National Association delegates in their efforts to elicit public sympathy for the Ashton spinners. As a result of this co-operation the turners "manifested an anxious desire that the laws, rules and regulations of the National Association should be fully understood by them as a body, in order that every member thereof might be satisfied of the utility of such an institution generally".[2] This "manifested desire" resulted in the turners calling a general meeting on February 28th, when, after satisfying themselves of the "utility of such an institution", they decided to join the National Association.[3] It seems impossible now to ever know how soon it was after this date that the potters in other branches of the industry organised themselves. Although the interest in combination had been revived, or, perhaps more truly, recreated, it was not all in favour of the National Association. From the beginning the opinion was expressed that a union of potters should be formed, and that it should be kept free from entanglements with combinations in other trades.[4] In August 1831 the National Union of Operative Potters was established, which took men of every branch in the pottery industry.[5] In the following month one hears incidentally of the existence of a Potters' Painters' Union, but such a society,

[1] *Staffordshire Mercury*, February 5, 1831.
The Voice of the People, February 12, 1831.
[2] *The Voice of the People*, March 5, 1831.
[3] *The Voice of the People*, March 5, 1831.
[4] *Staffordshire Mercury*, October 30, 1830.
[5] *Staffordshire Mercury*, August 17, 1833.

or societies like it, could not have lived long and would soon be absorbed in the larger body.[1]

After October 1831 the agitation of the National Association amongst the potters ceased, and no more mention of that body is made in the district. The organisation of the potters at the time was weak, a fact from which another and curious phenomenon emerges. For a year, from October 1830 until October 1831 the National Association had conducted under favourable circumstances an almost continuous propaganda. When the delegates first came to the potters they came to workmen who had already been roused from their apathy by another campaign. The year 1831 was one of good trade, and consequently in that respect favourable to the growth of combination. Moreover, judging from the newspapers, the potters' interest in trade unionism, and the National Association in particular, was sustained throughout this year of propaganda. Nevertheless, trade unionism amongst the potters was weak. The National Association claimed that its newspaper, *The Voice of the People,* attained a circulation of 30,000,[2] which, if true, makes the number that went to the potters look absurdly small, for North Staffordshire, combined with Leicester, took only 140 copies.[3] Judging by their achievements amongst the men of other trades, the National Association delegates must have been disappointed with the potters. Even in the potters' own district, and with less care spent upon them, the miners as early as May 1831 had 1,600 of their number in the Association.[4] Nevertheless, it would

[1] *The Voice of the People,* September 10, 1831.
[2] Webb: *The History of Trade Unionism* (ed. 1920), 123. ". . . All this activity lends a certain credibility to the assertion, . . . that *The Voice of the People* enjoyed the then enormous circulation of thirty thousand."
[3] *The Voice of the People,* August 22, 1831.
[4] *The Voice of the People,* May 14, 1831.

be a mistake to belittle the influence upon the potters of the National Association delegates. Certainly the result of their labour in their time was but small, but they had created anew an interest in combination, and had kept that interest alive. They left the potters comparatively weak, but they left them also with the machinery whereby they could make themselves powerful.

CHAPTER IV

THE NATIONAL UNION OF OPERATIVE POTTERS

The work of the National Association delegates in the rousing of trade union interest was well done, for, when left alone and free of all outside influence, the potters combination did not wither, but prospered and grew. The building up of this combination was the work of the potters alone, for, until the coming of Owen, by which time the work was done, there was no Union propaganda done amongst them by any outside person.[1] Even in the birth of the Union some credit must be given to that group of nameless potters who so willingly assisted the Manchester delegates.[2]

In apportioning the credit or discredit for the birth and growth of a movement, contemporary local historians are very unreliable.[3] If it is a movement of which the historian does not feel proud, then he is certain to ascribe its appearance in the district to the work of outsiders.

Left alone, the Potters' Union for a long time behaved

[1] There is no mention of any in the local newspapers, and for that matter there was no organisation or person to do any trade union propaganda.

[2] Not altogether nameless, but unknown. Jesse Buxton, John Rathbone, and Richards are the names of the three potters who were chairmen and movers of resolutions at different meetings. See *Staffordshire Mercury*, November 20, 1830; *The Voice of the People*, February 12, September 17, 1831. The names of the men who were prominent a few years later—Glasse, Stacey, Simpson Pratt, Lancaster and Miers—do not appear.

[3] J. Ward: *History of Borough of Stoke-on-Trent* (1846), 56. Trade unionism amongst potters attributed to work of outsiders.

J. Boyle: "An Account of Strikes in the Potteries in 1834–36," *Journal of Statistical Society*, London, vol. i (1839), 38. Formation of National Union of Operative Potters attributed to work of outsiders. This only partly true.

with a seemliness that is only possible to the contented or the weak. The hirings of 1831 and 1832 were passed over without dispute, and no attempt was made by the men in mass to hire on better terms.[1] During these years the Union was far from strong, and its activities were confined to the redressing of "truck" and "good from oven" grievances.[2] In 1833 the hard work of the pioneers began to show results. Interest in industrial questions, which had been kept alive amongst the potters by the efforts of the staunch few, now began to take concrete form, and the Union grew rapidly in membership and aggressiveness.[3] Relations were established between North Staffordshire and the "Out-Potteries", and in the latter districts out-lodges were established.[4]

At its height the Union had fifty-four lodges. A lodge was composed of the workmen of a particular branch in a particular district, though this probably did not apply to some of the out-potteries, where all potters of whatever branch would be in one lodge. Each lodge had its president and secretary, but there was little lodge autonomy, for the government of the union, including the holding of the funds, was vested in a central Board of Management. This board consisted of the lodge presidents, grand president, treasurer, secretaries and auditors.[5] It was a

[1] There is no attempt recorded in the newspapers.
[2] *Staffordshire Mercury*, July 21 and 28, 1832.
[3] *Staffordshire Mercury*, June 15, August 3, 1833. *Crisis*, October 19, 1833. Letters to Robert Owen, Holyoake House, Manchester. R. G. to the Editor of the *Crisis*, September 24, 1833.
[4] *Staffordshire Mercury*, August 17, 1833.
[5] *The Case of the Manufacturers of China and Earthenware in the Staffordshire Potteries, with some account of the Late Turn Out, its Origin, Proceedings, and Termination*, 1836–37, published by authority of the Chamber of Commerce (pamphlet) (N.D.).
Crisis, October 19, 1833.
Potters' Examiner, July 14, 1844.

favourite gibe of the masters that this governing body of the Potters' Society was a "secret board".[1] That this gibe was made was largely the fault of the potters themselves. Actually the deliberations of their Board of Management were no more and no less secret than those of a chamber of commerce at that time, or of a trade union executive committee in this, but it pleased the potters of the 'thirties to think that their policy and their plans of action were framed and decided in secret.[2] It was as if there were magic in the word "secret", and despite the fact that the potters must have known that, when used in connection with workmen's associations, the word had an evil sound in the ears of the middle classes, and that there was no particular point in offending these people, they still spoke of their "secret order". The only reason one can find for their so doing was that being connected with something secret appealed to their imagination or their sense of the theatrical.

Early in 1833 the Potters' Union felt itself strong enough to be active, and entered upon what proved to be a long campaign for the levelling up of piecework prices. No general action against the masters as a body was attempted, nor was it necessary, for many of them gave what even the workmen considered to be fair prices for their work.[3] It was to the standard of these better-paying masters that the Union tried to lift the others. The Union would request the master of a low-paid manufactory to lift up his workmen's prices to the level of those paid by his more reputable neighbours. If negotiations failed, or having begun, broke down, a few essential men were withdrawn from work,

[1] *The Case of the Manufacturers, etc.* (pamphlet) (N.D.). *Staffordshire Advertiser*, October 1, 1836.
[2] *Staffordshire Mercury*, August 3, 1833, March 1, 1834.
[3] *Staffordshire Mercury*, August 3, 1833.

and the employer forced to close his factory.[1] Such a strike, occurring at any other time than at Martinmas, was a clear case of violation of agreement, and the employer had his remedy before the magistrates. But, as the masters themselves complained, imprisoning the men did not restart the factory.[2] Moreover, in times of decent trade, the number of unemployed men from the ranks of whom the manufacturer could fill his vacancies would be very few. He would have to find men that were of the trade he wanted, for men skilled in some other branch would not do.

It was not the case, as in some other industries, of finding men who could work at any of several processes of manufacture. To break the strike by attracting men from other factories was again, under the circumstances, impossible. A man coming from another works would be necessarily breaking a contract and rendering himself liable to prosecution, and, in his case, there would be no union to support him or his family. The attempt of the Union to level up piecework prices was not viewed with disfavour by the reputable employers.[3] The same reason which caused many manufacturers to join in the campaign against "truck" made them approve of the action of the workmen in doing what was in effect the same thing.[4] On Saturday, June 8, 1833, 400 men from one manufactory joined the Union at the request of their employer.[5] It appeared that his fellow-manufacturers had tried to rob this particular master of a rather large order by offering to fulfil it at a

[1] *The Case of the Manufacturers, etc.* (pamphlet) (N.D.). *The Times*, November 15, 1836 (cutting from *Manchester Herald*).

J. Boyle: "An Account of Strikes in the Potteries in 1834–36," *Journal of Statistical Society*, London, vol. i (1839), 41.

[2] *The Case of the Manufacturers* (pamphlet) (N.D.).

[3] *The Case of the Manufacturers* (pamphlet) (N.D.).

[4] *Staffordshire Mercury*, June 15, July 13, 1833.

[5] *Staffordshire Mercury*, June 15, 1833.

much lower price. He retained the order, but he showed his resentment at these attempts at under-cutting by requesting his workmen to join the Union. Five weeks later another manufacturer, in a letter to the local newspaper, publicly expressed his sympathy with the workmen's organisation.[1] In this letter he pointed out to the working potters that, at the moment, ware was of a better quality and being sold more cheaply than at any former period, and, as pottery manufacturers had never at any time made large profits, it followed that, if this system of underselling were continued, there would be large reductions in wages at the next hiring. If this was not to happen, the letter continued, then the potters must make out a standard list of prices for the whole trade, and refuse to hire anywhere on less advantageous terms. If the potters did this, then the manufacturers who under-sold would be compelled to stop the guilty practice. In addition to the above sound advice, the letter included a little homily upon the immorality of violating written agreements—a sin, the writer regretted to observe, which was treated too lightly by the potters.

A few weeks later the Union published a letter in reply.[2] After thanking the manufacturer for the kindly spirit exhibited in his letter, it went on to say that the men had long been aware of the vice of under-selling which existed amongst the manufacturers, and, in so far as it affected wages, the Union intended to deal with it. In reference to the course of action which the manufacturer had advised the working potter to follow, the Union could say nothing; it was a secret body, and consequently could not impart any knowledge of its plans to an outsider. The Union took this occasion to publish a letter to the manufacturers in

[1] *Staffordshire Mercury*, July 13, 1833.
[2] *Staffordshire Mercury*, August 3, 1833.

the pottery industry which it had drawn up on June 5th, and intended freely to circulate throughout the trade, but for which, upon consideration, it had decided that the time was not ripe.[1] This letter contained a request to the manufacturers in the industry that they should combine for the purpose of getting a good return for their products, and should cease from their present practice of competing in selling prices to the ruin of the trade. It does not appear as though working potters were clear as to the principle upon which making prices should be arranged. They thought that wages should be high—that is certain, but it is not certain whether they believed that selling prices should rule wages or whether wages should be a fixed working cost, unaffected by the price obtained for the finished product. In their letter to the manufacturers they seem to incline to the belief that the selling price is a wage determinant, but upon other occasions they strenuously contended that labour should be treated as any other raw material, in which case it would not matter how high its price was, for the selling price would adjust itself to it as it did to the price of coal. In any case, the ideas of the potters at this time were not solidified into a doctrine: they were rather working beliefs that fitted the exigencies of the moment.[2]

On Monday, August 5, 1833, and on the three following days, the National Union of Operative Potters held their second annual meeting.[3] Delegates were present representing the lodges in the out-potteries of Bristol, Swansea, Newcastle-on-Tyne and different parts of Worcestershire, Derbyshire and Yorkshire. It was at this time that the

[1] *Staffordshire Mercury*, August 3, 1833.
[2] *Staffordshire Mercury*, March 1, 1834.
Staffordshire Potteries Telegraph, December 18, 1852.
[3] *Staffordshire Mercury*, August 17, 1833.

potters took a place of prominence, which they held for several years, in the world of labour, but which, once lost, was never regained.[1] The membership of the Union at the time of the August meeting is not known, but eight weeks later it was 8,000, 6,000 in North Staffordshire and 2,000 in the out-potteries.[2] This figure was never again reached after the 'thirties until comparatively recent times, despite the fact that the number engaged in the industry grew very considerably.[3] All classes of men engaged in the trade, including many black-coated workers, were in the Union.[4] It was claimed that all potters were members, with the exception of those whose conduct compelled the Union to reject them, a few who refrained from joining from scruples of conscience, and those who held confidential positions and therefore could not be members if they were honourably to serve their masters. That these last-named were exempt from membership is understandable, but it is not clear how the conscience and bad character clauses worked out in practice. In reference to those in the latter category, it was apparently the rule, if a potter wished to join the Union, for his name to be submitted to the lodge a week previously, so that his suitability for membership could be considered.[5] There is one case recorded of a workman whose application was

[1] G. D. H. Cole: *A Short History of the British Working Class Movement* (1925), vol. i, 126. "The five great Unions . . . the Builders, Spinners, Potters and Clothiers, and the Leeds, Huddersfield and Bradford District Union. . . ."

[2] *Crisis*, October 19, 1833.

Letters to Robert Owen, Holyoake House, Manchester, N.R. (or W. R.) Wood to Owen, June 14, 1834.

[3] Total persons in the pottery industry: 1841, 24,774; 1851, 36,512; 1861, 47,144.

[4] Letters to Robert Owen, Holyoake House, Manchester; Henry L. Pratt to Owen, November 12, 1833.

[5] *Staffordshire Mercury*, March 1, 1834.

refused, which perhaps throws light on what was meant by a "bad character". This particular potter was a radical, and his doctrine, "that the law of supply and demand was as absolute as the physical law of nature", was distasteful to his fellows, and he, because of his insistence upon it, was objectionable to them.[1] What the procedure was, and how the bad character and conscience exemptions operated in those cases where strikes occurred to compel men to join the Union, is difficult to understand. The only explanation is that the practice of trade unions, like the practice of other associations, or even of individuals, is so full of inconsistencies that it will not permit of rational explanation.

It is impossible to say now with accuracy how nearly the National Union of Operative Potters attained the ideal of 100 per cent. membership. To do this, not only must the trade union membership be known, but also the possible membership. The census of 1831 is not very helpful. It gives for North Staffordshire 4,400 men and their families engaged in the pottery industry, but there is nothing to indicate how many men eligible for trade union membership were included under "families";[2] nevertheless, the census figure, as it is, roughly corresponds to the trade union figure of 6,000 membership two years later. The 1841 census, which goes into details, gives the number of males over twenty years of age in North Staffordshire engaged in all branches of pottery manufacture as 8,000.[3] The number of potters would be larger in 1841 than at the time when the Union claimed to have 6,000 members, but this would be partly offset by the Union members under twenty, of whom there would always be a fair number. The state-

[1] *Staffordshire Mercury*, March 1, 1834.

[2] *Census*, 1831 (1833), vol. ii, 604 : "(the pottery factories) contain about 4,400 men and their families employed."

[3] Actual figures, 7,687 males over twenty years of age; 3,757 males under twenty years of age.

ments of the Union with reference to their membership cannot be disproved, and there are no good grounds for disbelieving them. As accurate figures appear to be unobtainable, the men's own statement that almost all potters were organised in the Union must be accepted.

On September 16, 1833, the pottery manufacturers of North Staffordshire held a meeting to consider the framing of a new list of selling prices, which, it was alleged, would be necessary if the advance in wages urged by the workmen was to be conceded. The most influential firms in the trade were represented at this meeting, and from many of the others notes were received expressing willingness to concur in all reasonable decisions that were made. A committee was appointed to prepare a list of selling prices, and to come to some arrangement with the Union respecting wages. A meeting of representatives from the Union and a deputation from this committee was arranged, at which it was agreed that the workmen should prepare a list of minimum working prices.[1] The list was prepared, given to the masters' committee, and on October 6th submitted to a general meeting of manufacturers. This meeting rejected it, but three weeks later a committee of six operatives and seven masters was appointed to settle all working-price disputes.[2] In the meantime the manufacturers had come to an agree-

[1] *Staffordshire Mercury*, September 21, 1833.

[2] *Staffordshire Mercury*, September 12, November 9, 1833.

Letters to Robert Owen, Holyoake House, Manchester; Henry L. Pratt to Owen, November 12, 1833.

J. Boyle: "An Account of Strikes in the Potteries in 1834–36," *Journal of Statistical Society*, London, vol. i (1839), 39. "This committee entered on its duties, and proceeded to effect the object in view, but it was soon brought to a termination by what the masters deemed a violation of faith on the part of the workmen. The general body of one important branch of the trade refused to sanction the acts of their delegates, and when this was communicated to the committee, the masters would not proceed further in the business."

ment respecting their selling-price list.[1] Throughout these negotiations both operatives and employers had kept in close touch with the out-potteries.[2] In reference to the facts of the "list" negotiations, the evidence of the manufacturers is to the effect that as "at this time the demand for goods was very brisk and the workers were fully employed, it appeared to the masters a favourable opportunity to respond to the feelings of the workmen and to make an advance in the price of workmanship. It was thought that such a course would allay the irritation and discontent which generally prevailed towards a certain class of manufacturers".[3] There is little more than a hint in this statement that there was pressure from the men's combination. It rather suggests that the masters favoured the idea of their workmen benefiting during a time of good trade, not only by more regular employment, but by better working prices. Indeed, later, when all thoughts of friendship between masters and operatives, whether true or pretended, had been dropped, the allegation was made from the side of the manufacturers that, at the time the "list" was being framed, certain manufacturers had been imprudent enough to encourage the men in their wild demands;[4] which is probably true if "certain" is meant to imply "few".[5]

The evidence of the men, though not more detailed, is more definite. According to them, the Union not only compelled the employers to agree to the framing of a list of working prices, but it interfered with selling to the

[1] *Staffordshire Mercury*, October 19, October 26, 1833.
[2] *Staffordshire Mercury*, September 21, October 26, 1833.
[3] J. Boyle: "An Account of Strikes in the Potteries in 1834-36." *Journal of Statistical Society, London*, vol. i (1839), 39.
[4] *Staffordshire Mercury*, August 23, 1834.
[5] Except the two mentioned no cases of manufacturers actively encouraging the Union, though of course there were many who did not oppose it, *supra*. 62-3

extent of prohibiting the sending abroad of manufactured goods on speculation; goods were only to be sent on order.[1] They admit, however, that the masters "had the good sense to meet their working dupes half-way".[2] To a much greater extent than the statements used the tone of the men's testimony suggests that the Potters' Union was the dictator of the pottery industry.[3] The masters are accused of adopting the "paltry expedient" of doubling the selling prices, as they thought, without the men's knowledge, so that when orders ceased to arrive, as would naturally happen, they would be able to say that the extravagant demands made upon them at the time of the formation of the list had led to a deprivation of trade.[4] There is one fact that powerfully strengthens the evidence of the men. During the whole of the negotiations the Union, by means of the strike, was insisting upon the adoption of its list, firm by firm.[5] These strikes were successful, which no doubt explained why many of the masters believed that the men's list was an equitable one. If the joint committee of employer and employees was created to prevent strikes, which, so the Union alleged, was the reason why the manu-

1 - 2 Letters to Owen, Holyoake House, Manchester; R. G. to the Editor of the *Crisis*, September 24, 1833.

3 As, for instance: "They [the masters] last Monday but one sent for a deputation from our lodge to the Swan Inn much compliments!" You can do anything you please. "Fudge."

Henry L. Pratt to Owen, November 12, 1833. (Letters to Owen, Holyoake House, Manchester.) "There is no section of the country where the march of intellect is making more rapid strides . . . this first solid proof of the disposition and ability of the people to look after their own interest." R. G. to Editor of *Crisis* (letters to Owen, Holyoake House, Manchester).

4 Letters to Robert Owen, Holyoake House, Manchester; Henry L. Pratt to Owen, November 12, 1833.

5 Letters to Robert Owen, Holyoake House, Manchester; Henry L. Pratt to Owen, November 12, 1833.

Staffordshire Mercury, October 19, 1833.

facturers pressed for its formation,[1] it certainly failed, for the men never desisted from their plan of enforcing the list by means of the strike.[2]

In the heyday of its power the National Union of Operative Potters came under the personal influence of the one man who, in any period, approached the nearest to the earning of the title of "monarch of the English labour world", Robert Owen.[3] The influence of Owen upon the potters' organisation can easily be wrongly estimated. Too much or too little importance can be given to it.[4] Owen influenced the Potters' Union and directed it along the lines of a certain policy, but his was an influence that was exerted by way of an active group, which included all the leaders, and not through the rank and file. He wielded great power over the Union leaders, but it is equally true that he had none over the potters in the mass.[5]

The foregoing statements need qualification, for the whole question of the relation between Owen and the potters was so involved that no generalisation is safe. Owen's conquests lay in the committee-room; he never captured the potters at their benches, but Owenism almost did.

[1] Letters to Robert Owen, Holyoake House; Henry L. Pratt to Owen, November 12, 1833.

[2] Letters to Robert Owen, Holyoake House; N. R. Wood to Owen, June 14, 1834.
Staffordshire Mercury, March 1834.

[3] *Crisis*, October 19, 1833.
Staffordshire Advertiser, November 9, 1833.

[4] The manufacturers overestimated and underestimated the influence of Owen (Boyle, op. cit., 38). They said that Owen stimulated Unionism amongst the potters, which he did not; also that many of the Union officials were *suspected* of being his followers; they *were* his followers.

[5] Letters to Robert Owen, Holyoake House; Henry L. Pratt to Owen, November 12, 1833.
Staffordshire Advertiser, October 26, 1833.

The relationship of Owen to the potters was almost the opposite from that which existed between O'Connor and the illiterate Yorkshire labourers, who followed their leader although they had but hazy notions concerning all the implication that lay in the acceptance of the Charter. The nearest parallel to Owenism and the potters is seen in the case of the non-political town councillor who believes in municipal tramways because he has become convinced, owing to the subtle efforts of socialists who have carefully hidden their politics, that municipal socialism is merely applied common sense. Using the same tactics as the subtle socialist, Owen's potter disciples preached co-operation and workers' control, but carefully hid the flag for which they fought.[1] Owen went to North Staffordshire on October 2, 1833, and met there a small group of the potters' leaders, to whom he explained certain of his ideas.[2] As there seems no reason to suppose otherwise, and the evidence points to the fact, it may be assumed that the men whom Owen met upon this occasion had for some time before been familiar with his doctrines.[3] With what imaginative decoration the officials at this meeting painted the picture of the victorious advance of the members of their trade will never be known, but they certainly succeeded in filling their visitor with enthusiastic admiration for the potter. This was seen a few days later at the Co-operative Congress, when Owen, in his speech to the assembled delegates, described the potters as being in spirit and intelligence far above the men of other trades. The builders, he said, came next in the scale of intelligence, which statement, if praise for the builder, was high commendation for the potter.[4] Three weeks after meeting their officials,

[1] Letters to Robert Owen, Holyoake House; Henry L. Pratt to Owen, November 12, 1833.

[2] *Staffordshire Mercury*, October 5, 1833.

[3] *Crisis*, October 19, 1833.

[4] *Crisis*, October 19, 1833.

Congress having occurred in the meantime, Owen addressed the potters of North Staffordshire on the subject of Trade Unionism and Co-operation.[1] Two meetings were held, one at Burslem and one at Hanley, but, although they were open to all potters, not more than two hundred attended.

Meanwhile, a definitely hostile movement against Owen and his teaching had arisen amongst a section of the potters, and the Union leaders had to use great skill to prevent it doing damage to their organisation.[2] The members of this movement were chiefly Methodists, and opposed Owen and Owenism on religious grounds.[3] This hostility was not to be despised, for the Methodists were strong in the district and had great influence;[4] the home of the potter was, in fact, the birthplace of a large Methodist sect. The Committee of the Potters' Union did not make the error of treating the power of the Methodists lightly. Simpson, the secretary, wrote to Owen, October 20th, as follows: "There is a great hue and cry against you; all the religious world, so called, are opposed to you. This is very natural, and I fear will do us much more mischief than any other subject."[5] The attitude of the Methodist potters to Owen, even if based upon misunderstanding was, at any rate, excusable. It cannot be lightly dismissed as fanaticism. The Methodists

[1] *Staffordshire Mercury*, October 26, 1833.
Staffordshire Advertiser, October 26, 1833.

[2] Letters to Robert Owen, Holyoake House; Henry L. Pratt to Owen, November 12, 1833.

[3] Letters to Robert Owen, Holyoake House; Simpson to Owen, October 20, 1833; Henry L. Pratt to Owen, November 12, 1833.

[4] Old Potter: *When I was a Child* (1903), 193. "Working potters who were not Methodists were yet under an influence which made them distrustful of all associations which were condemned by religious people."

The Potteries is the birthplace of Primitive Methodism, the first Conference of which body was held 1820.

[5] Letters to Robert Owen, Holyoake House; Simpson to Owen, October 20, 1833.

saw themselves, and perhaps truly, as fighters in a battle against almost overwhelming odds, to save the world from the devil. Life in the pottery towns in the 'thirties must have struck any decent person with horror. Drunkenness was common, and at week-ends almost general. Often the potters would have ale and spirits conveyed to the workshop, and begin a drunken spree, which would last all night. Sometimes upon these occasions the men would prevail upon their women attendants to stay with them, in which case the night would be one long abominable orgy. The Methodists probably confused effects with causes, but they certainly saw in their religion something that was destroying, though slowly, these horrors and miseries.[1] They heard that Owen opposed religion, so what more natural than that they should oppose him, since in their eyes religion was the one force that saved a pottery town from being a hell?

Had the potters' leaders been less skilful, the uncompromising hostility of the Methodists to Owenism would have led to a split in the Union. As it was, a rupture occurred. The warehousemen as a body refused to pay any more subscriptions until they were assured that no Union money was to be used for the furtherance of Owenite schemes.[2] The Board of Management made a promise satisfactory to the malcontents, and the threatened hurt to the Union was prevented.[3] The leaders were thus left in an akward position. They believed that the workers' salvation lay along the path that Owen had pointed out, but they also knew that, if they openly guided the potters in that direction, the break-up of the Union would follow.

[1] Old Potter: *When I was a Child* (1903), 50.

[2] Letters to Robert Owen, Holyoake House; Henry L. Pratt to Owen, November 12, 1833.

[3] Letters to Robert Owen, Holyoake House; Henry L. Pratt to Owen, November 12, 1833.

The difficulty was evaded by the adoption of a policy of deception. Owenite schemes were pressed forward by the potters' leaders, but special care was taken not to mention the name Owen or the word Owenism.[1] In a letter to Owen, written November 12th, Pratt, a member of the Potters' Board of Management, explained how this policy was practised. After stating that the Methodists, with all their sectarian bigotry, were opposing Owen, he goes on to say: "The seed you sowed when you were here has taken a deep root. We have been compelled, in order to keep the bigots with us, to separate it . . . from the Union and from you also. . . . I judged it prudent to let the fire you lighted go out, but kept at work with single individuals, where in a shop of a dozen or more they were opposed to it . . . by thus bringing the leading man over, it has brought the whole shop, that shop part of the manufactory . . . they others, so that the undercurrent is working."[2]

The scheme which Owen wished the potters to adopt was, in general terms, co-operative production instead of master and servant production, ownership of the industry by the trade union instead of by a group of capitalist manufacturers.[3] To Owen the pottery trade seemed singularly adapted to the easy working of such a scheme.[4] The Union was very powerful; the industry was practically localised, and the potters themselves were "far in advance of the rest of the trades in a right understanding of the proper means to be adopted for effecting their own deliverance".[5] In the absence of the wholehearted support of

[1] Letters to Robert Owen, Holyoake House; Henry L. Pratt to Owen, November 12, 1833.
[2] Letters to Robert Owen, Holyoake House; Henry L. Pratt to Owen, November 12, 1833.
[3] Letters to Robert Owen, Holyoake House; Simpson to Owen, October 20, 1833; Henry L. Pratt to Owen, November 22, 1833.
[4] *Crisis*, October 19, 1833. [5] *Crisis*, October 19, 1833.

the scheme by all the workers in the industry—had it been given it is not known what would have happened—it is a pity that the few who pressed for it were not able to take the same view of the capabilities of Owen as did many of the middle-class people at the time. The workers remembered New Lanark, but forgot New Harmony; the middle class, or, at any rate, that section of it which spoke through the newspapers, remembered both, but stressed the latter. The potters' officials write to Owen: "We need your advice . . . your practical experience."[1] The *Leeds Mercury* reports: "This projector, after twenty years of unsuccessful exertion to establish his favourite system . . . has at last discovered a fulcrum on which to place that co-operative lever which has to raise the world. . . . [He] . . . has been so obliging as to show us his scheme as formed for the operatives in the Staffordshire Potteries. . . . We strongly suspect that the fate of all Mr. Owen's other schemes to render men rich and happy awaits the one now promulgated".[2] Nothing could be more opposed than the two points of view as expressed in these statements. The innocent non-worldly trust that the potters had in Owen's ability is pathetic to the point of tragedy. It exhibits what is too often seen, the awe which a workman skilled in a craft has for a craft of which he knows nothing. Potters, like other workmen, knew nothing of business, and were awed by those who moved confidently and successfully amongst its mysteries. The middle class who lived with it may have worshipped business, but they did not revere it. A somewhat similar phenomenon is seen in the prestige with which poor people will endow a university person, or

[1] Letters to Robert Owen, Holyoake House; Henry L. Pratt to Owen, November 22, 1833; Simpson to Owen, October 20, 1833.

[2] *Staffordshire Advertiser*, November 16, 1833 (cutting from *Leeds Mercury*).

one that has the chief characteristic of a university training, a speech that is free of dialect.

The trust of the potters' officials in Owen's business ability appears the more pathetic when it is remembered that these men were not incautious dreamers believing without thought the good news that was preached to them. The Union secretary pointed out to Owen that the pottery trade was one which required a large outlay of capital before there were any returns, and asked him what the consequences would be if the masters made a "regular stand" against the scheme.[1] The weight of Owen's "practical experience" evidently crushed these doubts, for shortly afterwards a committee was formed for the projection of the scheme.[2] The Committee called a general meeting for November 13th, which all members of the Potters' Union were invited to attend. At this meeting a series of resolutions, which embodied the rules of the scheme, were put and carried.[3] All of them, in the opinion of a Potters' Union official who was present, were very tactfully worded.[4] The most important of these resolutions was the first, which laid down that measures be taken for the establishment of a co-operative factory for the production of pottery, but that it should be kept quite separate from the affairs of the Potters' Union and have no connection with it.[5] Further meetings were called to enable all the pottery

[1] Letters to Robert Owen, Holyoake House; Simpson to Owen, October 20, 1833.

[2] *Crisis*, December 14, 1833.
Letters to Robert Owen, Holyoake House; Henry L. Pratt to Owen, November 13, 1833.

[3] Letters to Robert Owen, Holyoake House; Henry L. Pratt to Owen, November 13, 1833.
Crisis, December 14, 1833.

[4] Letters to Robert Owen, Holyoake House; Henry L. Pratt to Owen, November 13, 1833.

[5] *Crisis*, December 14, 1833.

districts to be covered, and names were taken of all those who were willing to subscribe.[1] The fact that the scheme had no connexion with the Union was probably the reason why it did not meet with the opposition that its promulgators expected.[2] Had it not been for the danger of a split as already mentioned, the Union itself would have run this scheme. Some time before Stacey, the President of the Union, had been approached by dealers, who promised that, in the event of the Potters' Union manufacturing, they would pay ready money for its ware.[3] Evidently manufacturing by the Union was expected. The co-operative production scheme was not put into practical operation until the following June, and by December it had failed, with a loss eventually to the potters of £1,500.[4] Some confusion seems to have existed as to why the co-operative factory was started. The followers of Owen believed that it was a first step towards dispensing with the services of the master in the industry, whilst others believed that it was but an expedient for coping with unemployment, a profitable method of keeping those potters who otherwise would be idle out of the labour market.[5] The first reason—except probably by Owen—was never, so far as one knows, publicly stated in the pottery districts. The second was the more prevalently believed both by potters and outsiders. As the projectors of the co-operative scheme had to keep their ultimate ideals hidden, such confusion was inevitable.

[1] Letters to Robert Owen, Holyoake House; Henry L. Pratt to Owen, November 13, 1833.
[2] Letters to Robert Owen, Holyoake House; Henry L. Pratt to Owen, November 13, 1833.
[3] Letters to Robert Owen, Holyoake House; Henry L. Pratt to Owen, November 22, 1833.
[4] Letters to Robert Owen, Holyoake House; N. R. Wood to Owen, June 14, 1834.
[5] *Crisis*, October 19, 1833.

To what extent the National Union of Operative Potters became implicated in that greater project of Owen's, the Grand National Consolidated Trades Union, is not clear. When the idea was first broached, at the first Co-operative Congress, the potters' delegates frankly stated that their Union would not give up its independence or merge its identity in any larger body, but it could not object to entering into an alliance with other unions.[1] There the matter rested for a long time. In June 1834, by which time the Grand National Trades Union had been some months in existence, one of Owen's missionaries, who was doing propaganda work in North Staffordshire, wrote to him to the effect that, with a little trouble, the Potters' Union would probably be brought over to the idea of consolidation, and, further, that Simpson, the secretary, offered to get a number of men, such as himself, to form an auxiliary lodge.[2] It is not likely that any auxiliary lodges were formed, and it is less likely that the Union became part of the Grand National Consolidated, for the latter body was already at that time at its last gasp. Queerly enough, many in North Staffordshire must have thought that the Potters' Union was part of the Grand National, for, in a report of a meeting at Hanley, held in protest against the sentence of the Dorchester Labourers, the local newspaper speaks of Stacey, the Grand President of the National Union of Operative Potters, as the Grand Master of the Pottery Branch of the Trades Union.[3] This was a month before Owen's missionary was writing that "the Potters' Union could probably be brought over to the idea of Consolidation".

[1] *Crisis*, October 19, 1833.
[2] Letters to Robert Owen, Holyoake House; N. R. Wood to Owen, June 14, 1834.
[3] *Staffordshire Mercury*, May 24, 1834.

From this time onwards the personal interest of Owen in the affairs of the Potters' Union appears to have ceased. He came again to North Staffordshire, but to preach ideas other than militant trade unionism.[1] From the point of view of material comfort and prosperity Owen's work for the potters was not productive of much good. He came many times amongst them, but there is no reason to believe that he helped to increase the membership of their society, or in any other way to make them more powerful.[2] He brought ideas, but they were productive of dissension and not of unity. What his ultimate influence was cannot be known. One can only speculate whether such and such a workers' policy or action may not have been the result of ideas let loose at the time of Owen's campaign amongst the trade unions. But in that sense men of all trades, and potters no more than others, are his legatees.

[1] Lloyd Jones: *Life Labours of Robert Owen* (3rd ed., 1900), 359 to 364. This visit was in June 1840 and Owen was lecturing on religion.
[2] *Crisis*, October 19, 1833.
Letters to Robert Owen; N. R. Wood to Owen, June 14, 1834; number of members of Potters' Union given the same in both cases.

CHAPTER V

THE STRIKES OF 1834 AND 1836

In the words used at the time to describe the event, the list of minimum selling prices agreed upon by the manufacturers, October 21, 1833, was "stillborn".[1] The list had been drawn up because of the conviction that, unless selling prices were readjusted, the trade would be unable to bear the cost of the increased wages demanded by the men.[2] Agreement to adopt the list had hardly been made before it was dishonoured by its signatories.[3] The failure of the manufacturers to stand by their own selling agreement made the men's fight for the general adoption of the piece-rate list the harder. Many employers sold recklessly and, consequently, learnt experimentally that wages can trench upon capital; but, nevertheless, the men persisted in their campaign for the standard rate, using their only practical weapon, the strike.[4]

In the summer of 1834, almost at the same time as similar movements in other parts of the country, the revolt of the manufacturers against the power of the Union began. The first sign of this revolt was the refusal by three Tunstall employers to continue to pay the Union rate. The contention of the employers was that they had hired their men on Union rates, and that the understanding had been that all other firms were to be compelled to do the same.[5] That understanding had been falsified, and

[1] *Staffordshire Advertiser*, December 13, 1834; letter of "Civis". *Staffordshire Mercury*, October 26, 1833.
[2] *Staffordshire Mercury*, September 21 and 28, 1833.
[3] *Staffordshire Advertiser*, December 13, 1834; letter of "Civis".
[4] *Staffordshire Mercury*, October 19, 1833. *Staffordshire Advertiser*, December 13, 1834.
[5] *Staffordshire Mercury*, August 2, 1834. *Crisis*, October 19, 1833.

consequently they considered that the engagements that they had made were void. Their workmen refused to accept this reasoning and a stoppage occurred. The real blame for the stoppage did not lie with the potters. It is true that there were still many firms not paying Union rates, but their number was being lessened, and the mere fact that the Union had spent on strikes during the previous year no less than £6,223 2s. 11d. proved that it was serious in its efforts to get the list adopted.[1] That it had not fully succeeded was the reason given by the employers for their action, but this was only an excuse. The reason lay with the builders, the farmers, the magistrates and all others who had been stamping down the aspirations of the work-people. Trade unionism in different parts of the country had been receiving shattering blows, and the echoes of them had been heard by the master potters.[2]

From this time onwards the attitude of the manufacturers to the workman and his combination altered. In a space of little over two years their relations with the National Union of Operative Potters changed from genuine respect, and friendship, real or assumed, to undisguised hostility. In the previous winter a member of the Union Board could write of the masters, "They would be glad if we would consent to the foundation of a Council."[3] In the winter following the manufacturers could give as their opinion that unionism was "a system . . . which under the pretence of defending the rights of the workmen destroys their free agency, keeps them in conflict with the masters

[1] Letters to Robert Owen, Holyoake House; N. R. Wood to Owen, June 14, 1834.

[2] Notably in the case of the "Dorchester Labourers", March 1834, and in the "Lock-out of London Builders", July 1834; see Webb: *History of Trade Unionism* (ed. 1920), 138, 150.

[3] Letters to Robert Owen, Holyoake House; Henry L. Pratt to Owen, November 12, 1833.

. . . imposes upon them suffering . . . and [is] destructive to the best interests of the trade".[1] The final stage of hostility to trade unionism was reached toward the end of 1836, when, in reply to a letter sent to them by the Potters' Board of Management, signed by Mark Lancaster, the body representing the manufacturers wrote as follows to the local newspapers: "That the Chamber can only reply to Mr. M. Lancaster individually, as a workman, and not as agent of any secret Board, professing to represent the workmen at large; in which capacity the Chamber cannot recognise either him or them."[2]

It was the anti-unionist feeling throughout Britain which was the source of the Master Potters' assertive spirit and not the sins of the workmen's organisation. In the week following the stoppage at the Tunstall firms a circular was sent out which testified to the source from which the pottery employers derived their courage.[3] After stating that the increase in the wages of the potter was due to trade unionism, the circular goes on to suggest how the price of labour can be made to conform more nearly to the ability of the trade to pay. The suggestion is that trade unionism be destroyed, which, if the masters so willed, could be easily enough done, for, "whilst every other manufacture has successfully resisted Trade Unionism, the Potters alone are signalised by an indolent submission. In no part of the kingdom has a determined resistance to the domination of Unions failed." The circular closes by recommending the document as used by the London

[1] *Staffordshire Advertiser*, February 14, 1834.
[2] *Staffordshire Advertiser*, October 1, 1836.
The Case of the Manufacturers of China and Earthenware in the Staffordshire Potteries, with some Account of the Late Turn Out, its Origin, Proceedings and Termination (1836–37), published by authority of the Chamber of Commerce (pamphlet) (N.D.).
[3] *Staffordshire Advertiser*, August 23, 1834.

Builders to the consideration of the Master Potters. Too much weight should not be given to this circular, for it was not issued by an official body; but it is significant in that it expresses an attitude and ideas that were growing in strength.

Some few days before Martinmas 1834 almost all the Tunstall employers took up the same position as the three of their number already mentioned, expressing their determination to discontinue paying their workpeople the Union rate of wages. They offered to hire on the rates that existed before Martinmas 1833, which were from 30 per cent. to 35 per cent. lower than those fixed by the Union.[1] During the remaining weeks of 1834 no attempt was made to settle the dispute, each side trusting to its fortitude or obstinacy to win its case. Upon nomination day for the January 1835 election several employers hinted at the hustings that they would be willing to have the dispute settled by arbitration, but, when they were reminded of this afterwards by the trade union officials, they said they could do nothing without consultation with their fellow-manufacturers.[2] About the same time Mr. Mason, of Wetley Abbey, a country gentleman, offered himself as arbitrator upon the question at issue. Despite the horror of industrial conflict which they expressed, the employers declined Mr. Mason's offer.[3] The masters then proposed their scheme of arbitration, which was that the whole matter should be handed over for settlement to a body

[1] *Staffordshire Mercury*, November 1, December 6, 1834.
Staffordshire Advertiser, November 22, December 20, 1834.
J. Boyle: "An Account of Strikes in the Potteries in 1834–36", *Journal of Statistical Society*, London, vol. i (1839), 39.
There were also Burslem firms concerned in the dispute. *Staffordshire Mercury*, November 1, 1834; *Staffordshire Advertiser*, December 20, 1834.

[2] *Staffordshire Mercury*, February 28, 1835.

[3] *Staffordshire Mercury*, January 24, 1835.

composed of five manufacturers unconnected with the dispute.[1] This was not quite what the men had understood the word "arbitration" to mean. They thought, perhaps naturally, that their interests would not be adequately represented on a board composed wholly of employers. In their reply declining the offer, the men suggested that, as both employers and employees were concerned in the dispute, a board equally representing both parties would be more suitable. To such a board they would agree to submit their case, but not to one composed solely of employers.[2] Unfortunately this suggested board did not appear to the masters to be any more equitable in its composition than theirs had done to the men, and they rejected it on the stated grounds "that the men who might be selected would not feel themselves independent, but act on the direction of the Union".[3]

A deadlock having been reached and the next move being with them, the employers concerned in the dispute called a meeting for January 23rd, to which all the manufacturers in the trade were invited. This meeting, having first expressed its cordial approval of the offer rejected by the men to submit the case to the arbitration of five manufacturers, formed a committee to revise the list of prices which the employers in the dispute had submitted to it for consideration and revision. The committee revised the list and submitted it to another general meeting of manufacturers, which approved of it. It was then placed before the workmen and rejected by them.[4] At another

[1] *Staffordshire Advertiser*, January 31, 1835.
J. Boyle: "An Account of Strikes in the Potteries in 1834–36", *Journal of Statistical Society*, London, vol. i (1839), 39.
[2] *Staffordshire Advertiser*, January 31, 1835.
[3] *Staffordshire Advertiser*, January 31, 1835.
[4] *Staffordshire Advertiser*, February 14, 1835.
J. Boyle: "An Account of Strikes in the Potteries in 1834–36", *Journal of Statistical Society*, London, vol. i (1839), 39–40.

general meeting of the employers it was decided to ask the workmen to agree to the formation of a committee composed of equal numbers of men and masters, and, under the chairmanship of a retired master potter, to go over the late committee's list and make in it any alterations deemed desirable. The decisions of this body were to be binding upon both parties to the dispute.[1] This offer the men, in rather impatient language, refused, stating definitely that their own list was a fair one, and that they intended to have it accepted without modification.[2] This obstinacy on the part of the men is understandable when it is remembered that the chairman of the manufacturers' meeting, and the committee men appointed by that meeting, represented firms that paid better prices than those on the list of which they had approved. After all, it must have appeared ridiculous to the working potters that committee men should approve of less prices being paid by those whom they served than they themselves gave.[3] When some months before the Union had expressed willingness to defer the question at issue to arbitration, it would only have been because it was certain that any impartial umpire would have tried in his award to make working prices uniform throughout the trade.[4]

With the refusal of the workmen to accept any modification of their list, negotiations broke down, and shortly

[1] J. Boyle: "An Account of Strikes in the Potteries in 1834–36", *Journal of Statistical Society*, London, vol. i (1839), 39–40. *Staffordshire Advertiser*, February 14, 1835.

[2] *Staffordshire Advertiser*, February 14, 1835. J. Boyle: "An Account of Strikes in the Potteries in 1834–36", *Journal of Statistical Society*, London, vol. i (1839), 39–40.

[3] J. Boyle: "An Account of Strikes in the Potteries in 1834–36", *Journal of Statistical Society*, London, vol. i (1839), 39.

[4] *Staffordshire Mercury*, January 24, 1835.

afterwards the factories reopened on the Union's terms.[1] This successful strike checked the revolt of the employers, but it was only a temporary setback, for they were by this time definitely in line with the other members of their class throughout the country in being uncompromisingly and actively hostile to militant trade unionism. At their last general meeting before the close of the strike they made the threat that, if the present system of trade unionism continued, they would "employ every means which they may possess to counteract the efforts which may be made to dictate what prices they shall pay".[2] Although it does not appear that the Potters' Union pursued any different policy during 1835 than it had done during the previous year, yet it was accused by the employers of being elated at its victory and of thinking that nothing could withstand its will. According to the accusation it would make certain demands upon a particular firm, and if they were not immediately conceded the workmen would be withdrawn. Its leaders were charged with assuming to decide all matters relating to employer and employed.[3] But these things were not 1835 phenomena. The Union leaders had always deemed all matters concerned in the relationship between potter and master potter to be their business, and from the time of the birth of the Union the industry had never been free of strikes that violated agreements.[4] Naturally the Union felt elated after so great a victory, but the great change in the industrial relationship had been made by

[1] *Staffordshire Advertiser*, February 28, March 1, 1835.
J. Boyle: "An Account of Strikes in the Potteries in 1834–36", *Journal of Statistical Society*, London, vol. i (1839), 40.
[2] *Staffordshire Advertiser*, February 14, 1835.
[3] J. Boyle: "An Account of Strikes in the Potteries in 1834–36", *Journal of Statistical Society*, London, vol. i (1839), 40–1.
[4] Letters to Robert Owen, Holyoake House; Henry L. Pratt to Owen, November 12, 1833.
Staffordshire Mercury, July 13, 1833.

the masters. In 1833 they shared with their class in its fear and panic, and in 1835 they wished to share in its triumph.

In the beginnings of the Union the reputable manufacturers saw in the action of the men the laudable attempt to make the price of labour the same to all buyers.[1] A few years later the same manufacturers saw in the same action an attempt to interfere in the legitimate business of the master. "Any stick is good enough to beat a dog with" was now the implied belief of the employers respecting trade unions. The fact that Robert Owen had several times visited the potters was used as condemnatory evidence against the Union. The men were accused of extending and enforcing their organisation "upon the model of the Lanark system", which, though it means nothing, sounds impressive, and probably implied something which was thought wicked and desperate.[2]

In August 1835 some cases of dispute between potters and their employers were heard before Captain Powys and the Rev. J. Sneyd, two magistrates for the county, which are important as indicating the trend of affairs.[3] The first charge preferred was that of Messrs. Chetham and Robinson against eighteen of their workmen for leaving their work, and twelve of them were convicted. The next charge was brought by Mr. Hawley against twenty-eight of his men, who, though hired to serve until Martinmas, had left without just cause. Fifteen of these men had been com-

[1] *Staffordshire Mercury*, June 15, July 13, 1833.
Letters to Robert Owen, Holyoake House; R. G. to Editor of *Crisis*, September 24, 1833.

[2] *The Case of the Manufacturers of China and Earthenware in the Staffordshire Potteries, with some Account of the Late Turn Out, its Origin, Proceedings and Termination*, 1836–37, published by authority of the Chamber of Commerce (pamphlet) (N.D.).

[3] *The Times*, August 22, 1835 (cutting from *Wolverhampton Chronicle*).

mitted for three months for leaving Mr. Hawley's employ in the previous April, and they were now charged for not having returned to their work at the expiration of their imprisonment. The defendants refused to return to their work, and were sentenced to three months' imprisonment. After the above cases had been disposed of four other potters were charged with the offence of intimidation. It was stated in evidence that the firms of John Mayer, Goodwin, and Messrs. Knight and Elkin had raised the prices to their workpeople in consequence of the defendants who had "acted as plenipotentiaries of the men". It was pleaded that no threats had been used or acts of intimidation committed, but the Rev. J. Sneyd brushed the defence on one side and said that "it matters little whether the language was mild or otherwise when the intention was so apparent". Two of the men were sentenced to be imprisoned for two months, one for one month and one for fourteen days. In all thirty men were sentenced to imprisonment. Judging from these cases it would appear the Union was not the only party in the pottery trade making extravagant claims, for it is hardly possible to imagine a claim more extravagant than that made by the Rev. J. Sneyd, that the meaning of intimidation is apparent intent to intimidate.

In March 1836 the pottery manufacturers formed themselves into a Chamber of Commerce.[1] The formation of this body was avowedly a mobilisation of the employers' forces to fight the Union. The threat of 1835 had become a reality. In a statement of one of its members "the professed object [of the Chamber] was to protect the general

[1] Really a rebuilding of the 1830 Chamber.
The Case of the Manufacturers of China and Earthenware in the Staffordshire Potteries with some Account of the Late Turn Out, its Origin, Proceedings and Termination, 1836–37 (N.D.).
J. Boyle: "An Account of Strikes in the Potteries in 1834–36", *Journal of Statistical Society*, London, vol. i (1839), 41.

interests of the trade, but virtually to counteract the effect of the proceedings of the workmen".[1] It is a singular fact, and one which leaves itself open to cynical observation, that employers whose combination for the regulation of selling prices was "stillborn" formed an organisation to fight their employees which proved to be very efficient. Shortly after this the Union intimated its intention of abolishing the systems of "annual hiring" and "good from oven", substituting for the former engagements terminable with one month's notice on either side, and for the latter the system of "good from hand".[2] In an effort to realise these demands the men at thirteen manufactories in Tunstall and Burslem struck work during August of this year.[3] They were emboldened to do this because a short time before the Union had, by means of the strike, compelled Messrs. Adams, of Tunstall, a very important firm, to submit to those same demands.[4] Either there was some error in the carrying out of the Union's strike orders, and men were called out from firms where the Union had intended that no strike should occur, or, as seems more probable, the strike was called precisely as ordered, but, having begun, the Union discovered that

[1] J. Boyle: "An Account of Strikes in the Potteries in 1834–36" *Journal of Statistical Society*, London, vol. i (1839), 41.

[2] *Staffordshire Advertiser*, September 17, 1836.
J. Boyle: "An Account of Strikes in the Potteries in 1834–36", *Journal of Statistical Society*, London, vol. i (1839), 42.
The Case of the Manufacturers of China and Earthenware in the Staffordshire Potteries with some Account of the Late Turn Out, its Origin, Proceedings and Termination, 1836–37 (N.D.).

[3] *Staffordshire Advertiser*, September 17, 1836.
(*Staffordshire Advertiser*, September 10, gives eighteen firms; evidently some rapidly gave way to the men.)

[4] *The Case of the Manufacturers of China and Earthenware in the Staffordshire Potteries with some Account of the Late Turn Out, its Origin, Proceedings and Termination*, 1836–37, published by authority of the Chamber of Commerce (pamphlet) (N.D.).

the strikers from some firms were unreliable and likely to be a source of weakness, in which case it was better that they should be at work. But, whatever the reason, the Union ordered the hands at some of the firms to go back to work. This the masters would not allow, except on the condition that the men from all the striking firms went back, and to this the Union would not agree.[1] On September 9th the manufacturers, through their Chamber of Commerce, publicly intimated that hirings for the year commencing November 11th would be on an agreement containing a clause guaranteed to protect them in future from the aggressions of the Union. This clause, which to ensure its legality was drawn up under the advice of counsel and magistrates, gave the master power at any time to suspend his workmen. Thus the employers would be able to make a partial strike into a general lock-out by suspending their employees.[2]

The powers thus taken by the masters were such as, according to workaday ethics, it was quite legitimate for them to use in times of industrial war, but they could also be used, and unfairly, in a time of declared peace. The agreement offered too ideal an instrument for victimisation for it to be employed by any employer as he liked. Under it a master could suspend his workman, wait until he got another situation, recall him and suspend him

[1] *The Case of the Manufacturers of China and Earthenware in the Staffordshire Potteries with some Account of the Late Turn Out, its Origin, Proceedings and Termination*, 1836–37, published by authority of the Chamber of Commerce (pamphlet) (N.D.).

[2] *Staffordshire Advertiser*, September 17, 1836.

J. Boyle: "An Account of Strikes in the Potteries in 1834–36", *Journal of Statistical Society*, London, vol. i (1839), 42.

The Case of the Manufacturers of China and Earthenware in the Staffordshire Potteries with some Account of the Late Turn Out, its Origin, Proceedings and Termination, 1836–37 (pamphlet) (N.D.).

again. A master could thus keep a workman he did not like unemployed from one Martinmas to the next, when the man would be free and could hope to get engaged by a less unscrupulous employer. It is not surprising that the men spoke of this clause as being "Hell-invented".[1] Although thirteen manufactories were out at the end of August, it was known that the real struggle would not begin until November 11th, when all engagements of service expired. It would have to be decided then which form of agreement should rule throughout the trade—the Union's with its abolition of "good from oven" and "annual hiring", or that of the Chamber of Commerce with its suspension clause.

Shortly after their public declaration of September 9th the Chamber received a letter from the Union's Board of Management, suggesting that a conference of representatives of men and masters should be held and the questions at issue decided by conciliation.[2] In the public reply made by the Chamber to this communication the proposal for a conference was refused, and the statement made that, while the manufacturers could not have any dealings with a secret Board, they were quite prepared to deal with the workmen as individuals and give them any information that they might desire.[3] The workmen were silent regarding this offer, which fact the employers, with affected surprise, afterwards recorded as proof that they were all united in

[1] *The Case of the Manufacturers of China and Earthenware in the Staffordshire Potteries with some Account of the Late Turn Out, its Origin, Proceedings and Termination*, 1836–37 (pamphlet) (N.D.).
[2] *Staffordshire Advertiser*, October 1, 1836.
Report from the Select Committee on Masters and Operatives (*Equitable Councils of Conciliation*), evidence Maitland (1856), 219.
[3] *Staffordshire Advertiser*, October 1, 1836.
The Case of the Manufacturers of China and Earthenware in the Staffordshire Potteries with some Account of the Late Turn Out, its Origin, Proceedings and Termination (pamphlet) (N.D.).

the secret Board.[1] Very soon after the rejection of their offer to submit the dispute to conciliation the Union sent delegates into different parts of the country to solicit aid for the strikers. In some of the districts visited the delegates distributed handbills containing matter of a rather sensational kind. In one put forth at Liverpool the masters were said to be "starving their penniless men, to oblige their submission to the most arbitrary and diabolical laws ever conceived by Christians", and the public were exhorted "not to stand by and wink upon the bloody deed". Naturally the employers described these handbills as being disgraceful, of an inflammatory character and quite foreign to the facts.[2]

On October 13th the Chamber of Commerce issued a public statement in its defence.[3] This was followed on December 7th by another statement of a similar character, and with the same end in view, to prevent public sympathy with the potters.[4] In the interval between these two statements Martinmas had arrived, and as neither masters nor

[1] *The Case of the Manufacturers of China and Earthenware in the Staffordshire Potteries with some Account of the Late Turn Out, its Origin, Proceedings and Termination* (pamphlet) (N.D.).

[2] *The Case of the Manufacturers of China and Earthenware in the Staffordshire Potteries with some Account of the Late Turn Out, its Origin, Proceedings and Termination* (pamphlet) (N.D.).

The Times, December 6, 1836 (cutting from *Staffordshire Advertiser*).

The Case of the Manufacturers of China and Earthenware in the Staffordshire Potteries with some Account of the Late Turn Out, its Origin, Proceedings and Termination (pamphlet) (N.D.)

[3] *The Case of the Manufacturers of China and Earthenware in the Staffordshire Potteries with some Account of the Late Turn Out, its Origin, Proceedings and Termination* (pamphlet) (N.D.).

[4] *The Case of the Manufacturers of China and Earthenware in the Staffordshire Potteries with some Account of the Late Turn Out, its Origin, Proceedings and Termination* (pamphlet) (N.D.).

It is interesting to note that one of the gentry, Sir C. Wolseley, Bart., sent £2 to the strikers.—*Staffordshire Advertiser*, November 19, 1836.

men had agreed to the other's form of hiring, practically the whole industry was at a standstill.[1] Before the general stoppage of November 11th proved otherwise, it is fairly evident that the men did not think that the employers would hold together in the Chamber of Commerce.[2] Naturally it would be assumed that hatred of trade unions would not bind men of business together when arrangements of commercial advantage had failed to do so. In this the men were mistaken. The members of the Chamber showed an absence of self-seeking and a desire to work for the associated good which must have surprised the journeyman potter. The Chamber comprised numerically nearly three-quarters of the Staffordshire manufacturers and, in extent of business, a much greater proportion. All the large houses, with one or perhaps two exceptions, were included.[3] Those employers not in the Chamber yielded to the demands of the men and kept their factories at work. Through the whole course of the strike defections from the Union were occurring, and men were hiring on the Chamber of Commerce agreement.[4] Nevertheless, the employers who were combined refused to allow the factory of any one of their number to open until all were ready to start. The suffering of the potters was considerable, for the subscriptions and loans, large as they were, only permitted of a few

[1] *The Times*, November 15, 1836 (cutting from *Manchester Herald*). *Staffordshire Advertiser*, November 19, 1836.

[2] J. Boyle: "An Account of Strikes in the Potteries in 1834–36", *Journal of Statistical Society*, London, vol. i (1839), 43.

[3] J. Boyle: "An Account of Strikes in the Potteries in 1834–36", *Journal of Statistical Society*, London, vol. i (1839), 43.
Staffordshire Advertiser, September 17, 1836.
The Case of the Manufacturers of China and Earthenware in the Staffordshire Potteries, with some Account of the Late Turn Out, its Origin, Proceedings and Termination 1836–37 (pamphlet) (N.D.).

[4] *The Times*, November 29, December 6, December 13, 1836 (cuttings from *Staffordshire Advertiser*).
Staffordshire Advertiser, November 12, November 19, 1836.

shillings per week to each member of the Union.[1] Non-unionists, of course, got nothing. During the progress of the strike the number of non-unionists grew, for all men who signed the Chamber of Commerce agreement were immediately expelled from the Society.[2] Withdrawals from the Union were almost certainly encouraged by the publication of a statement to the effect that all those who, because of signing the Chamber of Commerce agreement, had been cast off by the Union, would, if the strike continued, be afforded relief by the employers.[3] Whether the publication of this statement was a subtle movement of the masters to promote disaffection amongst the working potters, or whether it was merely the putting into print of a journalist's invention, is not known. At any rate, the manufacturers did not contradict the statement nor "afford the relief", although the strike lasted for another month.

No negotiations of any kind took place between employers and employees from the beginning of the dispute until December 30th, when a conference took place between the three parties concerned: the unionists who were striking, the non-unionists who were locked out and the manufacturers.[4] Before the employers would consent to this meeting the Union had to give a pledge that no member of its Board of Management was to be amongst its representatives. That the Chamber of Commerce was able on the one hand to insist that non-unionists should be represented, and on the other that the unionists were not to be represented by any of their own officers, shows that

[1] *The Times*, December 6, 1836 (cutting from *Staffordshire Advertiser*)
[2] *The Times*, November 29, December 6, 1836 (cuttings from *Staffordshire Advertiser*).
[3] *The Times*, December 6, 1836 (cutting from *Staffordshire Advertiser*).
[4] *The Case of the Manufacturers of China and Earthenware in the Staffordshire Potteries, with some Account of the Late Turn Out, its Origin, Proceedings and Termination*, 1836–37 (pamphlet) (N.D.).

it had the powers of settlement well in its grasp. But that a conference should be held at all, even on terms so derogatory to the dignity of the Union, would lead one to suppose that the strikers were not completely beaten. It is not usual to discuss terms of settlement with a defeated enemy; they are dictated. In a pamphlet published by the manufacturers shortly after the termination of the stoppage,[1] the reason given for the holding of a conference was because of a request of the "independent" workmen to come to an understanding with the employers. On the face of it such a reason seems strange, for the "independent" workmen, by signing the Chamber of Commerce agreement, had already come to terms with their masters. There appears to be this much truth in it, that when hirings on the Chamber's agreement took place—and there were no other hirings—the promise to discuss grievances was given.

It was thus a case with the non-unionists of discussion after surrender, but that was a position never taken by members of the Union. J. Boyle, writing April 16, 1835,[2] makes no mention of the conference, but he was definitely partial and had purposes in view other than the recording of facts. He was out to persuade the 1838 Trade Union Commissioners to the belief that unionism damaged trade, irritated the manufacturers and was useless in fulfilling its avowed objects of protecting the workman and bettering his condition.[3] From the facts that are known it may be safely assumed that the Union, though sufficiently beaten as to acquiesce in the dictation by the Chamber of the conditions of procedure that were to rule the pro-

[1] *The Case of the Manufacturers of China and Earthenware in the Staffordshire Potteries, with some Account of the Late Turn Out, its Origin, Proceedings and Termination*, 1836–37 (pamphlet) (N.D.).
[2] J. Boyle: "An Account of Strikes in the Potteries in 1834–36", *Journal of Statistical Society*, London, vol. i (1839).
[3] *Weekly Herald*, May 6, 1838.

posed conference, had yet enough stubbornness to be able, if need be, to keep the industry at a standstill for some time longer. This the Chamber knew, and would propose a conference with the idea of hastening a settlement. It is hardly likely that a meeting of manufacturers and men would be proposed for any other reason than to get the industry restarted.

On December 29th, the day previous to the conference, a note was presented to the Chamber of Commerce, which was then sitting, signed by seven persons representing themselves to be delegates from Bristol, Sheffield, Birmingham, Worcester, Glasgow, Manchester and Huddersfield, and stating that they and many other delegates from various parts of the Empire had assembled at Hanley to investigate the position of the working potter, and adding that if something were not speedily done national means would be taken in aid of the workmen. As the signatories to the note were in attendance, they were called in, interviewed by the Chamber and told of the conference to be held at Betley the following day, an invitation to attend being given them.[1] At the hour arranged, on October 30th, eight manufacturers, six non-unionists and six unionist workmen met at Betley, in the presence of Francis Twemlow and George Tollet, county magistrates who were acting as mediators and had no power of arbitration. The legal adviser and the secretary of the Union came, but they were both compelled to withdraw. It appeared that the condition of conference, that the unionists should have no member of their Board of Management to represent them, had been evaded. All the unionist representatives were Board members who had vacated their office for the

[1] *The Case of the Manufacturers of China and Earthenware in the Staffordshire Potteries, with some Account of the Late Turn Out, its Origin, Proceedings and Termination*, 1836–37 (pamphlet) (N.D.).

day. Technically they were private members, and as such were allowed to remain. The seven delegates who had the day before interviewed the Chamber came to the conference accompanied by the rest of their number—forty in all. They were told that they would be allowed to be present, but only on condition that they were spectators and took no part in the proceedings.[1] Whether the presence of these delegates influenced the course of the conference it is impossible to say. That they were there at all seems rather singular. The end of 1836 is generally understood to have been a dead time for trade unionism, and that there should have been sufficient solidarity between the workers of different trades as to send delegates from the length and breadth of the land to watch over the interests of the potter seems to contradict the usual ideas concerning that period.[2]

At the close of the conference it was understood that the manufacturers were to report to the Chamber and the workmen to their fellows the results of the deliberations. The Chamber met on the following day—December 31st —and, after receiving the report of its representatives, immediately resolved on modifying its form of hiring agreement so as to meet, as far as possible, the objections urged by the men. The results arrived at by the conference were not satisfactory to the Union, and when the Chamber met on January 20th there were still nine factories unable to recommence work. At its next meeting on the 24th there

[1] *The Case of the Manufacturers of China and Earthenware in the Staffordshire Potteries, with some Account of the Late Turn Out, its Origin, Proceedings and Termination*, 1836–37 (pamphlet) (N.D.).

[2] G. D. H. Cole: *Organised Labour* (1924), 4. "By the end of 1834" the Trades Union "had vanished, leaving behind it only an increased number of local Trade Clubs and a few National Trade Unions on a craft basis which held together after the general collapse. The lock-out and the 'document' had forced the working class to its knees."

were only two factories unprepared, but it still adhered to its resolution that all members should be ready before any should start. The Chamber met again on the 27th, when it appeared that all its members were ready, so preparations to resume business were forthwith commenced.[1]

The concessions obtained by the men as a result of this strike were fairly considerable.[2] The hiring agreement was altered so as to guarantee the potter sixteen days' work per month at least, in place of the uncertainty which before existed, and, in case the employer from some cause was prevented from finding the stipulated amount of work, the man had the power to dissolve the contract by giving a month's notice. The "good from oven" system was retained, but with alterations. Ware for which the workman was not paid was to be broken. Before this a master was able to refuse to pay his workman for certain ware on the plea that it was badly made, and yet obtain the full price for it from his customers. All browned ware, and that damaged by others than the maker, was also to be paid for. Furthermore, the men were to be allowed to draw weekly on account a sum equal to two-thirds the value of the ware they had on the premises unfired, and a balance struck at stated periods, instead of, as previously, having low, high or no wages, as best suited the convenience of the employer.[3] These concessions were important, and

[1] *The Case of the Manufacturers of China and Earthenware in the Staffordshire Potteries, with some Account of the Late Turn Out, its Origin, Proceedings and Termination*, 1836–37 (pamphlet) (N.D.).

[2] *Potters' Examiner*, January 14, 1844.
Staffordshire Advertiser, October 13, 1850.
Report from the Select Committee on Masters and Operatives (*Equitable Councils of Conciliation*), evidence Maitland (1856), 219.

[3] *Pottery Mercury*, June 22, 1825.
Potters' Examiner, January 14, 1844.

it would seem that the Potters' Union in 1836–7 had conducted a successful strike. Actually the strike was disastrous; it had gained for the men certain objects, but it had lost them the Union;[1] for, with the resumption of work, the National Union of Operative Potters did not show signs of recovering from the weak state into which the costliness and long duration of the strike had inevitably thrown it, but on the contrary its members' confidence in it waned, dissension came, it grew feeble, staggered and died.[2]

Two questions force themselves to the front. First, how was a defeated Union able to gain concessions from the employers? and second, why, having obtained concessions, did the potters let the Union die? From the beginning of the struggle there seem to have been weaknesses in the Potters' Union. It was a good fighting machine for guerilla warfare, but when it was engaged in a campaign in which almost the whole army of the enemy was arranged against it, defects showed themselves. The controllers of the machine were conscious of these defects, but they did not appear to know how to remedy them.[3] In the preliminary engagement weaknesses in the Union had been shown, in spite of which its members entered into the larger struggle. The men counted upon the masters also having weaknesses, but to rely on that expectation was to place too much reliance upon good fortune. The struggle proper began on November 11th, and almost immediately there were losses in Union membership. It does not seem that these losses were occasioned by members deliberately

[1] *Report of Royal Commission on Trade Unions*, evidence Hollins (1867–68), 86.

[2] *Potters' Examiner*, December 28, 1844.

[3] *The Case of the Manufacturers of China and Earthenware in the Staffordshire Potteries, with some Account of the Late Turn Out, its Origin, Proceedings and Termination*, 1836–37 (pamphlet) (N.D.).

deserting, but rather by their being expelled. As the stoppage continued the Union found itself compelled to expel more and more of its members.[1] In an ordinary strike those workers who accepted the masters' terms would immediately commence work, but in this case the masters made that impossible. They had arranged that no firm should recommence business until all were ready, with the result that, so long as there were enough men in the Union to hold up one factory, the whole industry was at a standstill. The Union was thus at the time of the conference able to exact good terms from the masters, although numerically it was then very weak. That having obtained good terms it still kept on with the strike was folly on its part, for it obtained no further concessions, and further desertions from its ranks compelled it eventually to capitulate. The same circumstance that enabled the Union, though weak, to obtain concessions, also put it in bad odour with a large number of potters. For weeks before the resumption of work some men, although they personally had come to terms with their employers, had been kept idling and enduring starvation because of the obstinacy of the Union. That the Union had brought them misery was terribly apparent; that it had also brought them concessions was not so clearly seen.

To complete the answers to the above questions the objects of the strike must be kept in mind; it was for alterations in certain trade customs; there was no wage question at issue. Furthermore, only two branches of the trade came under one of the customs in dispute; other workers in the trade were unaffected.[2] Had the strike been for a rise in wages, an object applying to all, and one

[1] *The Times*, November 29, December 13, 1836 (cuttings from *Staffordshire Advertiser*).
[2] Hollow-ware Pressers and Flat Pressers.

which all could appreciate, its course and result would probably have been different. The Union's first error was in fighting for objects the attainment of which would not directly affect the pockets of its members.[1] The strike once started, a further error was made—that of keeping on in the face of huge losses in membership. Its first duty was to keep itself alive. Fighting to the last man may be glorious, but it is bad generalship.

Before closing this account of the 1836–7 strike a tribute should be paid to the way in which the officials of the Union conducted their publicity campaign, as it would now be called. It was admirably managed. Potters' delegates covered the whole of the country soliciting sympathy for the strikers, and the huge sums which were sent to their aid were a testimony to their hard work and ability.

[1] Good from oven affected the pockets of those who worked under that system, but even of those many would be affected very little. It was the fact that the workman was subject to losses when he ought not to have been, rather than the actual loss, which made of good from oven a source of permanent grievance.

NOTE:—The following extract from *A History of the English Poor Law*, 1904 ed., vol. ii., 327, Sir George Nicholls, is of interest in connexion with the strike of 1836–37.

"Stoke-upon-Trent was the first manufacturing town placed under a Board of Guardians. The order for that purpose was issued on the 31st of March, 1836. . . . The Guardians . . . thus found themselves . . . involved in difficulty, and . . . applied to the Commissioners for advice. They were told . . . that so long as there was room in the workhouse, no able-bodied applicant ought to be relieved out of it. . . . Whenever the workhouse was full, out-relief in kind might be afforded, . . . no break of the peace or serious disturbance took place . . . although the resources of the operatives were much reduced . . . and the stagnation of trade which afterwards took place, threw numbers out of employment, the machinery of the new law was equal to the emergency."

CHAPTER VI

THE UNITED BRANCHES

After the close of the 1836–7 strike little more was heard of the National Union of Operative Potters. It was shattered by the struggle, and killed by the atmosphere of suspicion which followed it.[1] Had the Union survived, it is almost certain that for many years it would, in any case, have been weak. In 1837 it learnt experimentally what afterwards became general knowledge, that a union with but purely trade benefits stands a great risk of collapsing in a time of adversity. A fighting union cannot expect to get recruits when those to whom it makes its appeal want above all things industrial peace. To appreciate the excessive war weariness of the potters at this time it must be remembered that thousands of them had been made to endure terrible suffering for weeks after they had been starved into surrender.[2] Had the struggle finished when the majority were wearied of it, the reaction against fighting would not have been so great. A relatively small number of men had kept the strike on long enough to obtain concessions from the employers. A small number had continued it in the hope of getting still better terms and failed. In the meantime, the majority of potters stood by suffering, and wanting nothing except to get back to work. How many men in the early days of the strike hired on the employers' terms it is impossible to say with accuracy, but on November 10th, the last day of the potters' year, the Chamber stated that out of a total of sixty-four seven of their members had fully hired their

[1] *Potters' Examiner*, December 28, 1844.
[2] *Children's Employment (Trades and Manufactures) Commission*, (1843), C.3, report by Scriven.

men, and twenty other members had partially done so.[1] By the first week of December the Union had but 1,400 members on its funds, which, if it is estimated that 1,300 were at work, means that since the beginning of the dispute it had lost over one-half of its members.[2] This was six weeks before the end of the strike, during which time the membership losses of the Union greatly increased. It is not surprising that when work was eventually resumed the men for whom peace had been too long deferred revenged themselves by smashing the Union.

The National Union of Operative Potters had to come to an end, but a gallant attempt was made by the few staunch men who composed its remnants to pay off the debts which it had incurred.[3] These debts were fairly considerable; the Sheffield trades had lent £2,193, the London trades £800, making, with the addition of a few smaller amounts owing elsewhere, a total of £3,383. Besides this sum there was £2,563 owing to various potters either for money lent to the Union or for claims withheld.[4] The few men who tackled the problem of clearing the debt went about the matter in a businesslike way. Public meetings were called, committees formed and a general and financial secretary appointed. Some hundreds of pounds were received by the debt committees and sent by them to local and outside claimants. Monthly printed reports, which gave satisfaction to both payers and

1 *Staffordshire Advertiser*, November 12, 1836.

2 *The Times*, December 13, 1836 (cuttings from *Staffordshire Advertiser*). Seven-ninths of the men were employees of members of the Chamber. The employees of non-members remained at work and presumably kept in the Union. A very rough calculation makes 2,700 in the Union out of an original 6,000.

J. Boyle: "An Account of Strikes in the Potteries in 1834–36", *Journal of Statistical Society*, London, vol. i (1839), 43.

3 *Potters' Examiner*, December 28, 1844.

4 *Potters' Examiner*, December 19, 1843; December 21, 1844.

receivers, were prepared and distributed by the secretary, Robert Glasse. After a short time the distrust and suspicion, which seem to be inevitably associated with the reaction from strife, strangled these committees. The bad depression in trade which came soon afterwards made their resuscitation impossible.[1]

With this depression the potters entered into what is perhaps the most hopeless period in their history. From the end of 1837 to the year 1842 trade was almost consistently bad, hosts of potters during that time were out of work, and almost all were thrown on short time.[2] The employers were now able to take a mean revenge for the indignities they had suffered at the hands of organised labour. This the more unscrupulous of them did. One man who, in the opinion of his employer, busied himself too much in labour questions was dismissed from his work, and, as other employers had agreed not to engage him, he and his family were driven into the Poor House. He obtained employment again, 'but it was for a master who was not a party to a Gentlemen's Agreement to watch dangerous men.'[3] Men who were known to be friends and adherents of Owen were dismissed from their employment.[4] In the June 4, 1842, number of the *New Moral World* there is a letter from a resident of the Potteries saying: ". . . our friends . . . will be glad to hear that I am no longer under the ban of proscription, but have obtained a situation at my former employment. . . ." In fairness to the employers

[1] *Staffordshire Advertiser*, October 15, 1836.
Staffordshire Mercury, August 3, 1833.

[2] *Potters' Examiner*, December 28, 1844.
Lloyd Jones: *The Life, Times and Labours of Robert Owen* (ed. 1900), 361.
J. Ward: *History of Borough of Stoke-on-Trent* (1846), 67.

[3] Old Potter: *When I was a Child* (1903), 90, 117.

[4] Lloyd Jones: *The Life, Times and Labours of Robert Owen* (ed. 1900), 361.

it must be remembered that the motives for dismissing Owenites were mixed. It is as likely that they were dismissed upon sincere, though bigoted, religious grounds as for revenge for previous labour activities.[1] It is hard to discover the motive, probably in some cases both operated, and, in any case, an unscrupulous employer would find it convenient to have a religious reason for dismissing a man who had disturbed the harmonious relationship of master and servant.

With the breakdown of unionism the concessions which were given to the men as a result of the 1836–7 dispute were in many instances withdrawn.[2] Many of the employers had from the first objected to making these concessions, and had only agreed to them after much wrangling with their fellows. Immediately it was possible to do so they reverted to the old practices of the trade.[3] If the greatest sorrow is the memory of happier things, then the thinking potters of 1838 were living in tragedy. It was not that their material conditions were particularly bad, though there was a great deal of unemployment, for wages compared very favourably with those of workers in other trades. The tragedy lay in the change which had taken place in the relation of the potter to his industry. In 1836 the potters had thought that workers' control of industry was near realisation, but in 1838 even the least pessimistic of their number must have thought that, despite the theorists, the control of industry was inseparable from ownership. It is probable that this change was more apparent than real, for it is unlikely that the potters at any time came as near to controlling their industry as

[1] Lloyd Jones: *The Life, Times and Labours of Robert Owen* (ed. 1900), 361.
[2] *Potters' Examiner*, January 14, 1844.
[3] *Potters' Examiner*, January 14, 1844.

many of them in the middle 'thirties had believed. The National Union of Operative Potters had opposed the claim of the employers to hire and discharge at their pleasure.[1] Its minor demands in the dispute of 1836–37, the equitable distribution of best work and the limitation of apprentices were attempts further to encroach in the sphere of control. But the more solid achievements of the Union had been in the field of wages. Attempts to "interfere with the business of the master", as workers' control was then called, were less successful. Nevertheless, the tragedy of the change remained. In 1836 the potter was firm in the belief that he had the right and the power to interfere with the conduct of his industry, but by 1838 he had become convinced that, whatever his rights, he was helpless before the power of the employer.

During this period of depression in trade and helplessness of the men, the "Allowance System" was extensively practised. Under this system the wages of the workman were reduced without, in theory, reducing the prices at which he worked. From his gross wage the workman "allowed" to his master 2d., 3d., or 4d. in the shilling.[2]

The Allowance System, though startling upon first acquaintance, and giving the appearance of being a subtle invention of the masters to reduce the wages of the individual without interfering with the collectively arranged price, is actually nothing more than could, from the conditions of the trade, under certain circumstances, be expected to happen. Although most flagrant in the late 'thirties and early 'forties, its practice is not peculiar to that period, for it persisted, though to a slight extent,

[1] J. Boyle: "An Account of Strikes in the Potteries in 1834–36", *Journal of Statistical Society*, London, vol. i (1839), 41.
Staffordshire Advertiser, October 15, 1836.
Staffordshire Mercury, August 3, 1833.

[2] *Potters' Examiner*, January 4, 1845.

almost to the present time.[1] The Allowance System was an evil which grew out of the conditions of apprenticeship. In the early days of the pottery industry the apprentice was indentured to serve his master for seven years, during which time he was paid a small weekly wage irrespective of the amount of work done. Long before the 'forties the system of giving the apprentice a fixed weekly wage had almost died out, and he was made, like the journeyman, into a pieceworker. After becoming a pieceworker the apprentice throughout his period of service, and as a condition of it, would allow a few pence to his master out of every shilling which he earned.[2] In some cases the apprentice allowed 4d. in the shilling throughout his seven years' service; in others he allowed 6d. in the shilling during the first few years, then 4d. and during his last year 2d. In the clay departments the former practice—4d. in the shilling throughout the whole term of apprenticeship—was the more general. It is obvious that under such a system the employment of apprentices was a very profitable business to the master,[3] the money allowed by the apprentice each week being a clear gain to him, for, like the journeyman, the apprentice was paid only for what he made. Occasionally a journeyman would be given well-paid work to make, or a small sum per week to look after all the apprentices in a particular department, but usually the master did not take even an indirect responsibility for the teaching of the trade to an apprentice. The apprentice was taught his trade by the journeyman with whom he worked; in return for which teaching the apprentice

[1] *Staffordshire Advertiser*, September 21, 1850.
[2] *Trade Societies and Strikes. National Association for the Promotion of Social Science* (1860), 283.
[3] *Trade Societies and Strikes. National Association for the Promotion of Social Science* (1860), 283.
Potters' Examiner, February 10, 1844.

did little services, such as lighting fires, running errands, etc. That the master took no responsibility for his training does not mean that the apprentice did not properly learn his trade. The evidence shows that he did. The point to make clear is that the money allowed by the apprentice was a gain to the master without any corresponding loss. Although the apprentice during his first years in the trade would not be able to make articles demanding a high degree of skill, in his last year he was capable of, and usually did, make the same class of articles as the journeyman.

The fact of the profitableness of the apprentice was taken advantage of by the masters in two ways. One, which held good throughout the century, but was more particularly flagrant towards the end, was that when a journeyman applied for a situation he was engaged on the condition that he brought an apprentice with him.[1] The other, which led to the allowance system, was to dismiss those apprentices who at the expiration of their term of service demanded to be paid the full journeyman rates.[2] In some cases an apprentice would be allowed to become journeyman and retain his situation by allowing from his wages an amount slightly less than the full apprentice deduction.[3]

Looking at the facts, but being unfamiliar with the industry, the Commissioner of 1841[4] drew different con-

[1] Letter from one-time potters' union official: "It was about the 1890's that . . . the large firms made a condition of employment that he brought an apprentice. I refer to pressers."

[2] *Trades Societies and Strikes. Report of National Association for Promotion of Social Science* (1860), 283.

Birmingham Daily Post, February 20, 1908. S. Clowes (Union, official), "as to apprentices he said that under present system had apprentices of 40 years of age working in some factories."

[3] *Children's Employment (Trades and Manufactures) Commission* (1843), evidence Scriven, C.5.

[4] *Children's Employment (Trades and Manufactures) Commission* (1843), evidence Scriven, C.5.

clusions from them than those given above. The facts, as he correctly observed, were, first, that many young journeymen were working for less than journeyman rates; and second, that, as the indenture system was no longer usual, apprentices were able to, and no doubt did, leave the firms where they were working and sought situations elsewhere as journeymen before they had completed the customary seven years' service.[1] The Commissioner wrongly concluded that the first fact was a result of the second. A third fact, had he noticed it, would have prevented him from making this error. This was that potters, whether young or old, apprentices or journeymen, working at full rates or not, were pieceworkers, and were only paid for those articles which were made to the satisfaction of the employer. It is, moreover, extremely unlikely that apprentices would seek situations as journeymen during such a period of depression, for the number of experienced journeymen seeking work must have been large. Actually it was more common for men to be working as journeymen before they had completed their full time of service to the trade during the boom years when labour was in great demand. Writing in 1844 and pleading for the limitation of apprentices, the editor of the potters' trade union journal said that "in Glasgow, Derby, Worcester and other out-pottery districts shoals of apprentices are poured into the pottery business from the depressed families of the cotton, woollen and gloving departments of industry, and which apprentices at the age of maturity are discharged from their employ, for the purpose of giving place

[1] *Staffordshire Mercury*, January 16, 1847, meeting of pottery manufacturers resolved to memorialise Chancellor asking for indenture duty to be reduced to 2s. 6d. Not more than one apprentice in forty was legally bound. *Trade Societies and Strikes. National Association for Promotion of Social Science* (1860), 283. Government on application reduced it to 2s. 6d., but yet no change followed.

to younger and less expensive labour, and are thus compelled periodically to swarm into the Staffordshire potteries . . . to seek that employment denied to them elsewhere. . . ."[1]

The reduction of the indenture duty was not followed by the reform in conditions of apprentice labour anticipated by the Commissioner of 1841.[2] The Social Science Report of 1860 speaks of master potters dismissing apprentices at the end of their seven years' service unless they consented to work for two more years at apprentice rates.

It is easy to see how under such conditions an allowance system could become general. In a time of trade depression and unemployment it would be moderately easy for an employer to refuse to allow an apprentice to become a journeyman unless he agreed to work for less than the recognised journeyman rates. This system would then extend itself so as to include many other journeymen who had hitherto been paid at the full rates. The spreading of the system would be aided by the fact that the masters could give the work upon which the most wages were earned to the men who made allowances, and it could happen that the men who made no allowance would be actually getting less wages than their workfellows with weaker principles.[3] The idea sometimes put forward that potters worked for less than full rates because they were only partly skilled and unable to make the best ware,

[1] *Potters' Examiner*, February 10, 1844.

[2] Scriven: *Children's Employment (Trades and Manufactures) Commission* (1843), C.5.

[3] *The Case of the Manufacturers of China and Earthenware in the Staffordshire Potteries, with some Account of the Late Turn Out, its Origin, Proceedings and Termination*, 1836–37 (pamphlet) (N.D.). Good work to be equally distributed was one of the minor demands of the men in 1836.

will not stand examination. Plausible as it may appear, it is unrelated to the facts.

Widespread as the allowance system was in the late 'thirties and early 'forties, it is unlikely that it would have survived a period of good trade, apart from any question of an organisation amongst the men to resist it. There was no chance of the system ever being officially recognised as a trade custom; the best masters never practised it and it was a purely individual arrangement. The settling of piecework prices in the pottery industry was, and is, always a collective affair. The amount of money that a man will "allow", and whether he will "allow" at all, is an individual arrangement. The making price of an article is settled by the men of the trade in which that article is made who are working in the factory at the time it is introduced. It may happen sometimes that the maker of the article will settle the price of it without the aid of his fellow-workers, but they, in that case, acquiesce in the settlement. In all cases a price once settled is binding upon all concerned. Allowances are different. If a man agrees to make a certain allowance the agreement is not binding upon his fellows or upon the man who follows him. In short, price-settling is collective bargaining, but the making of "allowances" is not, although its prohibition may be.

The United Branches of Operative Potters' Society was established on September 6, 1843, its professed chief object being to stamp out the allowance system.[1] Trade was now reviving, and consequently the new Union accomplished its object with moderate ease. This Union, as its name implies, was a federation of branch unions. The powers of its governing committee, which consisted of representatives from the component branch unions, were very limited. It had very little executive power, being

[1] *Potters' Examiner*, January 4, 1845.

merely a convenient vehicle whereby the branches were able to act in unison. The branches retained full power to conduct their own business, including the right to strike.[1] They levied when they pleased, and fixed their own membership subscription. There was thus a wide difference between the United Branches Society and the National Union of Operative Potters. The latter, though composed of branches, each with its several lodges, had kept the funds and full executive power in the hands of its central committee, while the United Branches was a federation whose central committee had neither funds nor power.[2]

The establishment of the United Branches Society was not the rebirth of unionism in the pottery industry; it was the coming together in federation of unions already in existence.[3] It is difficult to say whether or not these unions had survived the dissolution of the National Union of Operative Potters. There is no definite proof of their existence between the end of 1837 and February 1842, but there is no reason to suppose that there was none during that period. It is certain that if they did exist they were insignificant and weak, for even after the revival of unionism amongst the potters in 1843 only two-sevenths were organised.[4] At no time in its history was the United Branches Society strong from the point of view of numbers. It never claimed to have more than 2,000 members, which number compares very unfavourably with the 8,000 on the membership roll of its predecessor. Nevertheless, it was virile and active. It successfully opposed the allowance system and made strenuous efforts to raise wages, in which it succeeded so far as to secure, during

[1] *Potters' Examiner*, July 14, 1844.
[2] *Potters' Examiner*, July 14, 1844.
[3] *Potters' Examiner*, January 24, February 10, 1844.
[4] W. Evans: *Art and History of the Pottery Business* (1846), 9.

its first two years, rises equal in amount to at least $7\frac{1}{2}$ per cent. on weekly earnings for all members of the trade.[1] Soon after its inception the Union organised a system for taking up collections from its members in order to remove the debts incurred by the National Union of Operative Potters during the dispute of 1836–7. It is true that these collections were started at the request of the late Union's principal creditor, the Sheffield Trades, but the response made is a clear indication that the committee of the United Branches was taking its mission seriously, for the business of debt liquidation is no light task for an association to grapple with in its infancy.[2]

Attempts were also instituted to organise the out-potters, and were in most cases successful.[3] Sick and burial funds were run in conjunction with the Union, and a trade journal of a high literary standard, the *Potters' Examiner*, was established.[4] The editor, William Evans, a man of marked ability, had great influence upon the policy of the Union. As might be expected, after the dispute of 1836–7 the potters favoured an anti-strike policy for their Union. The representative to the National Conference of Trades, March 1845, stated definitely that his constituents were opposed to strikes.[5] A year later the writer of a small book on pottery manufacture gave the reason for the non-militant policy of the Union when he said: "The disastrous turnout of 1836–7 should stand as a warning to all future combinations of working potters".[6]

1 W. Evans: *Art and History of the Pottery Business* (1846), 9. *Potters' Examiner*, December 19, 1843; January 1, 1844.

2 *Potters' Examiner*, December 19, 1843; January 1, 1844.

3 *Potters' Examiner*, February 10, 1844; August 6, 1844; March 22, 1845.

4 *Potters' Examiner*, June 1, 1844. The first number of the *Potters' Examiner*, Saturday, December 2, 1843; price 1d.

5 *Northern Star*, March 29, 1845.

6 W. Evans: *Art and History of the Pottery Business* (1846), 9.

The increase in wages of 1844–5 was obtained by peaceful methods; trade was good, and concessions came easily from the masters. Indeed, several manufacturers behaved so liberally towards their employees that the Central Committee of the Union expressed a desire to thank them for their "honourable conduct".[1] There was one exception to this anti-militancy, where a long-drawn-out strike took place over a matter relative to prices.[2] As an alternative to militant action the Central Committee placed its faith in the restriction of supply of labour.[3] The other possible alternative, the formation of Boards of Arbitration or Conciliation, did not meet with their approval.

During a discussion at the National Conference of Trades, Easter 1845, upon the advisability of establishing "Boards of Trade" (Arbitration Boards), Evans, for the potters, stated that the establishment of such Boards would be useless so long as the evil of "surplus labour" remained, and, in any case, he did not think that working men could be found with sufficient courage to give evidence before their employers.[4] The United Branches Committee considered emigration to be the best expedient for the removal of surplus labour. For the furtherance of this idea it decided, February 1844, to form a Joint Stock Emigration Society.[5] Shortly after its formation interest in this society received a tremendous fillip because of the introduction of machinery in certain branches of the trade, which created a panic amongst the potters.[6] These men

[1] *Potters' Examiner*, October 26, 1844.
[2] *Potters' Examiner*, December 9, 1843.
Northern Star, March 29, 1845.
[3] *Potters' Examiner*, February 10, 1844.
[4] *Northern Star*, March 29, 1845.
[5] *Potters' Examiner*, February 24, 1844.
W. Evans: *Art and History of the Pottery Business* (1846), 9.
[6] *Potters' Examiner*, August 3, 1844.

could see themselves in the future in the condition of the handloom weavers, and the evil of surplus labour became a more real problem to them. Their faith in emigration as a remedy for this evil became active, as was shown by the enthusiasm with which they turned to the society established for the purpose of furthering that object.[1] Had this machinery scare not arisen, in all probability the Union would have continued along its smooth path, which would have led it eventually to the "New Model" unionism of the 'fifties.

In August 1844 a machine was introduced by J. Ridgway for the making of "paste" or "patch" boxes, and in the following October C. J. Mason introduced another one for the making of plates and saucers. In neither case were they successful, and after short trials were abandoned. Both machines met with great opposition from the Union. Of J. C. Mason's machine, which to the men appeared the more dangerous as it affected a much larger number of operatives, the editor of the *Potters' Examiner* said: ". . . the spirited opposition of the operatives, together with some defects in the machine itself, caused Mr. Mason to abandon it after a few weeks' trial."[2]

The apparent success of the Union in the fight against the machines of Messrs. Ridgway and Mason stimulated it to oppose the printing machines which had been used for a long time by one or two firms; but this second struggle was unsuccessful, chiefly owing to the fact that the printing machines had shown no defects as had the others. It is interesting to note that at one factory the women who worked with the printers went on strike upon the introduc-

[1] *Potters' Examiner*, March 22, 1845.

[2] *Potters' Examiner*, August 3, August 17, November 2, November 14, December 14, 1844.
Northern Star, March 29, April 5, 1845.
W. Evans: *Art and History of the Pottery Business* (1846), 11.

tion of this machine, and were rewarded for their altruism by a tea-party and concert given by the Printers' Society.[1]

The potters' printing machine, which is merely an adaptation of newspaper printing rollers to the uses of the pottery industry, was introduced in 1833. On its introduction, beyond letters to the newspapers from two workmen who were fearful for the future of the hand-press printers, it caused little comment.[2] From that time until the machine scare of the 'forties, when it was described as a "Rolling Monster . . . crushing the interest of the Printing Branch", its use appears to have passed unnoticed.[3]

In January 1845 some hundreds of potters in one of the largest of the pottery towns divided into parties and waited upon the manufacturers of the district with the object of persuading them not to introduce machinery into their factories. With one exception all those interviewed were of the opinion that, apart from its probable effect upon the workmen, machinery would injure them as manufacturers, and they seemed anxious that the men should resist it wherever it was introduced.[4] Commenting upon the fear of machinery entertained by many of the manufacturers, a Methodist parson who had worked as a potter during the 'forties wrote: ". . . even some of the largest employers fled from the introduction of machinery as from a ghost."[5]

The panic into which the potters were thrown by the very timid invasion of machinery into their trade is in amusing contrast to the philosophical and statesmanlike attitude adopted by them to the problems arising out of the displacement of manual skill by machinery at a time

[1] *Potters' Examiner*, March 8, 1845.
[2] *Staffordshire Mercury*, May 18, May 25, 1833.
[3] *Potters' Examiner*, March 8, 1845.
[4] *Potters' Examiner*, January 25, 1845.
[5] Old Potter: *When I was a Child* (1903), 186.

when they were of the opinion that their own crafts would be for ever unaffected by mechanical inventions. In November 1830 the potters of North Staffordshire presented a petition to the House of Commons praying for the opening of the trade to China, and giving as their "solemn conviction that the distress under which a large portion of the community was suffering was not owing to the invention of machinery, but to the monopolies which existed in various branches of trade". The presenter of the petition praised the potters for not "joining in the ignorant cry which was raised against the employment of machinery in many of the agricultural and manufacturing districts".[1] Except for the printing rollers, which were in fairly extensive use by the 'fifties, and cup-making machines, used in one or two of the small out-potteries,[2] it was many years after the scare of the 'forties before machinery came to be used in the manufacture of pottery. Nevertheless, although in 1845 handwork was not being displaced by other methods of pottery manufacture, the machinery scare remained and exerted great influence.

Instead of taking a minor place in the affairs of the Union, as an experimental arrangement for the removal of surplus labour, in which case it would probably have died as it did in other trade societies where it was tried, the emigration scheme grew in importance. A fund of £5,000 was started for the purpose of buying land in America, on which the victims of machinery were to be settled.[3] That there were no "machinery victims" at the time the fund was started made no difference to the plans of the potters, for in their panic they could see all handicrafts doomed.

[1] *Staffordshire Advertiser*, November 27, 1830.

[2] W. Evans: *Art and History of the Pottery Business* (1846), 11. *Staffordshire Advertiser*, September 21, 1850.

[3] *Potters' Examiner*, November 30, 1844.

The attitude of the potters to machinery, and their subsequent enthusiasm for emigration, offended the delegates of the Sheffield trades.[1] The delegates were at that time in the Potteries endeavouring to recover the money lent by them to the potters during the dispute of 1836. They contended that the potters were foolish in attempting to prevent the introduction of machinery, and protested that debts ought to be paid before an emigration fund was raised. In reply the potters pointed to historical cases of grievous harm done to hand-workers through the invention of machinery, and in reference to the emigration fund, before any debts were paid, their duty was to preserve their trade.[2] The potters at the time owed £1,600 to the Sheffield Trades.[3]

The launching of the emigration scheme brought the Central Committee of the United Branches into collision with the Chartists. In November 1846 the Potters' Union published a handbill designed to show that its emigration scheme was more sound and businesslike than was the land scheme of the Chartists. The handbill contained the statement that the Chartists' Society, through O'Connor, was paying £50 an acre for land. This sum, as was intended, appeared outrageously high in comparison with the few shillings per acre paid by the Potters' Emigration Society for land in America. The Hanley branch of the Chartist Land Society published a letter in reply to the handbill

[1] *Staffordshire Mercury*, January 4, 1846.
[2] *Potters' Examiner*, December 28, 1844.
The Sheffield delegates described the opposition of the potters to machinery as "monstrous nonsense". (*Potters' Examiner*, January 4, 1845.) But in April 1843 the committee of the Sheffield Trade Societies published an address in which they attributed the evils under which they laboured to (1) the increase of machinery, (2) the manufacture of cheap articles. See *Trade Societies and Strikes. National Association for the Promotion of Social Science* (1860), 542.
[3] *Potters' Examiner*, September 22, 1844.

in which it was stated that, although O'Connor had paid as much as £50 for an acre of land, it was the best land in the best situation, and for inferior land a much less price had been given. The letter concluded by accusing the chief advocate of the Potters' Emigration Society, William Evans, of "juggling" and using "machinery dodges" to cajole money for emigration out of the potters.[1]

The Chartists had been brought into bad odour with the potters by a succession of stirring and troublesome events. From the time of the first convention the Potteries had contained small groups of Chartists,[2] but it was not until 1842 that the whole district became involved in the movement. The Potteries received visits that year from O'Connor, Cooper and other Chartists of less prominence.[3] The pottery district at the time was an excellent field for the sowing of the seed of Chartism. Trade unionism was at an exceptionally low ebb, and appeared to be of little use. Economic conditions, which were bad, were suddenly made worse in July by the North Staffordshire miners' strike. The strike was accompanied throughout by acts of violence and sabotage. Many "blacklegs" were severely maltreated and much damage was done to the pits. In the case of one particular mine "everything destroyable on the pit-bank and [in] the engine house was destroyed".[4]

Coal is an essential raw material of the pottery industry, and this sudden cutting down of supplies caused very

[1] *Northern Star*, December 5, 1846.

[2] T. Cooper: *The Life of Thomas Cooper* (ed. 1873), 192.
M. Hovel: *The Chartist Movement* (ed. 1918), 130.

[3] T. Cooper: *The Life of Thomas Cooper* (ed. 1873), 187–95.
Staffordshire Advertiser, May 21, 1842.
W. Payne: *Staffordshire Gaol and its Associations* (1887), 145.

[4] W. Payne: *Staffordshire Gaol and its Associations* (1887), 145.
Old Potter: *When I was a Child* (1903), 33.
J. Ward: *History of Borough of Stoke-on-Trent* (1846), 584. Actually it was a lock-out. The miners were resisting a reduction in wages.

many pottery manufactories immediately to close down. Coal and pottery were, and still are, the two main, and almost the two sole, industries of the district, and the effect upon the North Staffordshire towns of the sudden stoppage of both industries can easily be imagined. The miners were striking and were in a combative mood.

The potters were unemployed and penniless, for the stoppage came to them after a long period of trade depression. At this singularly inopportune time—or opportune, according to the point of view—for the preaching of disruptive doctrines, when a spark would be expected to cause a conflagration, William Cooper visited the Potteries. He held a meeting on Crown Bank, Hanley, on Sunday, August 14th, and at its close he announced that he would hold a meeting the next morning at nine o'clock for the purpose of addressing the colliers who were on strike. The meeting took place as announced and, according to Cooper, it consisted of a crowd of more than eight thousand people.[1] At the close of his address Cooper, who had received his instructions from Manchester, proposed the resolution that all work should cease until the Charter became the law of the land. The meeting ended with a unanimous vote in favour of the resolution, but the assembled people did not disperse. There was a cry of "Follow me", and the crowd, still under the influence of Cooper's oratory, marched to the neighbouring town of Longton, stopping on its way to turn out the potters from the few factories which were working.[2]

[1] T. Cooper: *The Life of Thomas Cooper* (ed. 1873), 191.
[2] T. Cooper: *The Life of Thomas Cooper* (ed. 1873), 192.
Old Potter: *When I was a Child* (1903), 158.
W. Payne: *Staffordshire Gaol and its Associations* (1887), 145. Cooper's account slightly varies from the one given here. He says after the passing of the resolution the meeting broke up. As he went immediately to his inn at the close of the meeting he would not be aware that the crowd had not dispersed.

For two days the district was in a state of fierce riot. Besides committing other damage the houses of the following gentlemen were sacked and burnt down: Mr. Forrester, who was the agent of Lord Granville, the chief coal-owner in the district; the Rev. R. E. Aikens and the Rev. Dr. Vale; Mr. Rose, the stipendiary magistrate; and Mr. Parker, a lawyer. The rioting was eventually put down by the military, at a cost to the mob of one man killed and many injured. Repressive measures were used to restore order in the district and 800 people were arrested for being concerned in the rioting.[1]

It would be a mistake to suppose that this violent outbreak of the mob was due to enthusiasm for the Charter. The Chartists brought the people together, but any group of men, with any plan for the reformation of society, could have got a crowd under such circumstances. The crowd once gathered, the speeches of Cooper were not calculated to soothe it, nor to put it into good humour with those in authority.[2] One of the incidents of the riots gives a glimpse of the mind of the mob. A large number of men marching into the Potteries from the surrounding villages were met by Captain Powys and asked by him for their reason in assembling together. The reply came quickly, "The Charter, and more to eat".[3] The last three

[1] Old Potter: *When I was a Child* (1903), 158–66.
W. Payne: *Staffordshire Gaol and its Associations* (1887), 145.
T. Cooper: *The Life of Thomas Cooper* (ed. 1873), 195 seq.
J. Ward: *History of the Borough of Stoke-on-Trent* (1846), 558. As a result of the riots 54 men were transported, and 146 sentenced to imprisonment with hard labour.

[2] T. Cooper: *The Life of Thomas Cooper* (ed. 1873), 188–9. Cooper spoke from the text "Thou shalt do no murder". In his address he asserted that those who were responsible for the passing of the new Poor Law, and those who were trying to reduce wages, were guilty of murder. He himself says that he filled his hearers with a desire to avenge their wrongs.

[3] Old Potter: *When I was a Child* (1903), 163.

words of the answer to the question put by Captain Powys almost explain the Pottery Riots.

It would appear that during the riots the miners were far more violent in their conduct than the potters.[1] The magistrates at the time took this view, for long after order had been restored they anxiously watched the district, being of the opinion that "a finger raised would draw hundreds out of the pits where work had been resumed".[2] The explosive elements in the industrial atmosphere came from the mines and not from the pot-banks.

As far as the potters were concerned, the chief result of the rioting was to strengthen the feeling against conflict which the reaction from the 1836 dispute had already created. Their reluctance to oppose the employers was increased, with the result that it was reported of the Potteries that "in no part of the country has the terrible power of the capitalist been more severely felt".[3]

Established some few months after the riots, the United Branches of Operative Potters reflected in its policy the anti-militant sentiments of the potters.

[1] Old Potter: *When I was a Child* (1903), 182.
[2] *New Moral World*, September 17, 1842.
[3] *Northern Star*, June 7, 1845.

CHAPTER VII

CONFLICTING IDEAS

Their costly struggle with the employers in the winter of 1836–7 turned the potters from the rugged path of militant reform into the smooth highway of cautious defence and pacific aggression. In place of an ardent determination to control the trade the organised potters merely wished to improve conditions of labour and safeguard their interests as employed artisans. With such a modest conception of the functions of a trade union the potters could legitimately have expected to enter into, if not prosperity, at least placidity and contentment. At one time it seemed as if all things were working together to bring that happy state of affairs to pass. Trade was good, wages were moderately high, the policy of the Union was pacific and, lest party politics should cause dissension in its ranks, the Union kept its journal closed to political discussion.[1] It is uncertain how far Methodism helped to tone down the character and policy of the potters' unions, but it is evident that its influence was exerted to that end.[2] Distrust of all organisations and movements that tended to subvert law and order was deep-rooted in Methodism.[3]

Of all the Methodist connexions the Wesleyans were probably the most zealous in their opposition to worldly politics. The annual address of this body expressed sentiments of such loyalty to the Crown and regard for the law that only in the utterances of the most subservient of a State's subjects could they be rivalled. In their address to the King, August 1830, the Wesleyan Methodists claimed

[1] *Potters' Examiner*, December 2, 1843.

[2] Old Potter: *When I was a Child* (1903), 193.

[3] H. Faulkner: *Chartism and the Churches* (1916), 24.

that their ministers "sedulously endeavoured to inculcate the principles of civil order, subjection to the laws and affectionate loyalty to the Throne".[1] In the following year Wesleyans were requested by their Conference "not to let worldly politics engross too much of their time".[2] The Conference address of 1833 was aimed directly at the trade unions. Trade unionism was not mentioned, but Wesleyans were told to "keep at the utmost distance from all associations which [were] subversive of the principles of true and proper liberty, employing unlawful oaths and threats and force to acquire new members, and to accomplish purposes which would tend to destroy the very framework of civil society".[3] Although other Methodist bodies probably did not take so strong a line as the Wesleyans, the general trend of their views was the same. At a Primitive Methodist Conference held at Tunstall, one of the pottery towns, gratitude to George IV was shown for passing the Act of 1812, and a nervous fear exhibited lest camp meetings should be put down by the expulsion of one of the delegates on the grounds that he was a "speeching radical".[4] The Methodism of the early 'forties in the pottery districts "frowned upon trade unionism as much as on poaching". A working man, if he were a class leader or local preacher, would warn his fellows against the "wiles of the devil".[5]

[1] *Minutes of Methodist Conference from the first held in London,* by the late Rev. John Wesley, A.M., vol. vii. (1838), 74.
[2] *Minutes of Methodist Conference from the first held in London,* by the late Rev. John Wesley, A.M., vol. vii (1838), 74.
[3] *Minutes of Methodist Conference from the first held in London,* by the late Rev. John Wesley, A.M., vol. vii (1838), 306.
[4] H. B. Kendal: *The Origin and History of the Primitive Methodist Church* (1905), vol. i, 339. (Skevington in Leicester put out of Primitive Methodists for being a Chartist. Jefferson wrote "Lion of Judah", a Methodist hymn to metre and tune of "Lion of Freedom", to outdo, if possible, that hymn of the Chartists.)
[5] Old Potter: *When I was a Child* (1903), 192.

These wiles were often supposed to be found in trade unionism.[1] Methodism was strong amongst the potters, and even those who were outside its ranks were under its influence.[2]

A character in one of Arnold Bennett's short stories testified to the power of the Methodists in the Potteries, though his remark that the Five Towns were all chapels and public-houses was probably inaccurate as a complete description.[3] Consciously or unconsciously the force of Methodism must have greatly influenced the Potters' Union and encouraged it along the path of respectability into which it had already turned its steps. The conflict of loyalty to Church with loyalty to class would naturally result in the Methodist workman trying to make of his trade union an organisation to which his fellow-religionist could unashamedly belong.[4]

The organised potters were shaken out of the placid state into which they were settling by the machinery scare.[5] In its reactions to that scare the Society of the United Branches of Operative Potters laid itself open to attacks from the National Association of United Trades for the Protection of Labour.[6] This association, and its sister organisation, the National Association for the Employment of Labour, were products of the ideas of the time, and, although neither in themselves was vastly important, yet both in their aims and policy mark a new era in the development of British Trade Unionism. The

[1] Old Potter: *When I was a Child* (1903), 192.
[2] Old Potter: *When I was a Child* (1903), 193.
[3] A. Bennett: "The Long Lost Uncle," *The Argosy*, January 1927, vol. i, no. 8. "Her says Hanbridge is dirty and too religious for her. Says its nowt but chapels and public houses and pot banks."
[4] Old Potter: *When I was a Child* (1903), 193.
[5] *Potters' Examiner*, August 3, 17, 1844.
[6] *Northern Star*, April 25, 1846.

promoters of these associations aimed at the substitution of friendliness for hostility in the relationship of master and servant. The well-being of the workers was to be sought and their interests to be forwarded, not by means of the crude, bludgeoning strike, but by humane and reasonable methods. Except where the autocratic tyranny or obstinacy of the employer left no alternative, the strike weapon was not to be used, neither to enforce the claims of the men nor to resist those of the masters, but all matters in dispute were to be settled by conciliation or arbitration. Reason and justice were to decide between the rival claims of employer and employed, not brute-force and famine.[1]

These associations were the outcome of the National Conference of United Trades, held during Easter Week, 1845.[2] The Conference had been called by the London Trades for the purpose of discussing the advisability of forming a bond of association between the many trade unions of the country. The discussion resulted in the Conference deciding that the establishment of a close relationship between the various unions was desirable. A committee was appointed to draw up a plan of organisation to that end, and the Conference adjourned until August, when it was expected that the committee would be ready to submit its report. At the adjourned Conference only fifty delegates were present, as compared with one hundred and ten at the previous one.[3]

[1] Webb: *History of Trade Unionism* (ed. 1920), 187.
Northern Star, March 29, April 5, 1845.
Report from the Select Committee on Masters and Operatives (*Equitable Councils of Conciliation* (1856) 1; evidence Winter.

[2] Webb: *History of Trade Unionism* (ed. 1920), 188.
Northern Star, April 5, August 2, 1845.

[3] Webb: *History of Trade Unionism* (ed. 1920), 191. The Conference was for six days, beginning July 28th.
Potters' Examiner, April 5, 1845. Resolution passed at Trades Conference held Easter, 1845: "That the next general conference . . . take place in London on the first Monday of the coming August."

In the interval between the two meetings many of the unions had been reviewing their position, and the larger ones had come to the conclusion that a close alliance of unions was not desirable. The memories of the disaster which followed the 1834 attempt to build up a General Trades Union were still distinct, and union leaders feared that a similar fate would overtake the new experiment. The consequence was that, in the main, the adjourned Conference represented only the smaller trades.[1] At this Conference the National Association for the Protection of Labour and the National Association for the Employment of Labour came into being. The two associations were designed to be mutually helpful. On the whole the object of the National Association for the Protection of Labour was to improve the conditions of work of the men in the trades which it represented, and to negotiate for the men in cases of dispute between employer and employed. If, during a dispute, negotiations broke down and the National Association for the Protection of Labour decided that a strike was both necessary and justifiable, the National Association for the Employment of Labour was to be called in to find work for the strikers.[2] In thus finding work for strikers the National Association for the Employment of Labour was not aiming eventually to obtain workers' ownership of industry. Its aim was much more modest, being merely to make strikes less costly to the men.[3] During the first year of its existence many more trades were persuaded to join the National Association for the Protection of Labour, and at its Conference, June 1846, as many as one hundred and twenty-six delegates were

[1] Webb: *History of Trade Unionism* (ed. 1920), 191.
[2] *Report from the Select Committee on Masters and Operatives* (*Equitable Councils of Conciliation*) (1856), 1; evidence Winter.
Webb: *History of Trade Unionism* (ed. 1920), 192.
Webb: *History of Trade Unionism* (ed. 1920), 190.

present.[1] Paid organisers were appointed and much missionary work was done. It found itself, however, unable effectively to pursue its policy of peaceful mediation between masters and men. With the depression in trade, reductions in wages were pressed for by the employers, and the Association was unable to prevent the men from defending their standard of living by means of the strike.[2]

The Association for the Employment of Labour was, in the attainment of its objects, even less effective, for, except in a few cases of trades which were based upon handicraft, it was unable to find work for the men who were on strike.[3] In 1848 the two associations were merged into one, and an attempt was made to restart as one organisation.[4] The new association survived until 1861, but it did not occupy an important place in the trade union world. It never included any but the smaller, and, from a trade union point of view, unimportant trades.[5]

For the first five years after the establishment of these associations the history of the organised potters is intermingled with that of the National Association for the Protection of Labour, and, to a less extent, with that of the National Association for the Employment of Labour. The potters were represented at the first Conference of the United Trades, and their delegate was made chairman of the committee which the Conference appointed to draw up a scheme for the establishment of a permanent

[1] Webb: *History of Trade Unionism* (ed. 1920), 192.
[2] *Report from the Select Committee on Masters and Operatives* (*Equitable Councils of Conciliation*) (1856), 2; evidence Winter.
Webb: *History of Trade Unionism* (ed. 1920), 193.
[3] Webb: *History of Trade Unionism* (ed. 1920), 194.
[4] Webb: *History of Trade Unionism* (ed. 1920), 194.
[5] *Report from the Select Committee on Masters and Operatives* (*Equitable Councils of Conciliation*) (1856), 1; evidence Winter.
Webb: *History of Trade Unionism* (ed. 1920), 195.
G. Howel: *Conflicts of Labour and Capital* (ed. 1890), 394.

association.[1] When the two National Associations came into being after the adjourned Conference, July 1845, the United Branches of Operative Potters took out one hundred shares of 25s. each in the National Association for the Employment of Labour, to the directorate of which body a potter was elected.[2]

The United Branches of Operative Potters did not join the National Association for the Protection of Labour, for from the first moment of the Association's existence it was apparent that the organised potters were not in agreement with its policy. This disagreement was none the less because the policy of the National Association and that of the Potters' Union had the same parentage. Fear of strikes and hostility to the revolutionary sentiments of the previous decade formed the source from which both policies sprang: but, though possessing a common origin, they had become different things; the policy of the National Association was idealistic and progressive, but that of the Potters' Union had developed into a paralytic cautiousness. At no time had the United Branches of Operative Potters been in real sympathy with the aims of the National Association for the Protection of Labour. At the Easter Conference of United Trades the potters' delegate spoke against the establishment of Boards of Conciliation and Arbitration, the advocacy of which afterwards became identified with the National Association, and with a caution which the leaders of the United Potters always displayed when any but the most fantastic schemes were being discussed, urged the delegates to hesitate before they pressed for the adoption of such Boards.[3] Most of the unions outside the National Association for

[1] *Northern Star*, March 29, April 5, 1845.
[2] *Northern Star*, January 3, 1846; May 1, 1847.
[3] *Northern Star*, March 29, 1845.

the Protection of Labour agreed with it on many things, and only abstained from joining because of their objection to an association of unions. The lesson they had learnt from the past, rightly or wrongly, was that general unions ultimately led to disaster;[1] but it was not for such a reason that the United Potters refused to join. Its leaders expressed no objections to a general union, but, being completely enthralled by a "work fund theory of wages", they could see little point in many of the ideas stressed by the National Association. In the opinion of those who spoke for the potters' society the main object of a union was to keep down the supply of labour by hindering the development of the use of machinery.[2] It was hoped that the result would be a job always for every man in his own trade. Compared with such an ideal, other unions' aims appeared unimportant.[3]

The incompatibility of the ideas of the United Potters with those of the National Association was startlingly shown at a Conference of the latter body in June 1846. Although not entitled to be there, a potters' representative was present at this conference. After some demur on the part of the delegates present, he was allowed to address the Conference. He told the delegates that the "original intention of the Association had been to render strikes unnecessary by giving employment on the land or in the manufactures". The society he represented, he went on to say, had purchased land in America, and in doing so had obtained for its members several rises in wages. His speech concluded with an attempt to persuade the delegates to establish a weekly newspaper "from which with a small outlay great profits could be made".[4]

[1] Webb: *History of Trade Unionism* (ed. 1920), 191.
[2] *Northern Star*, April 5, 1845. [3] *Northern Star*, May 1, 1847.
[4] *Northern Star*, June 6, 1846.

It is not clear that Evans, the potters' delegate, was hopelessly incorrect in his statement concerning the original intention of the National Association. He was the chairman of the committee which had drawn up the plans for the two sister National Associations, and he should therefore have known its intentions. He was probably of the opinion that at the time when the Conference decided to have two Associations the National Association for the Employment of Labour was intended to be far more important than it afterwards proved to be. He had some justification for thinking that his speeches to the delegates at the Easter Conference, urging the acceptance of plans for emigration and the ownership by the workers of stores and workshops, and grudgingly favouring schemes of home colonisation, fairly interpreted the sense of the meeting.[1] But in any case, whatever the National Association of Labour was intended to become, Evans showed by his speeches that he was unable to appreciate or to have a sympathetic understanding of the ideas for which it later came to stand. The National Association did not have a particularly long life, and for many years before its final disappearance it was in a moribund condition;[2] but the chief ideas for which it stood had vitality, and were taken over by other bodies. It was these vital ideas which the United Potters never held, and upon which they disagreed with the National Association.

In April 1846 the National Association for the Protection of Labour began its missionary work amongst the potters. John West, of Macclesfield, conducted a four days' cam-

[1] *Northern Star*, April 5, 1845.

[2] Webb: *History of Trade Unionism* (ed. 1920), 195.

Report from the Select Committee on Masters and Operatives (*Equitable Councils of Conciliation*) (1856); 1–2, evidence Winter.

Report from the Select Committee on Masters and Operatives (1860), 6; evidence Humphries.

paign in the pottery district of North Staffordshire, which met with encouraging success. At his meetings the necessity to the potters of allying themselves to a national organisation was stressed, and, although the problems arising from the development of handicraft by machine production—a matter much discussed by the potters at that time—was not touched upon, the kindred question of "surplus labour" was dealt with. According to West, the National Association would remove surplus labour by shortening the working hours of all those in employment, and he tried to show the superior advantages such a system possessed as compared with emigration. At Burslem, the stronghold of the emigration movement, no opposition was made to the National Association meeting, although West expected it. It was at these meetings that Humphries, then a young potter, but later to become Secretary of the National Association, first came forward.[1]

It is significant of the trend of feeling at the time that of the three chairmen mentioned in connexion with these meetings one was the most noted Chartist in the district, Richards, and another was Mark Lancaster, a one-time member of the Board of Management of the old National Union of Operative Potters, and the only man who was prominent in that society whose name, after the disasters of 1837, reappears in Union history.

Some months previous to West's missionary effort Lancaster had written, on behalf of the potters of Burslem, to the Central Committee of the National Association, and there is no doubt that his influence had much to do with the visit of West.[2] It is not surprising that an old

[1] *Northern Star*, April 25, 1846.

[2] *Northern Star*, February 28, 1846. ". . . The central Committee (of the National Association) met at the Trades Office . . . Bloomsbury. . . . A number of letters were read; among others . . . from Mr. Lancaster on behalf of the potters of Burslem."

National Union leader should feel dissatisfied with the United Branches, for to him then ewer body would appear to be effete and devitalised.

By the middle of 1846 the United Branches was in an exceedingly bad way. It had withstood attacks from the delegates of the Sheffield Trades; it had been, and still was being, opposed by the Chartists, and now, aided by its other opponents, the National Association was beginning to attract the allegiance of the potters.[1]

The United Branches was by this time completely identified with the Emigration Society, and the doctrine of emigration was the only one which it could preach.[2] This pessimistic doctrine, that the well-being of the worker could only be secured by sending all the unemployed out of the country, reached its culminating point in a speech by Evans, the United Branches' chief spokesman, to a meeting of potters.[3] In this speech Evans "assured the meeting that any attempt to raise the wages of the great staple manufacturers of this country would be attended with most alarming effects to the commercial prosperity of England, as it would drive these trades to the continent". Considering that its strongest man held such views, it is not to be wondered at that the United Branches fell back before the attacks from the National Association.

Although their main concern, when speaking to the potters, was to draw attention to the advantages which the National Association for the Protection of Labour offered to its members, the agents of that organisation did not leave the claims of the National Association for the Employment of Labour unstated. It is usually understood that the latter association was too modest in its

[1] *Northern Star*, April 25, October 3, 1846.
[2] *Northern Star*, May 1, 1847.
[3] *Northern Star*, May 1, 1847.

aims to be correctly described as "Owenist", yet those who spoke of it to the potters claimed for it definite Owenist ideals.[1] Either the missionaries themselves believed that the aims of this association were as ambitious as was the scheme projected by Owen, or they were of the opinion that Owenism had survived amongst the potters to such an extent that an appeal along the same lines would be effective. But, whatever the reason, it was pure, though pacific and mild-mannered, Owenism which was preached to the potters by the advocates of the National Association for the Employment of Labour. The potters were told that from its profits the Association was to "gradually extend [its] sphere of action until the working classes eventually [became] . . . their own employers".[2] Except for the style, such a statement could have been used by Owen in 1834.

The immediate results of the National Association campaign amongst the potters, which began in April 1846, were rather encouraging. One branch union, the Painters' and Gilders', joined the Association, and several local committees were formed with the object of enrolling the potters of other branches.[3] Too much importance should not be given to the fact of the Painters' and Gilders' Union joining the National Association, for it was a comparatively new society and represented a trade the members of which seemed to lack a strong will to combine, and never possessed a long-lived union.[4] Some few months later another branch of potters, the crate-makers, formed themselves

[1] Webb: *History of Trade Unionism* (ed. 1920), 190.
Report from the Select Committee on Masters and Operatives (*Equitable Councils of Conciliation*) (1856), 1; evidence Winter.
[2] *Staffordshire Advertiser*, May 8, 1847.
[3] *Northern Star*, April 25, 1846.
[4] The old Painters' and Gilders' Society had dissolved April 1844.
Potters' Examiner, December 21, 1844. Painters' and Gilders' Unions later in the century were short-lived.

into a society, and came into the National Association.[1] Like the Painters' and Gilders', but with greater excuse, they were of a trade which was not easy to organise. Crate-making was carried on in small workshops, and being a trade in which it was moderately easy for a man to become a master, a strong employees' union could not be expected. Of potters other than painters, gilders and crate-makers, the numbers that joined the National Association appear to have been rather small. In October 1846 Humphries, the potters' secretary to the National Association, wrote enthusiastically of one hundred and fifty paying members, and the expected addition to that number of fifty others.[2] During the following months the number of potters in the Association increased, but not to any great extent. Attempts were made from North Staffordshire to bring the out-potters into the Association, but without success, except in the case of South Stockton.[3] On the whole, despite its encouraging start, the National Association did not succeed in filling the general run of potters with enthusiasm for combination.

The Potters' Emigration Society tried hard to obstruct the work of the National Association. One method used was to circulate a rumour to the effect that the agents of the National Association were emissaries of Chartism, and as the Chartists were disliked and distrusted by many people, such a rumour was calculated to make the work of the Association agents more difficult.[4] The tactics of those who worked for the National Association were no less mean. Towards the price of one hundred shares at

[1] *Northern Star*, February 20, March 6, 1847.
[2] *Northern Star*, October 3, 1846.
[3] *Northern Star*, May 8, December 25, 1847. *Staffordshire Advertiser*, May 8, 1847.
[4] *Northern Star*, May 8, 1847.

25s. each, which it had taken out in the National Association for the Employment of Labour, the United Branches of Operative Potters had only paid £1 5s. 0d. Speakers from the National Association alleged that a considerable sum of money had been subscribed for the purchase of the shares, but except for the £1 5s. 0d. which was accounted for, it had been misappropriated, the probability being that it had been flung into the potters' "Bottomless Pit", the Emigration Society. The officials of the United Branches stated that £1 5s. 0d. was the whole sum which had been subscribed, and there is no reason to suppose that they were not speaking the truth.[1]

The Chartists took part in the squabbling and tried by ridicule to damage the Potters' Emigration Society. They made malicious puns out of the name of the area in America in which the Emigration Society had purchased land—Dodge County—which were very pointed and personal.[2] Although the Chartists at the time belonged to a minority movement and were unpopular, their enmity was not to be despised. In November 1847 there were in the Potteries one thousand members of the National Land Campaign, which fact suggests that Chartism was sufficiently strong in the district for their influence to be worth courting and their enmity to be feared.[3]

As a result of the conflict of aims and policies, and the rivalries and squabbles amongst those who professed to lead them, unionism amongst the potters was in a hopeless muddle during the few years following 1846. During these years of disorganisation trade on the whole was bad, reaching its lowest point in the summer of 1847, when it was reported that the depression in the pottery

[1] *Northern Star*, May 1, May 8, 1847.
[2] *Northern Star*, December 6, 1847.
[3] *Northern Star*, November 27, 1847.

trade was greater than at any time during the previous twenty years.[1] Had trade been better, probably the course of events would have run differently, but, as it was, bad trade tended to change the "disorganisation" of the men into "no-organisation".

There was no concerted action on the part of the masters during this period to take advantage of the men's weakness and recuperate trade losses out of wages, but, nevertheless, many masters, without reference to their fellow-manufacturers, made cuts in the wage rates of their employees.[2] It would appear that there was but little alteration made in the wage rates at the time when hiring agreements were being made. At the 1847 hirings, a time of the worst depression, there were but "few cases of masters and men at variance". In some cases slight reductions in working prices were made, and in others advances were given, but for the principal articles in the trade there was no change made in the price of workmanship.[3] Nevertheless, reductions in wages were made at times other than the Martinmas Hiring Owing to the depression in trade men would be prevailed upon, despite their agreements, to submit to reductions in wage rates under the threat of losing their employment. In addition to reductions in piece-work prices the practice of journeymen working for less than journeyman rates became once more a common feature of the trade.[4] This state of affairs—weak trade union organisation and a downward tendency in wages—continued until the 'fifties, when, aided by improved trade, the potters made an attempt to better their conditions.[5]

In 1850 the potters were weakly organised in branch

1 *Northern Star*, May 22, 1847.
2 *Staffordshire Advertiser*, September 21, 1850.
3 *Staffordshire Mercury*, November 14, 1847.
4 *Staffordshire Advertiser*, September 21, 1850.
5 *Staffordshire Advertiser*, September 21, 1850.

unions which had survived from the United Branches of Operative Potters. The Potters' Emigration Society was no more. In 1848 it had resolved to admit to its membership men of any trade, thus ceasing to be a potters' organisation, and it consequently passes out of this history.[1] The National Association for the Protection of Labour, its importance gone and no longer carrying the boastful prefix of "Monster", did not represent any organised body of potters.[2] The disruptive ideas of "Emigration", "Home Colonisation" and "Workmen's Ownership of Industry", which had been projected by the different claimants to the sympathies of the potters, were no longer thought of as having a practical application.[3] Terribly weak, but still alive, the potters' organisations had clambered out of the muddle into which, by their own folly and the accident of circumstance, they had been thrown.

In the late summer of 1850 the potters at several manufactories sent in to their employers demands for an increase in wages. The demands were not issued generally throughout the trade, but were, unfortunately, sent, in the main, to those manufacturers who had been the least guilty of reducing their employees' wages during the periods of depressed trade, and who did not employ journeymen at less than journeyman rates.[4] The demands were resisted and a strike occurred which was, on the whole, favourable to the men.[5] During the whole course of the dispute, both

[1] *Staffordshire Mercury*, May 13, 1848.

[2] At one time usual for *Northern Star* to speak of National Association as "this Monster Association".

[3] United Branches for "emigration"; the Chartists for "Home Colonisation"; and the National Association for Employment of Labour for "Workmen's Ownership of Industry".

[4] *Staffordshire Advertiser*, September 14, September 21; October 13, 1850.

[5] *Report from the Select Committee on Masters and Operatives* (*Equitable Councils of Conciliation*) (1856), 213; evidence Maitland.

before and after the cessation of work, the representatives of the men pressed for the formation of a Board of Arbitration and Conciliation to which the question at issue could be referred. In this they were unsuccessful, but their efforts were not altogether wasted, for some time later the Chamber of Commerce, which was established soon after the dispute of 1850, intimated its willingness to discuss, on behalf of the masters, the idea of arbitration with the unions.[1]

The year 1850 is in many ways a great landmark in the history of the wage-earning potter. It was the end of an old and the beginning of a new order. The distinguishing marks of this new order were the existence of numerous small and unimportant potters' unions, the great importance given to the idea of arbitration and the gradual but enormous change in the manufacturing processes of the industry owing to the development of the use of mechanical power. All these points are of great importance, and need full and detailed treatment. To ignore any of them would be to present an incomplete picture. Misunderstanding would result from a treatment of the subject which dealt only with the numerous unions into which the potters were organised, and the allegiance which they all gave to the idea of arbitration, and ignored the fact that the pottery industry was passing through a change which, except that it was more gradual, affected the potter in the same way that the textile inventions of the early nineteenth century affected the spinner and weaver. These points indicate the lines along which the history of trade unionism in the pottery industry will be traced in the following chapters.

[1] *Staffordshire Advertiser*, October 13, 1850; November 20, 1852. *Report of Royal Commission on Trade Unions* (1867–68), 87; evidence Hollins.

CHAPTER VIII

ARBITRATION

The readiness of the potters, from the 'fifties onwards, to discuss and adopt schemes of arbitration and conciliation was due, in no small measure, to the work of the National Association of United Trades. That organisation stood wholeheartedly for arbitration or conciliation as a means of remedying industrial grievances,[1] and it is no mere coincidence that from the time of its propaganda work begins the reign of the arbitration idea in the pottery industry.

Arbitration and conciliation, as methods of terminating industrial disputes, had long been known to the potters, but never before the 'fifties had any serious importance been attached to them. In 1833 an arbitration and conciliation board had been formed in the pottery industry, but it had been short-lived, for the operatives felt themselves at the time too strong to be in need of any method other than the strike in order to secure their aims, and consequently they were not concerned in keeping an arbitration board alive.[2]

During the 1834 strike both masters and men asked that the questions at issue should be settled by arbitration or conciliation, but, as neither side could agree to the other's proposed personnel for a board, nothing came of the requests.[3] The dispute of 1836 was settled by conciliation, if such a term can be used to describe proceedings in which the complete dominance of the masters' representatives over those of the men was so obvious.[4] Earlier

[1] Webb: *History of Trade Unionism* (ed. 1920), 190.

[2] J. Boyle: "An Account of Strikes in the Potteries in 1834–36", *Journal of Statistical Society*, London, vol. i (1839), 39. *supra* (69, 81).

[3] *supra* (83–5).

[4] *supra* (94–7).

in the same dispute the men had proposed arbitration as a means of settlement, but the masters would not agree to the proposal.[1]

In neither the 1834 nor the 1836–7 dispute could it be said that the men were keen upon settlement by arbitration, their faith in both cases being placed in the strike weapon. Suggestions for arbitration or conciliation came merely as afterthoughts. In the 'forties, when it might have been expected that the potters' reactions to the disaster of 1837 would have led them to advocate schemes of conciliation, emigration held the field. With their tragic experience the potters were naturally timid of strikes, but they had no faith in conciliation or arbitration as methods to be used to maintain or improve the conditions of their working lives. They were obsessed with the idea of surplus labour. To improve the bargaining power of potters by reducing their number was a problem with which they were so much occupied that they had no time to consider the further problem of how potters should conduct their bargaining. In 1845 Evans stated the position of the potters at that time in regard to these questions when he said: ". . . the great evil was surplus labour, and so long as this continued, notwithstanding the establishment of boards of trade, their condition would not be much bettered."[2]

The ambition of the potters to give a scarcity value to labour died with the passing of the United Branches of Operative Potters, and its place was taken by ideas of conciliation and arbitration implanted in their minds by the delegates of the National Association.[3]

[1] *supra* (91).
[2] *Northern Star*, March 29, 1845.
[3] *Report of Royal Commission on Trade Unions* (1867–68), 86; evidence Hollins.
supra (126, 131).

It has already been stated that after the close of the 1850 dispute the masters intimated their willingness to discuss with the unions plans for the formation of a Board of Arbitration.[1] As a result of this intimation informal conferences took place between representatives of the Chamber of Commerce and representatives of the unions, the outcome of which was the addition in 1851 of an arbitration clause to the hiring paper which workmen signed when they entered upon their contract of service.[2] Under this clause it was provided that in the event of any dispute arising between workman and master such dispute should be referred to an arbitration Board of six persons, three of whom were to be pottery manufacturers chosen by the masters, and three working potters chosen by the workmen. The arbitration clause was not intended to, and did not in practice, deal with disputes arising at the time when contracts were being made. It was designed to deal with disputes which arose after the annual hiring contract had been effected.[3]

In the chapter dealing with the peculiar conditions of the pottery industry it was pointed out how easily disputes could arise, and how difficult they were, under the annual hiring system, to settle.[4] The introduction of new shapes and patterns was liable to be followed by a dispute, for often the employer and the operative would differ concerning the prices at which they were to be made. It could easily happen that upon the introduction of an article the operatives would object to the masters' assumption that it should be made at the same rate as existing articles, which were nearest to it in shape and size. If, for instance,

[1] *supra* (139).
[2] *Report from the Select Committee on Masters and Operatives* (*Equitable Councils of Conciliation*) (1856), 49, 201.
[3] *Report from the Select Committee on Masters and Operatives* (*Equitable Councils of Conciliation*) (1856), 49.
[4] *supra* (45).

the article was a ewer, and ewers at that particular factory were paid for at a poor rate, then the men would try to lift up the price of ewers by getting a better price for each new ewer which was introduced. The position adopted by the men in such circumstances is understandable. They would argue that the fact that they had worked for low wages on ewers was no reason why they should not get good wages on the next ewer to be introduced.[1] On the other hand, a dispute upon the introduction of a new shape could arise through the master offering the workmen a less price for it than the prices of similar articles made by his men would appear to warrant. The conduct of the master in this case is as understandable as the conduct of the men in the instance mentioned above. Men making certain articles would be getting more than the customary rate of wages, and the master had decided that the prices of those articles was to come down by the same process as that mentioned in the case of the ewers.

The most fruitful source of dispute, however, was the working of the system of "good from oven". New shapes were only introduced a few times during the year, but the system of "good from oven" was operating all the time that the factory was running. In the majority of cases, with good employers, there would be no dispute over ware which came imperfect from the oven.[2] Both master and man would be in agreement as to the cause of the imperfections. If the fault in the ware were due to the unskilfulness of the workman, payment would be refused him. But there arose many cases of real injustice to the workmen. Ware, after it had left the maker's hands, would be kept in the storeroom for a long time before it went into the oven, and the damage done to it during that

[1] *Report on Strikes and Lock-outs*, 1891 (1893–4), 394.
[2] *Report of Royal Commission on Trade Unions* (1867–68), 87.

period, although having nothing whatever to do with the workmen who had made it, had to be borne by them. Often, too, unscrupulous employers, or, as was more usual, their warehousemen, would refuse payment for ware in which the imperfections were manifestly not caused by the workman.[1]

For all these grievances of "good from oven" the arbitration clause offered a remedy, and for all disputes arising either from the introduction of new shapes or from other causes it provided an honourable means of settlement. In the past a master and his men either arrived at the settlement of a dispute as best they could amongst themselves, or they referred the matter to a magistrate for his decision.[2] For the workman who suffered under the "good from oven" system the only remedy had been to sue through the Courts, and that was a course which he, perhaps naturally, had felt disinclined to take.[3]

After the introduction of the arbitration clause the workman knew that should he, during the time of his contract, feel himself wrongfully suffering losses in his wages under the "good from oven" system, or be in disagreement with his employer over the price of a new article, he would be able to refer the matter to a tribunal upon which, equally with his employer, he was represented.

The Board of Arbitration provided for under the new clause in the hiring agreement was not a permanent one, but only to be called into existence when its services were

[1] *Trade Societies and Strikes. National Association for the Promotion of Social Science* (1860), 282.
The Beehive, March 11, 1872.

[2] *Report from the Select Committee on Masters and Operatives* (*Equitable Councils of Conciliation*) (1856), 203.

[3] *Report from the Select Committee on Masters and Operatives* (*Equitable Councils of Conciliation*) (1856), 55.
Trade Societies and Strikes. National Association for the Promotion of Social Science (1860), 282.

required. When a dispute arose, the master, or masters, and men concerned, would appeal to their organisations, and the matter would then pass out of their hands. The Chamber of Commerce and the particular union concerned would each appoint three persons, and thus the Board of Arbitration would come into being. The Board could, if it wished, appoint an umpire, but in practice this was never done. The Chamber's representatives would usually be nominated by the manufacturers involved in the dispute, and the union's representatives would be men of the same trade as those who were disputing. Thus, if the dispute was between a master and his hollow-ware pressers, the Hollow-ware Pressers' Society would send three of its members to represent the men. If it were flat pressers who were disputing, then three members of the Flat Pressers' Union would sit on the Board.[1] As at that time there was a separate union for each branch of the trade, it was easy to ensure that men involved in dispute were represented by workfellows in their own trade.

Hiring agreements containing the arbitration clause were first issued November 1852, and were used on all factories, the owners of which were members of the Chamber of Commerce. This body contained the bulk of the manufacturers and almost all those who were in a large way of business.[2]

To what extent the Chamber of Commerce agreement was used by outside manufacturers is not known, and it does not appear that there was any pressure exerted by the men to insist that the agreement should be used by all in the trade. During those years in which the arbitration

[1] *Report from the Select Committee on Masters and Operatives* (*Equitable Councils of Conciliation*) (1856), 213.

[2] *Staffordshire Advertiser*, November 20, 1852.

Report from the Select Committee on Masters and Operatives (*Equitable Councils of Conciliation*) (1856), 203.

clause operated, the services of a Board were only rarely called upon; nevertheless, there is no doubt that the fact of it being possible to refer a dispute to arbitration caused employers and operatives to settle their differences with greater ease.[1]

One decision given under the arbitration clause was of great importance, for it affected the whole trade and not merely those who were involved in the dispute to settle which a Board had been called. This was a decision given by a Board which had been called to settle a "good from oven" dispute between Messrs. Heath, of Tunstall, and some of their employees.[2] After hearing the evidence of both parties the Board laid down as a principle for the governing of the "good from oven" system that when ware was bad through faulty workmanship, then the maker should bear the loss, but for ware that was faulty from any other cause the workman should be paid. This decision of the Board was an acknowledgment by the employers of a principle to govern the system of "good from oven" and was a victory for the operatives, for the "good from oven" system had for many years had no governing principles. Actually the Board's decision was but a restatement of the principle for the governing of "good from oven" as laid down by the conference of masters and men in 1837, but the decisions of that conference had long been forgotten.[3]

Unfortunately the system of arbitration operating under the arbitration clause was bound up with a system which was detested by the men, that of annual hiring.[4] Nevertheless, for the period it was a great experiment and fully

[1] *Report of Royal Commission on Trade Unions* (1867–68), 87.
[2] *Report from the Select Committee of Masters and Operatives* (*Equitable Councils of Conciliation*) (1856), 55–6, 215.
[3] *supra* (98).
[4] *The Beehive*, April 23, 1870.
Report of Royal Commission on Trade Unions (1867–68), 87.

deserving of the praise which it received from all quarters. Credit for its introduction should be given to the delegates of the National Association of United Trades, and to M. D. Hollins, of the firm of Minton & Co. The former persistently pointed out to the potters that the annual hiring agreement ought to contain a mode of settlement for disputes which might arise during the twelve months, and that it should not be left entirely to whatever the master might choose to say he was willing to pay for any fresh article which he manufactured.[1] The latter, M. D. Hollins, worked hard from the side of the masters to introduce arbitration into the trade.[2]

In November 1866 the potters of North Staffordshire intimated their intention to abolish the system of annual hiring. The reason for this intimation was that, during the previous two years, the conduct of the masters in relation to annual hiring had been such as to make that system doubly irksome to the men. The practice of annual hiring had been gradually becoming less general, and the probability is that it would have eventually died out, but many of the masters in 1864 made an effort to reinstate it in its old position when they resisted the growing practice of terminating employment by the giving of a month's notice.[3]

[1] *Report of Royal Commission on Trade Unions* (1867–68), 86.

Trade Societies and Strikes. National Association for the Promotion of Social Science (1860), 282.

Lord Elcho, in the House of Commons, April 12, 1870: ". . . the fame of the Hon. Member for Sheffield [Mundella] rests upon this . . . that he has, or rather claims to have, invented . . . a system of reconciliation between workmen and employers, which was . . . in operation in agreement clauses in the Potteries for some twenty years before."

[2] Michael Daintry Hollins, of the firm of Minton & Co. He gave evidence before several inquiries. In the *Report from the Select Committee on Masters and Operatives* (*Equitable Councils of Conciliation*) (1856), his name is wrongly given as Magill Daintree Hollands.

[3] *Report from the Select Committee on Master and Servant* (1866), 62.

From the beginning of the century there had always been some few men fortunate enough to get a written stipulation added to their agreement, giving them the right to give and the obligation to take one month's notice to leave their employment.[1] The number of men working under these short-notice agreements remained very small until the late 'fifties, when there appears to have been a large and rapid increase in their number. There is, moreover, no doubt but that by the 'sixties even those who had no such stipulation added to their agreement believed that their contracts could be terminated upon the giving of a month's notice on either side.[2]

In the evidence collected by the Social Science Association for their report of 1860 it is stated that "in the Potteries the men are hired at Martinmas for a year, with a notice of one month in the case of either party desiring to be free".[3] A potters' union representative, giving evidence in 1866 before the Master and Servant Commission, said that up to two years previously it was customary for potters' contracts of service to be for one month.[4] During the years 1864–5 numbers of employers had insisted upon agreements being kept. Many men who left their employment upon the expiration of what they believed to be a legal month's notice found themselves summoned for breach of contract.[5] Those who had taken care to obtain

[1] *Report from the Select Committee on Master and Servant* (1866), 62. In 1825 there were some workmen on a week's engagement. *Pottery Mercury*, April 2, 1825. *Birmingham Daily Post*, November 15, 1866.

[2] *Staffordshire Mercury*, July 12, 1845. "Wood and Adams, potters in the employ of Messrs. Alcock . . . were charged with absenting themselves from work without leave . . . the defendants laboured under the impression that they might leave the Messrs. Alcock's employ by a month's notice. This they had done. . . ."

[3] *Trade Societies and Strikes. National Association for the Promotion of Social Science* (1860), 281.

[4] *Report from the Select Committee on Master and Servant* (1866), 62.

[5] *Report from the Select Committee on Master and Servant* (1866), 61.

a written stipulation giving them the right were, of course, able to leave legally at the end of a month, but during the two years mentioned these stipulations were hard to obtain.[1] Those who made no annual agreement, as, for instance, women and children, could legally leave at any time, but the custom of the trade was such that if an employer complained of an employee leaving him before the expiration of the trade year, no other master would employ that person until the new trade year began, irrespective of the fact that no written agreement had been broken.[2]

The desire of the workmen to have the practice of annual hiring discontinued was opposed by the masters, with the result that a stoppage of work of ten days' duration occurred. At the end of that time work recommenced upon the understanding that if men did not wish to sign annual hiring agreements they need not do so.[3] After this few men hired themselves for the year, and, although its reintroduction was threatened, the annual hiring paper disappeared from the trade.[4] The fact that the masters did not make a more determined opposition to the demand of the men for the discontinuance of the custom leads one to suppose that, despite the actions of many of their number during the few years previous to the stoppage, they had become less keen upon retaining the hiring system. One feature of the hiring system was retained; piecework prices and conditions of work were still fixed at Martinmas for the year.

The disappearance of the hiring agreement meant the disappearance also of the arbitration clause which was

1 *Report from the Select Committee on Master and Servant* (1866), 62.
2 *Select Committee on Masters and Operatives (Equitable Councils of Conciliation)* (1856), 203.
3 *Royal Commission on Trade Unions* (1867–68), 87.
Birmingham Daily Post, November 15, 16, 19, 1866.
4 *Potteries' Examiner*, August 12, October 14, 1871.

part of it, but its place in the trade was soon taken by an arbitration scheme of a more ambitious character.

At the end of 1867, just one year after the break-up of the annual hiring system, the workmen, through their unions, asked M. D. Hollins, the Chairman of the Potteries Chamber of Commerce, to use his influence with the manufacturers to obtain their consent to the establishment of a Board of Arbitration for the pottery industry on similar lines to that which was working so successfully in the hosiery industry in Nottingham. Hollins brought the matter before the pottery manufacturers and obtained their consent to co-operate with the unions in the establishment of such a Board.

A code of rules, based largely upon those of the Nottingham Board, was agreed upon, and in July 1868 a Board of Conciliation and Arbitration for the pottery industry definitely came into existence.[1] It was a permanent Board, and consisted of twenty members, ten of whom represented the men and ten the masters. From these twenty members four were elected to act as a working committee to which all questions in dispute had to be referred before they could be taken to the Board.

The Committee endeavoured in a conciliatory way to bring all matters referred to it to a settlement satisfactory to both parties, but if it failed such matters were to be sent to the Board. The Committee had powers of conciliation only and could not arbitrate. It could assist the parties in a dispute to come to an agreement, but it could not give an award. The Board met quarterly, unless there was urgent business to discuss, when its meetings were held as thought desirable. The officers of the Board consisted of a President,

[1] *Royal Commission on Trade Unions* (1867–68), 57.
The Beehive, April 23, 1870.
Royal Commission on Labour, vol. iii (1893–94), 397.

Vice-President, two Secretaries—one for the operatives and one for the employers—and a Referee.[1]

The establishment of the "Board of Arbitration and Conciliation for the Staffordshire China and Earthenware Manufacturers", to give it its full title, was largely due to the work of W. Owen, the editor of the *Potteries Examiner*, and M. D. Hollins, the Chairman of the Potteries Chamber of Commerce.[2] The former had been in correspondence with Mundella concerning the possibility of establishing a Board of Arbitration for the pottery industry similar to the one at Nottingham with which he was associated, and from him had received every encouragement.[3]

There is a great contrast between the 1868 arbitration scheme and the provision for arbitration under the old hiring agreement. The new Board was permanent and made provision for the regular holding of meetings. Its powers were sufficiently wide to enable it to deal with all disputes from the one between the individual workman and his employer to the one which affected every employer and employee in the trade. Under the old hiring agreement there was no permanent Board, and no provision for arbitration in the case of difference between the employers and employees as collective bodies. Arbitration was only provided for the settlement of disputes which occurred after prices and conditions of work for the year had been fixed. For example, the case of a general demand from the operative potters for a rise of wages could be dealt with under the 1868 Board, but it would not have come within the scope of the arbitration provision in the old hiring agreement. Both schemes were alike in that they depended

1 *Royal Commission on Trade Unions*, vol. ii (1868–69), 334.
2 *Royal Commission on Trade Unions* (1867–68), 87.
Royal Commission on Labour, vol. iii (1893–94), 397.
Birmingham Post, October 14, 1890.
3 *The Beehive*, April 23, 1870.

for their working upon the existence of organisations of employers and organisations of workmen. When the 1868 Board was first established it had power to deal with all questions which were brought before it.[1] No old-established usages were considered to be so vital to the existence of the trade as to be above discussion. Matters of difference between potter and master potter which may have developed into disputes were brought before it and amicably settled.[2] In the first year the men brought the question of "good from oven" before the Board with a view to the abolition of that system. In this they were unsuccessful, but they did get the Board to agree that in future the system of "good from oven" should be governed by the principle that the man should be paid for all ware which could not be proved to be imperfect because of faulty workmanship.[3] From the point of view of the men this was the best ruling which had been given upon the question of "good from oven", although it is doubtful if in practice it favoured them more than less generous rulings.

During the first few years of its existence far more use was made of the Board by the men than by the masters.[4] In the second year of the Board's office the secretary for

[1] *Royal Commission on Trade Unions* (1867–68), 88.
[2] *Royal Commission on Labour*, vol. iii (1893–94), 397–8.
[3] *Birmingham Daily Post*, August 30, 1869.
It will be noticed that this ruling was different from the one under the old "arbitration clause" (*supra* 146), which was that when ware was bad through faulty workmanship, then the maker should bear the loss, but for ware faulty from any other cause, the workman should be paid. The difference in the two is that whereas under the 1869 ruling it was the masters' business to prove that the flaws in bad ware were due to faulty workmanship, under the "arbitration clause" ruling the master could say to the man: "You claim to be paid for this bad work: you must clearly prove to me that it is not your fault." *Select Committee on Masters and Operatives* (*Equitable Council of Conciliation*) (1856), 207.
[4] *Royal Commission on Labour*, vol. iii (1893–94), 397.

the men wrote that he did not know of one case in which the employers had first appealed to the Board, although he declared that he knew several in which they had refused or wanted to refuse arbitration.[1]

These repeated appeals from the men for the redress of grievances without corresponding appeals from the other side soon led to consolidation in the ranks of the masters. Instead of questions being discussed by twenty members of a Board, often men voting with masters and masters voting with men, they were discussed by ten men and ten masters, each member voting consistently with his own class.[2] It was thus impossible to transact business without the presence of a referee.

In recognition of the necessity of the presence of a referee the Board, in the third year of its life, 1871, was reconstituted with that end in view. At the same time it was adopted as a principle to govern all disputes that work should be carried on pending settlements by the Board.[3] The rules of the Board provided for the presence of the umpire if he were required, but often settlements had been arrived at independently of him. As the Board became less deliberative and more contentious, and the impossibility of arriving at any settlement other than by the help of the umpire became apparent, it was necessary that he should be present during the whole proceedings of the Board, otherwise all the pros and cons of argument would have to be recapitulated for his benefit.[4]

The newly constituted Board was immediately called upon to settle disputes between certain branches of potters and their employers. These disputes had developed into

[1] *The Beehive*, March 26, 1870.
[2] *Royal Commission on Labour*, vol. iii (1893–94), 398.
[3] *The Beehive*, October 21, 1871.
[4] *Royal Commission on Labour*, vol. iii (1893–94), 398.

strikes and affected a large number of potters. In all cases they were the result of claims by the men for advances in wages. Both men and masters involved agreed to submit their differences to the Board, and an amicable settlement was arrived at which, upon the whole, was favourable to the men.[1]

In the following year, 1872, some few weeks before Martinmas, the men from most of the pottery branches in North Staffordshire sent in notices for advances in wages to begin in the new trade year, and from the two branches involved a demand was made for the abolition of the "good from oven" system.[2] The men were strengthened in their demand for the abolition of the system of "good from oven" by the fact that the leading house of Minton & Co. had just previously consented to pay their workmen "good from hand", but, nevertheless, almost all other manufacturers were determined to resist the radical change in the customs of the trade which acceding to the men's demand would have meant.[3]

The men refused to withdraw their demand for the abolition of the system of "good from oven", and the masters refused even to discuss the matter.[4] At the end of the trade year, November 11th, the manufacturers locked their men out. During the week of the lock-out the masters agreed to submit the men's demand to arbitration, and on Tuesday, November 19th, this was done. The umpire, H. T. Davenport, decided that alteration of a trade custom was a matter which fell outside the province of the Arbitration Board. The workmen submitted to this decision and the lock-out was lifted.[5]

[1] *The Beehive*, December 2, 9, 23, 1871.
Potteries Examiner, October 28, 1871.
[2] *The Beehive*, August 24, September 7, November 16, 1872.
[3] *The Beehive*, November 16, 1872.
[4] *The Beehive*, November 23, 1872.
[5] *The Beehive*, November 23, 1872.

The masters had not objected to discussing the claims sent in by the men for advances in wages, and after work had recommenced they were considered by the Board and fairly good advances were awarded.[1]

Four years later, September 1876, the pottery manufacturers of North Staffordshire gave notice that they would from Martinmas of that year reduce their workmen's wages by 10 per cent. The matter was referred to the Arbitration Board and J. E. Davis, who for the first few years of its existence had been umpire to the Board, being at that time Stipendiary Magistrate in the Potteries, but who was in 1876 Police Magistrate in London, was asked to act as umpire.[2] The case for the Manufacturers was:

1. The depressed state of trade;
2. The increased foreign competition;
3. The greatly reduced prices at which goods were selling;
4. That while from time to time when trade was good advances had been made in the prices paid to workmen, yet on no occasion had any reduction been made when trade had been depressed.

These grounds for a reduction were met by the workmen in written statements from each branch, some of which also contained counter claims. The statements from the men's branches differed in some cases. The hollow-ware pressers agreed with the manufacturers that trade was depressed, but claimed that it was no worse in the pottery than in any other large industry. The printers declared that trade with them was better than in 1871 and 1872, when advances had been awarded them, and that, in

[1] *The Beehive*, November 23, 1872.
Royal Commission on Labour, vol. iii (1893–94), 398.

[2] *Royal Commission on Labour*, vol. iii (1893–94), 398.

fact, it was better than it had been for over twenty years. The turners and handlers denied that there was any depression in trade in their branches. The ovenmen, kilnmen and saggar-makers declared that trade was as good with them as a year ago, but, even if this were not so, they contended that their wages ought not to be reduced as they were not pieceworkers but day-wage men.

All branches were agreed in ridiculing the fear of foreign competition. No country, it was declared, could surpass England in the production of pottery either in prices or quality. To the third point put forward by the Manufacturers, that the selling price of ware had been greatly reduced, the hollow-ware pressers replied that the advances in selling prices which had taken place during the previous years, and the reductions in the price of materials, would enable the manufacturers to make reductions without interfering with wages, which had never been governed by the fluctuations of the markets. The statement of the ovenmen and kilnmen was, in effect, that selling prices had never governed producers' prices, and, even if they had, they were still sufficiently good that they did not warrant wages being reduced. The printers contented themselves with pointing out that, since they had received advances in wages, selling prices had been risen several times, and, although some reductions had taken place, they were still high enough to cover wages.

In support of their counter claim for an advance of 10 per cent., the hollow-ware pressers contended that the coming of machinery had taken away from them the easy shapes upon which good wages could be earned and left them with only difficult ones to make. The flat pressers made a claim for 10 per cent. on the grounds that owing to Factory and Education Acts the wages of the children they employed had greatly risen.

The umpire decided that, although the evidence for depression in trade, foreign competition and reductions in selling prices was overwhelming and made it impossible to consider the applications for rises in wages, as it was inexpedient that workmen's wages should be made to move up or down with the fluctuations of the market, he could not recommend a reduction. He therefore awarded that wages for the coming year should be the same as if no notice for alteration had been given on either side.[1]

The workmen's evidence before this Arbitration Board enquiry contained a statement which was not wholly true. This was that selling prices had never governed wages.[2] It was true in the sense that wages had not fallen or risen with every change in selling price, but the rises in wages in 1872 were in part the result of rises in selling prices. In the *Beehive* for August 24, 1872, the following notice appears:

> "The China and Earthenware manufacturers in the Staffordshire Potteries have added 10 per cent. to prices, and the workpeople have given notice of a demand for a large increase in wages in November."

Moreover, there had been occasions when the unions had declared their desire for the linking of wages to selling prices.[3] However, the case put forward by the men in '72 was that house rent and other items in the cost of living had risen.

The matter of reduction in wages was taken up by the

[1] *Royal Commission on Labour*, vol. iii (1893–94) 398.
Award on the Dispute between China and Earthenware Manufacturers of North Staffordshire and their Workmen, 1876–77.

[2] *Award on the Dispute between China and Earthenware Manufacturers of North Staffordshire and their Workmen*, 1876–77.

[3] *Staffordshire Potteries Telegraph*, December 18, 1852. Letter from Hollow-ware Pressers' Union Executive: ". . . what we wish is to associate inseparably certain rates of prices with certain states of the market." (By 'prices' the potter understands 'making prices' or piece rates.)

employers again in 1879, and they issued a notice saying that from Martinmas of that year the wages of all their employees would be reduced by 10 per cent. The notice was taken before the Arbitration Board and Lord Hatherton was appointed umpire. The case for the masters was practically the same as the one put forward by them in 1876: depression in trade, foreign competition and their inability to pay the existing rate of wages. The evidence for the trade depression was indisputable, and in the opinion of the umpire it was a sufficient reason for a reduction in wages. He accordingly gave as his verdict that all directly employed workpeople should suffer a reduction in their wages of 8⅓ per cent., or one penny in the shilling.[1]

As would be expected, this award caused great dissatisfaction amongst the potters of North Staffordshire, and its application was the immediate cause of many small disputes between employers and employed.[2]

The Longton China Manufacturers, who were not represented on the Board, also met with much opposition in their attempt to enforce the award on their workpeople. In the month following Lord Hatherton's decision the throwers of Tunstall successfully struck for an advance in piece-rates to the level of those paid in Hanley, and in February the printers and transferrers at a large firm in Longton struck unsuccessfully for an advance in wages.[3]

The potters were in a turbulent mood, which did not lessen as the year advanced. In April the flat pressers threatened to strike for a rise in wages and for the changing of the price-fixing date from November 11th to June 1st,

[1] *Royal Commission on Labour*, vol. iii (1893–4).
Pottery and Glass Trades Review, June 1897. "It is but uttering a truism to say that 1878 has been a bad year for master potters."
[2] *Pottery Gazette*, January 1, 1880.
[3] *Pottery Gazette*, January 1, 1880.

and the throwers, turners and handlers intimated their intention to withdraw from the Board and to give notice for a rise in wages and an alteration in the price-fixing date from November to August.[1] Early in June of that year, 1880, the operative potters held a meeting and decided that instead of striking, which they would have done had the flat pressers pursued the course they threatened, they would abide by Lord Hatherton's award until Martinmas (November 11th).[2]

At Martinmas, 1880, the potters appealed to the Board for a return to the piece-rates existing before the Lord Hatherton reduction, T. Brassey at this time being umpire. The employers took the stand that the industry was unable to pay more wages and the workmen were not in a position to disprove that assertion. The umpire agreed with the employers that the trade could not pay more wages and gave a verdict accordingly.[3]

The men smarted under the disappointment caused by T. Brassey's adverse award and agitated for the break-up of the Board. A mass meeting of potters was held in December 1880, the month following the award, and resolutions were passed declaring that it was desirable to abolish the Board as then constituted, and that the time for price-fixing should undergo alteration, contracts to be entered into at midsummer instead of November.[4] Each of the operative potters' societies represented on the Board sent in a formal resignation, but at the request of the manufacturers these were withdrawn, and a meeting

[1] *Pottery Gazette*, June 1, 1880.
[2] *Pottery Gazette*, July 1, 1880.
[3] *Pottery Gazette*, December 1, 1880.
Royal Commission on Labour, vol. iii (1893–94), 398.
Board of Arbitration, Staffordshire Potteries, November 1880. Award of Thomas Brassey, M.P.
[4] *Pottery Gazette*, January 1, 1881.

of the Board was called to discuss the men's grievances.[1] The Board met on April 25, 1881, and the men's proposals were discussed and sent to the manufacturers' association for their consideration.[2] The employers held a meeting on May 2nd, when the following resolution was passed: "That the manufacturers consider that no proposal can be entertained that would constitute a breach of the contract entered into in November."[3] At a meeting of the workpeople a few days afterwards this breaking off of negotiations was accepted.[4]

In November of the same year, 1881, the operatives made an attempt to get by a strike what they had failed to get by arbitration. The china workers were not affected by the quarrel, and in the earthenware trade several of the leading firms, amongst whom were Messrs. Minton, of Stoke, and Messrs. Wedgwood, of Etruria, came to an amicable arrangement with their workpeople without the latter striking. Altogether thirty thousand persons were involved in the dispute, this number being equal to about two-thirds of those engaged in the earthenware manufacture.[5]

Many operatives' meetings were held during the course of the strike, and it was obvious from the remarks of the union leaders addressing these meetings, and from the interjections of the men, that the rank and file were tired of arbitration and had forced the leaders to countenance the strike.[6] The leaders, William Owen in particular, still advocated arbitration, but an arbitration which was

[1] *Pottery Gazette*, March 1, 1881.
[2] *Pottery Gazette*, May 2, 1881.
[3] *Pottery Gazette*, June 1, 1881.
Royal Commission on Labour, vol. iii (1893–94), 398.
[4] *Pottery Gazette*, June 1, 1881.
[5] *Royal Commission on Labour*, vol. iii. (1893–94), 398–9.
[6] *Birmingham Daily Post*, December 1, 7, 1881.

"fair" to the men. By "fair" arbitration they meant the establishment of a Board of Arbitration, the rules of which would give the umpire the right to appoint an accountant to examine the books of representative manufacturers, for, they argued, if, as the last two arbitration awards had demonstrated, the operatives' wages were to be determined by the ability of the trade to pay such wages, then the umpire ought to be in a position to know what profits or losses manufacturers were making.[1] The unions asked the manufacturers to agree to the dispute being settled by arbitration along these lines, but, although the manufacturers expressed their willingness to submit the case to an Arbitration Board, they were not prepared to agree to any scheme which meant the disclosure of their private business to an umpire.[2]

The strike dragged on for six weeks, and ended by the men going in to work on the employers' terms.[3] It does not appear to have been conducted very ably. At several of the firms concerned men were allowed to remain at work to finish up orders. The strikers were greatly distressed by lack of money, although the men still at work subscribed liberally to a fund for their aid.[4]

After a few years' interval the Arbitration Board was re-established and the rule pressed for by the operatives' unions incorporated in its constitution. This was: "That the umpire shall have full opportunity to verify any figures or statements made in evidence providing that such investigation be not allowed to interfere with or expose the private business of any firm; such verification shall be made through the sworn accountant appointed by and

[1] *Birmingham Daily Post*, November 25, December 1, 1881.
[2] *Birmingham Daily Post*, December 13, 15, 17, 1881.
[3] *Royal Commission on Labour*, vol. iii (1893–94), 399. *Birmingham Daily Post*, December 20, 1881.
[4] *Birmingham Daily Post*, November 18, 22, December 1, 6, 1881.

responsible to the umpire, and shall be disclosed to no other person."[1]

In 1890, full of hope that under the new rule the umpire would be forced to give them a favourable award, the operatives appealed to the Board for an advance of 10 per cent. in wages. The employers countered by sending in an appeal for a reduction of 10 per cent.[2] There was some delay before these appeals could be dealt with. First the employers objected to the operatives' representatives on the Board,[3] and, second, after it had been decided to form a special Board of one nominee of the masters and one of the men—the two to appoint an umpire—the masters' nominee, Frank James, of Walsall, objected to serve with the men's nominee, James Mawdesley, on the ground that the latter person was a trade union official, and therefore biased in favour of the operatives.[4] As the men insisted upon retaining J. Mawdesley as their nominee, the masters were compelled to appoint someone else in the place of F. James. Eventually the Board was formed—J. Mawdesley for the men, B. Suart for the manufacturers, and H. T. Hinckes as umpire—but owing to so much delay it was May 1891 before it could commence work.[5]

After the details of the dual requests had been considered the men pressed for the umpire to order an investigation of the manufacturers' books under the new rule. It then appeared that the masters had anticipated this move on the part of the men, and had privately appointed an accountant to examine the books on their behalf. They now brought forward his evidence to the effect that the books of ten firms had been examined and showed trade

[1] *Royal Commission on Labour*, vol. iii (1893–94), 399.
[2] *Royal Commission on Labour*, vol. iii (1893–94), 399.
[3] *Birmingham Daily Post*, October 14, 21, 22, 1890.
[4] *Birmingham Daily Post*, December 30, 1890.
[5] *Strikes and Lock-outs*, 1891 (1893–94), 341.

to be in an unremunerative condition. The men urged the umpire to appoint an accountant, to be responsible to him and to the two arbitrators, to investigate the statements made in evidence by the manufacturers, but, though at first favourable, the umpire did not press the matter, and no investigation was made along the lines desired by the operatives.[1]

The arbitrators and the umpire compromised between the claims of the masters and the men, and gave as their award that no alterations should be made in the rates of wages.[2] The men, dissatisfied with the result of the arbitration, and annoyed by the way in which the new rule, to which they had pinned their faith, operated in practice, obeyed the award for the period covered—May 1891 to March 1892—and then withdrew from the Board.[3]

The end of this period saw two strikes in progress amongst the potters of North Staffordshire, both of which were in the ovenmen's branch of the trade. One, at a Hanley firm, was for an advance in wages, and dated from January 4th, and the other, at a firm in Tunstall, against payment at less than the accepted rate, and dated from February 8th.[4] These two strikes being still unsettled, and the operatives' unions and the employers' association failing to agree as to whether the custom of fixing workmen's wages once a year should still continue or whether it should be substituted by a twenty-eight days' notice to terminate contracts, the employers decided to settle matters by locking their workmen out, which they did on May 2nd.[5]

1 *Royal Commission on Labour*, vol. iii (1893–94), 399.
2 *Strikes and Lock-outs*, 1891 (1893–94), 341.
Royal Commission on Labour, vol. iii (1893–94), 399.
3 *Royal Commission on Labour*, vol. iii (1893–94), 399.
4 *Report on Strikes and Lock-outs of* 1892 (1894), 70.
5 *Report on Strikes and Lock-outs of* 1892 (1894), 86.

The lock-out was lifted on May 21st, and the men recommenced work on the understanding that the custom of fixing wages once a year should continue, but that the trade year should no longer begin in November but on March 25th, the latter date being more favoured by the men as coming at a time when the weather was usually better than in November—a matter of some moment if a strike was in contemplation. A Joint Committee of Conciliation was to be established for the settling of general trade disputes, but the reconstruction of the Arbitration Board was to be left until an emergency should arise. The two ovenmen's strikes were settled at the same time as the lock-out.[1]

It was fairly obvious to all observers in 1892 that the arbitration idea was not held in favour by the operatives. They were tired of it in 1881, but partly owing to the fact that the strike of that year failed, and to the persuasion of their leaders that with a rule giving the umpire right to investigate the employers' books they would get reasonable demands granted under an Arbitration Board, they consented to give it another trial. The rule which their union leaders had striven for had been tried, and in the eyes of the men had proved a failure, so the last hope in arbitration had been destroyed.[2]

The Joint Committee of Conciliation which survived the death of the Arbitration Board lasted but a few years before that also died. This Committee was intended to deal with disputes which occurred at individual factories during the trade year, but as both employers and employees showed a lack of readiness to avail themselves of its services it lapsed from lack of employment. In 1893 it dealt with nine cases, but in 1897 only one case was brought

[1] *Report on Strikes and Lock-outs of* 1892 (1894), 86.
[2] *Royal Commission on Labour*, vol. iii (1893–94), 400.

before it, and in the following year, none. The one case in 1897 appears to be the last case dealt with by this body.[1]

In 1894 and 1895 the pottery manufacturers of North Staffordshire endeavoured to re-establish a Board of Arbitration, but their attempts failed.[2] In the years immediately following several small disputes were settled by arbitration, but it was not until 1908 that any further attempt was made to form an Arbitration Board.[3] In this year a dispute regarding the wages and conditions of employees led to the formation of the Board of Conciliation and Reference for the Staffordshire China and Earthenware Manufacturers and Operatives.[4] The constitution of this Board was based largely upon the model of its predecessor.

The period between 1892 and 1908, when there had been no Board, was sufficiently long to allow of the resentment felt by the operatives towards Arbitration Boards to die down. Moreover, whereas in 1892 the potters had been organised in numerous single branch unions, bound together in time of dispute in a loose federation, in 1908 almost all organised potters were in one union.[5] Their representatives to a Board, therefore, were more powerful, for they were not hampered by having to reconcile the differing policies and aims of many unions. The days of enthusiasm

[1] *Report on Strikes and Lock-outs*, 1896 (1897), lxxi.
Report on Strikes and Lock-outs, 1897 (1898), 112.

[2] *Pottery Gazette*, January, March, 1895.

[3] *Report on Strikes and Lock-outs*, 1908 (1909), appendix ii.
Report on Rules of Voluntary Conciliation and Arbitration Boards (1910), xviii.
Birmingham Post, February 12, 1908: "... attitude of operatives to conciliation uncertain ... leaning towards antagonism ... manufacturers generally in favour...."

[4] *Birmingham Daily Post*, February 20, 1908: "... operatives agree to ... refer all matters to Board of Conciliation...."
Report on Strikes and Lock-outs, 1908 (1909), appendix ii.

[5] *infra*, 177.

for the arbitration idea had, however, on the men's side, at any rate, long since passed, and it was inevitable that the Board would be unable to withstand any great strain imposed upon it. The testing of its strength and its breaking came with the raising of the century-old grievance of "good from oven". The rules of the Board laid down that "it is understood and agreed that under these rules neither employers nor operatives shall be entitled to appeal to the Board on the following questions, except as provided by the trade rules. (1) Good from Oven. (2) Limitation of Apprentices." The trade rules referring to these questions were: (1) The trade usage should be "that the operatives be paid for all ware that is spoiled through causes that do not come under their control or that cannot be traced to their bad workmanship", and "that any branch of operatives that is paid from oven and which is dissatisfied with the check provided by its employers as regards the loss and breakage of ware shall be entitled to have the question referred to the Committee", and (2) "that any body of journeymen who feel aggrieved by the action of any particular firm regarding the employment of apprentices shall be entitled to have the matter brought before the Committee".[1] The employers, when they agreed to the rules of the Board that "whereas grievances arising concerning 'good from oven' or the employment of apprentices could properly be submitted to the Board", clearly intended that there should be no alteration in trade usages, that, in fact, these customs should remain outside the scope of the Board's jurisdiction. The operative potters naturally chafed under these restrictions to the Board's activity, and early in 1911 they gave notice to the employers that they desired an alteration in the rules so as to enable the Board to consider the questions of

[1] *Report on Strikes and Lock-outs*, 1908 (1909), appendix ii.

apprenticeship and "good from oven". In this the operatives acted constitutionally, for the Board rules permitted of alterations and additions after due notice had been given. The employers proved as tenacious as ever for the retention of the custom of "good from oven". They pointed out what was perfectly true, that at the time of the formation of the Board they had insisted that the points now raised by the men should be expressly excluded from its jurisdiction, and, as their views upon the matter were unchanged, they felt bound to resist the alteration of rules as proposed by the operatives. Many communications passed between the manufacturers and the men, but neither side would move from the position which they had taken up. There was no desire on the part of the men or their leaders to preserve the arbitration principle at all costs, and, failing to widen its scope, they withdrew from the Board a few months after their notice requesting a change in the rules had been given.[1]

[1] *Monthly Journal* (*Potters'*), August 1911.

CHAPTER IX

THE CHANGE

The years 1850 to 1870 form a distinct period in the study of unionism in the pottery industry. This period saw the break-up of the annual hiring system and the establishment of an Arbitration Board.[1] But, more important in many ways, it saw also the end of that stage in the history of pottery manufacture which could be described as one of handicraft.

From 1850–70 the potters' unions were small and jealous of their independence. So far as North Staffordshire was concerned each branch of the trade had its own union, and, in some instances, more than one.[2] All of them were weak in membership,[3] although not conspicuously so when compared with the period following. Membership figures are obtainable for a few societies only, but, scanty as the information is, it is sufficient to indicate the strength of labour organisation amongst the potters during the period under review. The chairman of the Pottery Manufacturers' Chamber of Commerce, M. D. Hollins, in his evidence before the Select Committee on Masters and Operatives, April 1856, gave as his opinion that unionism existed amongst the potters of North Staffordshire to a greater extent than it did amongst workmen in any other district.[4] On the other hand, W. Maitland, a hollow-ware presser, giving evidence before the same Committee, declared

[1] *supra*, 149–50.

[2] *Royal Commission on Trade Unions* (1867–68), 88.

[3] *Select Committee on Masters and Operatives* (*Equitable Councils of Conciliation*) (1856), 217–18.

[4] *Select Committee on Masters and Operatives* (*Equitable Councils of Conciliation*) (1856), 204.

that many journeymen potters were not connected with any union.[1]

In 1867 the Hollow-ware Pressers' Society had a membership of eight hundred, roughly about half the number of journeymen of that trade in the district.[2] This number, however, must not be taken as indicating the normal membership of the society during the period 1850–70, for the year 1867 was the one following a successful strike and a good union membership is to be expected.[3] In 1868 the membership of this society had fallen to five hundred, which number may be taken as more nearly representing the average membership at that time.[4] The Ovenmen's Society in 1866 had a membership of seven hundred, out of a total number in the trade of one thousand, seven hundred.[5] In 1867 the Printers' Union numbered one hundred and forty.[6] In 1868 the Flat Pressers' Society had a membership of ninety-eight.[7] Ten years later, 1876–8 the membership of the Hollow-ware Pressers' Society was greater than that of 1868, but less than that of 1867.[8] The number of organised ovenmen was exactly the same in the later period as in 1866, but the membership of the Flat Pressers' Society had increased threefold.[9] The numbers of organised printers unfortunately cannot be compared, for while in the 'sixties and earlier their society

[1] *Select Committee on Masters and Operatives* (*Equitable Councils of Conciliation*) (1856), 217.

[2] *Royal Commission on Trade Unions* (1868–69), vol. ii, 58.

[3] *Royal Commission on Trade Unions* (1868–69), vol. ii, 58. *supra*, 149.

[4] *Royal Commission on Trade Unions* (1868–69), vol. ii, 324.

[5] *Birmingham Daily Post*, November 22, 1866.

[6] *Report of the Trades Conference*, St. Martin's Hall, London, March 5–8, 1867.

[7] *Royal Commission on Trade Unions* (1868–69), vol. ii, 324.

[8] *9th* (1876) *and 11th* (1878) *Reports of Trade Union Congress*.

[9] *8th* (1875) *and 9th* (1876) *Reports of Trade Union Congress*.

included only men, in the 'seventies and later it also included women.[1] It will be seen that, except for the Flat Pressers, organisation of potters in the 'sixties compared fairly favourably with that of the 'seventies. The years 1872 and 1873 have been deliberately excluded for purposes of comparison, for those were years of trade union revival,[2] and membership of all the societies during them was high and not at all typical. The years taken are good average ones for the 'seventies and 'eighties, excluding 1872 and 1873. Although no figures are obtainable for the earlier period, the 'fifties, there is no reason to suppose that unionism was either weaker or stronger then than in the 'sixties. In 1850, it will be remembered, the unions were strong enough to prosecute a successful strike,[3] and in 1852 to get an arbitration clause introduced into the annual agreement.[4]

In spite of the fact that the organised potters were in small single branch unions, and gave the impression of caring only for the interests of the members of a particular section of the trade,[5] they made efforts to keep in touch with the larger labour world. In 1866 arrangements were made for their various societies to join the United Kingdom Alliance of Organised Trades, though it does not appear that their negotiations fructified.[6] In 1867 two of the branch unions sent delegates to the Conference of Trades, St. Martin's, London—the assembly out of which grew the Trades Union Congress.[7] Apparently the potters theoretically believed in the unity of the producing classes, but found in practice that the unity of their own branch societies was too difficult to achieve.

[1] *infra*, 175. [2] *infra*, 172. [3] *supra*, 138. [4] *supra*, 142.
[5] As, for instance, their inability to come to a common agreement before an arbitration enquiry. *supra*, 155–6.
[6] *Birmingham Daily Post*, November 15, 1866.
[7] The Printers and the Crate-makers. *Report of the Trades Conference*, St. Martin's Hall, March 5–8, 1867.

The potters' unions of the 1850–70 period were based upon low subscriptions and few benefits. The Hollow-ware Pressers' Society, which is a typical example, received a weekly subscription of 3d. from its members, and had the power, in the event of a dispute, to call a levy. The benefits given were allowances to men out of work and strike pay.[1] The Turners' Society was exceptional in that it gave funeral benefits in addition to allowance for strike and out of work.[2] It does not appear that any of the societies gave sick benefit to their members.

Except in the case of Scotland, trade union organisation in the out-potteries apparently did not exist during the third quarter of the nineteenth century.[3] It should be remembered that the out-potteries, in most cases, were very small, often comprised of but one or two firms,[4] and, although there were good reasons why the potters employed there should ally themselves with a national union, the incentive to form a local independent society hardly existed. A few men working in one place, having problems which must be dealt with collectively, form almost a natural union, and this was the case with the out-potteries (Scotland excepted). Not until they felt kinship with the potters of other districts or with men of other trades would the desire for union arise.

Under the National Potters' Unions of the 'thirties and 'forties most of the out-potteries were brought into the organisations, but in both periods such organisation was short-lived.[5] Scotland, containing as it did the largest of

1 *Trade Societies and Strikes. National Association for the Promotion of Social Science* (1860), 143.
Royal Commission on Trade Unions (1868–69), vol. ii, 58.
2 *Royal Commission on Trade Unions* (1868–69), vol. ii, 328.
3 *Trade Societies and Strikes. National Association for the Promotion of Social Science* (1860), 141.
4 *Children's Employment (Trades and Manufactures) Commission* (1843), L.3.
5 *supra*, 64–5, 113.

the out-potteries, had by far the best and longest-lived potters' organisations outside North Staffordshire. The Scottish potters in the 'fifties and 'sixties were organised in branch unions with a central executive, but they had not a union for each branch of the trade.

Had all the out-potteries been centred in one district the actions of the operatives might have influenced the pottery industry from the side of trade unionism, but such was not the case. The operatives of the smaller out-potteries organised themselves in the 'seventies, 'eighties and 'nineties, but until they came under the national organisation they were weak. Light is thrown on the poor bargaining power of the out-potters by the fact that their wages were always lower than those of workmen in the same trade in the Potteries. Moreover, although they were probably just as averse to having their manual skill displaced by machinery as were their fellows in North Staffordshire, it does not appear that any manufacturer in the out-potteries had difficulty in bringing it into use.[1]

The 'seventies brought to the potters a short period of trade prosperity, the beginnings of an industrial revolution and a revival in trade unionism. The last, and, in part, probably the second, were the results of the first-named. The trade union revival took, amongst the potters, the form of a complete reorganisation of their societies, and also a great increase in all of them. The most extraordinary case of increased membership was that of the Hollow-ware Pressers' Society, which rose from five hundred in 1868 to fourteen hundred in 1873, but in the following year it dropped to eight hundred, the same membership figure as for 1867, and it was not until 1891 that this society

[1] *Staffordshire Advertiser*, September 21, 1850.
W. Evans: *Art and History of the Pottery Business* (1846), ii.

again reached a membership of over eight hundred.[1] The 1873 membership figure was not surpassed until 1900.[2]

Between 1870 and 1872 the Hollow-ware Pressers, the Flat Pressers, the Printers and the Crate-makers re-organised their societies; or, more correctly, built up new societies.[3] The Hollow-ware Pressers' and the Flat Pressers' societies adopted the policy of high subscriptions and many benefits. Although long tried in the unions of other industries, such a policy, except for a short period in the 'forties, was new to the potters.[4] In the case of these two societies the subscriptions, benefits and rules were the same.[5] Subscriptions were a shilling a week, and sick, funeral, no-situation, out-of-work, victimisation, lock-out and strike benefits were given. As it may appear strange that there should be both "no-situation" and "out-of work" benefits, it should be explained that to the potter the two terms meant different things. "No-situation" meant exactly what the words imply, but "out-of-work" meant that the person so described had a situation, but the firm by whom he was employed had no work for him to do for the time being.

The rules of the new Flat Pressers' and Hollow-ware Pressers' societies were very similar to those of the old societies. Both the old and the new emphasised the importance of settling disputes by means of conciliation, but both recognised that strikes may sometimes be necessary. They took away the power to strike from the

[1] *Royal Commission on Trade Unions* (1868–69), 11th Report, vol. ii, 58, 324.
5th (1873), *6th* (1874) *and 24th* (1891) *Reports of Trade Union Congress.*
[2] *33rd* (1900) *Report of Trade Union Congress.*
[3] *Potteries Examiner*, March 17, 1871.
Third Report on Trade Unions, 1889.
Fourth Report on Trade Unions, 1890–91.
[4] *supra*, 113.
[5] *Potteries Examiner*, June 24, 1871.

disputing workmen, or the lodge to which they belonged, and vested it in the executive committee.[1]

The old rules had a long paragraph, not included in the new, dealing with the protection and help given by the union to its members in cases where disputes between employer and employed were brought to the County Court.[2] The reason for the exclusion of this paragraph from the new rules was not that the new societies gave no legal assistance to their members, but that they were faced with different problems from those of the old societies. Members of the old societies worked under an annual hiring agreement which often brought them into conflict with the law, and this fact had had to be reckoned with. Under the annual hiring agreement it was no uncommon thing for a sentence such as the following to appear in the Press, showing the importance of County Court proceedings to the unions: ". . . the cases of summonses of workmen before the magistrates for neglect of work were exceedingly numerous, and generally speaking the alleged 'neglect' arose out of disputes respecting prices, in which the defendants were supported by the unions".[3]

Unlike the Flat Pressers' and Hollow-ware Pressers societies, the Printers' and Transferrers' Trade Protection Society, established 1871, had low subscriptions and purely trade benefits.[4] The reason for this was not a belief that a trade union was a fighting organisation and that too

[1] *Trade Societies and Strikes. National Association for the Promotion of Social Science* (1860), 135–6.
Royal Commission on Labour. Rules of Associations of Employers and Employed (1892), 237.
[2] *Trade Societies and Strikes. National Association for the Promotion of Social Science* (1860), 136.
[3] *Staffordshire Advertiser*, November 20, 1852.
[4] *Royal Commission on Labour. Rules of Associations of Employers and Employed* (1892), 238.
Third Report on Trade Unions (1889), 128.

many benefits were an encumbrance, but that the society was one of mixed membership, containing both men and women, and it was expedient that subscriptions should be low, on account of the poor wages paid to women, from whom it would have been useless to expect high subscriptions. As it was, a woman paid half only of the subscription of a man, 2d. a week to his 4d., her benefits being in proportion.

The rules of this society were of an ordinary character, containing one item only of special interest, this being that "apprentices must serve for five years and not more than one is allowed to five journeymen".[1] The latter part of the rule, the limitation of apprentices, is understandable, and was common in trade union rules, but the first part, the insistence upon a five years' apprenticeship, is misleading, for, on the face of it, it would appear to be a praiseworthy attempt on the part of the printers to keep up the standard of their craft, but such was not the case. Printing was the least skilled of the pottery trades, and it was possible for a man of mature years to take his place as a journeyman a short time after entering it. Thus the whole clause, the first as much as the second part, was aimed at restricting entrance to the trade.

Of the Crate-makers' Society little is known, except that it gave dispute and unemployment, but not sick and funeral, benefits. It was formed in 1872, some months after a successful strike (in 1871) conducted by the previous crate-makers' society. Its membership was good until 1879, when it collapsed owing to the depression of that year.[2]

[1] *Third Report on Trade Unions* (1889), 128.
[2] *Fourth Report on Trade Unions* (1890–91).
The Beehive, September 16, 23, 1871.
Potteries Examiner, September 30, 1871.

The enthusiasm of the potters in the early 'seventies for trade unionism quickly waned, and membership of their societies declined accordingly. In the case of the largest union, the Hollow-ware Pressers, as has already been noted, membership fell very rapidly.[1] Speaking in later years of this decline in membership, the union leaders blamed the Arbitration Board. In their opinion the potters reasoned that with the existence of an Arbitration Board there was no necessity for a strong trade union, for differences between employer and employed would be settled by the Board whether the unions were strong or weak.[2] If this were so, one would have expected a growing membership after the break-up of the Arbitration Board in 1881, but this did not occur. An increasing or decreasing membership does not always admit of a simple explanation. Bad trade and the existence of an Arbitration Board were probably contributory causes of the decline, but whatever the reason trade union membership in the pottery industry, except for occasional spurts, which usually coincided with improvements in trade and the effects of which were quickly and almost wholly lost, remained comparatively low until 1907 and 1908, when a revival of trade unionist enthusiasm occurred. But the enthusiasm of 1908 soon waned, though its effect was not lost up to the outbreak of the European War, when conditions surrounding trade unionism became entirely different.

Although in the generation before the war "there was the stamp of futility on everything the unfortunate potter touched",[3] his schemes failing and his job taken from him by women and machinery, he yet succeeded in, from the point of view of trade union organisation, two important respects, namely, in the organisation of the potters of the

[1] *supra*, 169. [2] *Royal Commission on Labour* (1893–94), vol. iii, 399.
[3] Old Potter: *When I was a Child* (1903), 184.

"out-districts" and in the formation of the numerous small unions into three organisations. These three unions were:

1. Packers' Association, an organisation for pottery ware packers;
2. The United Ovenmen's Society, which catered for ovenmen, kilnmen, dippers and saggar-makers;
3. (The largest.) The National Amalgamated Society of Male and Female Pottery Workers, a union for all potters not included in 1 and 2.

The two main factors in the building up of the National Amalgamated Society were the amalgamation of various unions and the taking over of the members of several small unions which had dissolved.

In 1883 the National Order of Potters was established, and operatives from any branch of the pottery trade were eligible for membership.[1] For some years this society kept up a roll of a thousand members, but by 1898 its number had fallen to five hundred and fifty, and in the following year it joined the Hollow-ware Pressers' Union, a much larger organisation.[2] The Amalgamated Society of Hollow-ware Pressers and Clay Potters soon became the only organisation for mould-makers and earthenware clay potters, for in 1899 the Throwers', Turners' and Handlers' Society dissolved, in 1900 the Operative Sanitary Pressers' Association, in 1902 the Jet and Rockingham Workmen's Society, whilst the Mould-makers' Society had dissolved as far back as 1885.[3]

[1] *Royal Commission on Labour. Rules of Associations of Employers and of Employed* (1892), 236.

[2] *9th Report on Trade Unions*, 1896 (1897), 126–7.
11th Report on Trade Unions, 1898 (1899), 94–5.
12th Report on Trade Unions, 1899 (1900), 100–1.

[3] *4th Report on Trade Unions*, 1889, 1890 (1891), 278.
9th Report on Trade Unions, 1896 (1897), 126–7.
12th Report on Trade Unions, 1899 (1900), 100–1.
15th Report on Trade Unions, 1902–4 (1906), 78–9.

In 1906 the Amalgamated Society of Hollow-ware Pressers, the China Potters' Federation, and the Printers' and Transferrers' Society united to form the National Amalgamated Society of Male and Female Pottery Workers,[1] and by 1914, except for those in the two unions mentioned elsewhere, the United Ovenmen's Society and the Packers' Association, all organised potters in North Staffordshire were in this union. (The China and Earthenware Gilders' Union had dissolved in 1894; the Potteries China and Earthenware Decorators' Union in 1907; whilst the China Furniture and Electrical Appliance Throwers' and Turners' Society joined the National Amalgamated Society in 1907 and the Society of Operative Pottery Engravers in 1908.)[2]

Soon after its establishment in 1906 the National Amalgamated Society began to extend its influence to the out-pottery districts. In that year the National Amalgamated Operative White Potters of Scotland joined it, and in 1908 the other Scotch Potters' Union, the Associated Stoneware Throwers, did likewise.[3] The National Amalgamated Society sent an official to Bristol in 1906, who there established a branch of the society amongst the general earthenware potters. Two years later the Bristol Stoneware Society joined the National Amalgamated Society. In 1907 a branch of the National Society was established in London.

Except that these were the larger and more important, they are typical of many other out-pottery districts in which lodges of the National Amalgamated Society were formed.

[1] *16th Report on Trade Unions*, 1905–7 (1909), 58–9.
[2] *16th Report on Trade Unions*, 1905–7 (1909), 58–9.
9th Report on Trade Unions, 1896 (1897), 126–7.
[3] *16th Report on Trade Unions*, 1905–7 (1909), 58–9.
17th Report on Trade Unions, 1908–10 (1912–13), 58–9.

CHAPTER X

THE PROBLEMS OF THE LAST GENERATION

It is the purpose of this chapter to study the conditions of the working potter during the period 1870–1914. From the point of view of the potters of to-day it is a period of great importance, for the fathers of the present generation were then engaged in the industry, and the way in which they met the circumstances of the time and their methods of either evading or tackling new problems is of practical interest.

Throughout the period under review the amount of trade done by English pottery manufacturers substantially increased. The home trade expanded and the value of exports grew considerably. The high import duties of U.S.A. obstructed trade with that country, but English manufacturers found other countries willing to receive their goods. The black side to this otherwise bright period of England's expanding pottery trade lay in the fact that the expansion was accompanied by very severe competition amongst the manufacturers.

Attempts to check competition by price agreements failed, with the result that selling prices dropped, to what was alleged to be an unreasonably low level. The Report on Pottery under the Profiteering Act 1919–20 makes the statement that in the twenty years before 1914 the English Pottery Industry was not remunerative. Her biggest foreign market, U.S.A., had, by the adoption of the McKinley Tariff in 1896, raised the duties on imported pottery from 40 to 60 per cent., erecting excessively high barriers, which resulted in a lowering of the export trade. At the same time the home market was threatened by the importation of cheap German and Austrian ware. This produced cut-throat competition amongst the English manufacturers and costs were brought down to the minimum.[1]

The conclusions of the Profiteering Committee were based upon the findings of the U.S.A. Commission upon the cost of Pottery Manufacture in Europe 1913–14.[2] This Commission found that, so far as England was concerned, the industry was subjected to foreign competition, and, owing to the price-cutting policy pursued by the manufacturers, it had become an unremunerative trade.

Concerning the practice of price-cutting at this time, the comment of the Profiteering Committee is: "This [the raising of tariffs in foreign countries] coupled with increased importation of cheap German and Austrian ware to this country, brought about cut-throat competition."[3] This comment would carry more weight had cut-throat competition been a new thing, but it appears to be a charge that can be levelled against English pottery manufacturers at almost any period during the previous hundred years. Underselling took various forms. It could mean that a manufacturer offered his goods for sale at a price avowedly less than that of his fellow-manufacturers in the same market, or that he sold them at agreed or customary rates, but offered substantial rebates or discounts. Another and common method was the selling of ware the actual size of which was larger than the nominal, i.e. a 10-inch plate would be sold as an 8-inch, an 8-inch as a 6-inch, etc. All these methods were practised during the nineteenth century.

1 *Profiteering Acts*, 1919–20. *Report on Pottery* (1921), 5.
2 *U.S.A. Bureau of Foreign and Domestic Commerce.*
The Pottery Industry Report on the Cost of Production in U.S.A., England, Germany, Austria, Washington, 1915.
U.S.A. Bureau of Foreign and Domestic Commerce.
Miscellaneous Series, No. 21.
3 *Profiteering Acts*, 1919–20. *Report on Pottery* (1921), 5.

In 1813 certain of the North Staffordshire manufacturers formed themselves into a Chamber of Commerce with the express object of regulating prices. A price list covering the chief varieties of ware was drawn up, but it did not answer the purpose for which it was made, for, by the giving of discounts and rebates, underselling was enabled to go unchecked.[1] Some years later, in 1825, the North Staffordshire manufacturers again formed a Chamber of Commerce, this time for the purpose of checking competition in the sizes of ware. This organisation persuaded the manufacturers of North Staffordshire and of several of the out-potteries to agree to the adoption of certain sizes for ware, and even went so far as to petition Parliament to fix legal sizes. The petition was not granted and a few years later the Chamber went to pieces, having failed to accomplish the object for which it was intended.[2] Al forms of underselling practices again became rife, and by 1830 manufacturers were complaining that the trade was being ruined by unfair competition.

Three years later another scale of selling prices was set up. It was but a short-lived attempt to stop illegitimate trading, for by the 'forties the old practices had once more returned. In 1846 the North Staffordshire manufacturers agreed to a selling-price list giving an advance of 10 to 15 per cent. over previous prices, but by 1850 this was generally ignored.[3] Competition in sizes was also taking place at the same time. In 1860 it was stated before a Parliamentary Committee that pottery-ware sizes had greatly increased during the previous few years.[4]

In the period dating from the middle 'sixties to the

[1] J. Ward: *History of Borough of Stoke-on-Trent* (1846), 66.

[2] J. Ward: *History of Borough of Stoke-on-Trent* (1846), 66, *supra* 32.

[3] *Staffordshire Mercury*, April 18, 1846.
Staffordshire Advertiser, October 13, 1850.

[4] *Report from the Select Committee on Masters and Operatives* (1860) 14.

middle 'seventies, which, on the whole, was one of prosperity for pottery manufacturers, there does not appear to have been any complaints of unfair competition, but with the lull in trade which followed that period came a reversion to old practices. The latter months of the year 1879 saw an advance in the price of potters' materials, coal, borax and lead, and the manufacturers, meeting in January of 1880, decided to increase the prices of the cheaper class of goods for the home trade to the extent of about 10 per cent. Hardly had the new list come into force when it was discovered that many manufacturers, members of the Masters' Association, who pretended to adhere to it, were underselling.[1]

What happened in 1879 and 1880 was true of almost every year for the remainder of the period ending 1914, when conditions changed substantially. Of 1894 the pottery trade organ was able to report "that there was less illegitimate trading than several years ago", but in April 1895 it was saying: "On all sides the potters complain of prices, and no doubt not without cause, for they fight one another in a triangular duel against the buyer, viz. in sizes, prices and discounts, giving the buyer three shots to their one."[2] A year later, April 1896, the same journal remarks that, "as to underselling, that is how some manufacturers live".[3]

It is thus seen that the cut-throat competition of the era beginning 1896 was no new feature in the English pottery industry. The difficult times which undoubtedly began then were met with a policy which was already traditional. There were no methods of underselling practised in the period following the McKinley Tariff which were new or had not been common at other times in the century. To break this traditional policy it was

[1] *Pottery Gazette*, February 1880.
[2] *Pottery Gazette*, January 1895. [3] *Pottery Gazette*, April 1896.

necessary that there should be a strong association of manufacturers, but here again the past handicapped the present. If it is true that nothing succeeds like success, it is equally true that nothing fails like failure, and certainly, if the past were considered, the outlook in the 'eighties and 'nineties for the building up of a strong pottery manufacturers' organisation was not hopeful.

The manufacturers' associations of 1813 and 1825 have already been mentioned.[1] Both of them were short-lived. The aggressiveness of the employees' trade union stimulated the employers into forming a vital and active combination in March 1836, probably one of the strongest of any pottery masters' associations of the nineteenth century, but with the removal in the New Year of 1837 of all fear to their interests from the men's union the cohesion of the masters weakened and their organisation, the Chamber of Commerce, dissolved.[2] It was revived again in 1852, however, and for some years was very flourishing, although, even at its strongest, some of the largest manufacturers were not members.[3]

From the 'eighties onwards pottery manufacturers were organising themselves into other bodies, leaving to the Chamber the broad function of watching over the trading and commercial interests of North Staffordshire. The

[1] *supra*, 181. [2] *supra*, 88.

[3] *Report of Select Committee on Masters and Operatives (Equitable Councils of Conciliation)* (1856), 203.

(In 1859 the Chamber of Commerce was responsible for the opening of an Exchange for North Staffordshire, an institution which was very short-lived. The Chamber became reorganised in 1874 and its name was changed from "Potteries" to "North Staffordshire" Chamber of Commerce. In the following year the Exchange was reopened under the auspices of the Chamber. This appeared at first to be a promising venture, but by 1881 the attendance had so fallen off that it was decided to suspend the Exchange for two years. The suspension was the end of the institution.)

earthenware manufacturers, by far the most considerable body, formed the Staffordshire Potteries Manufacturers' Association. Later, the china manufacturers formed a similar organisation. From this time onward, as fresh branches of pottery were developed and came to the fore, additional associations were formed, but at no time up to 1914 were the manufacturers in the main branches of the trade strongly organised.

The policy of the association which covered the interests of the largest branch of the trade, earthenware, in relation to the regulation of selling prices was decidedly weak. According to its constitution, as laid down in 1887,[1] it aimed to secure the united action of the manufacturers and to determine a course of action in regard to selling prices and terms of payment, but such decision was not to be binding on its members. Of this association it was said: "What has the Manufacturers' Association done for the trade? It has been in existence many years, and has several times arranged for an increase in prices which has never been maintained. The only point upon which action has been possible has been in resisting any advance in wages."[2] It may here be remarked that the constitution which laid down that decisions in regard to selling prices should not be binding on members made no such proviso in respect to its other objects, most of which bore direct reference to the relation of employer and employed: to maintain the usages of the trade, to regulate the custom respecting the discharge and engaging of workmen, to maintain the usage of good from oven, etc.

In 1898 certain earthenware manufacturers made an attempt to apply the "Bedstead Smith" scheme, "Birmingham Alliance" or "New Trades Combination Movement",

[1] *Royal Commission on Labour. Rules of Associations of Employers and Employed* (1892), 320. [2] *Pottery Gazette*, December 1898.

as variously called, to the industry. A feature of the scheme was the institution of a system of scientific stock-taking by which the average cost of production of all articles could be ascertained, but the key idea was that the unions of the men and the masters should form an alliance to keep up both wages and prices. The scheme had been practised and had come into prominence in the Birmingham Bedstead trade, under the guidance of E. J. Smith.[1] There already was an alliance such as described above in the China, Furniture and Electrical Fittings Trades (two small branches of the pottery industry), which had been working successfully since 1895.[2] In 1898 the earthenware manufacturers and operatives decided to try an alliance in their own trade. With this end in view they held a meeting on November 28th, to which E. J. Smith was invited to explain exactly the aims, objects and working of an alliance.[3]

The meeting decided to form an alliance in the earthenware trade, but, although a Wages Board was immediately formed, it was agreed not to raise either prices or wages until the whole of the trade had come into the scheme. Several manufacturers organised an opposition and the proposed scheme fell through.[4] Only a little over a year afterwards the idea of an alliance between masters and operatives was so far forgotten that the workmen were striking against their employers for advances in wages.[5]

There are certain special reasons why pottery manufacturers were unable with any measure of success to

[1] H. W. Macrosty: *British Industries*, edited by W. J. Ashley (1907), 202.

[2] E. J. Smith: *The New Trades Combination Movement* (1899) (footnote to introduction).

[3] *Birmingham Daily Post*, November 30, 1898.
Pottery Gazette, February 1899. [4] *Pottery Gazette*, March 1899.

[5] *Pottery Gazette*, March, April, May, June, 1900.

combine to keep out the illegitimate trader and make the industry more remunerative. Of the first importance is the fact that there is a wide field of variety of products in the industry. A very large catalogue would be required to enumerate all the articles which are made in but one of its branches, though that the largest, general earthenware.

In addition to this, which is true of all branches of the industry, there is a big difference in the quality of ware of the same description. Manufacturers give a greater or lesser degree of finish to their goods according to their standing in the home or foreign markets. Thus, although there are staple articles in the pottery as in every other trade, those staples differ as to quality of clay, colour and glaze, workmanship and character of ornamentation, to a degree which make the fixing of selling prices, according to classification of goods, a very difficult matter indeed. Anyone wishing to appreciate the fact of the extreme variety of pottery products has but to walk into a high-class china store, which, despite its name, is almost certain to stock more earthenware than porcelain, and observe the number and variety of articles exhibited. This visit should be followed by one to a shop which caters for more slender purses, and later to the stalls of the cheap stores, and, finally, to the booth of the "cheap-jack" auctioneer. The visit concluded, it is well to remember that samples of some only of the branches of pottery products have been seen, and those made expressly for the home market. As big a variety exists in the ware sent out to cater for the differing tastes of the U.S.A., the Argentine and Colonial buyers.

Along with this fact of variety in pottery products there operated throughout the whole period, from the beginning of the Industrial Revolution to the European War of 1914, a strong feeling of individualism amongst the masters. This individualism can probably be explained by the conditions under which the trade was conducted, and, possibly, by the geographical position of North Staffordshire. One of its causes, the variety of products, has already been mentioned, but it is a point which needs enlargement in this connexion. It could easily happen that a pottery manufacturer, whether in a large or a small way of business, was, and still is, the sole maker of the particular goods which he places upon the market. His clay bodies and glazes will be mixed according to his own receipts, which may or may not be the same as those of any other manufacturer. He will also probably make certain shapes of articles peculiar to his own factory, and some of his ware will be decorated in patterns designed by some member of his establishment.

In clay bodies alone the room for variation is almost illimitable. The same, but to a less extent, is true of glazes and colours. With the big scope for variety thus afforded in class of article, quality, shape and pattern, it can readily be understood how individualism is fostered. Normally a manufacturer would be making ware differing in some respect or other from that produced by any other firm, a circumstance which, although it should not have prevented him from co-operating with his fellows, would certainly tend to make him feel an individual manufacturer, with conditions to meet and problems to face slightly different from those of other master potters. This would not have been the case had conditions existed in his industry similar to those obtaining in most other industries.

Another difficulty in the way of schemes of organisation for the regulation of the trade was the fact that, in the nineteenth century at any rate, the bulk of the pottery manufactories were family concerns, owned by families which in many cases had very recently left the employed classes.[1] A manufacturer who had risen from the ranks would naturally tend to stress the importance of self-help, and, while the factory he controlled was kept within the family, he was able to assert those views. Many of these factories were old-fashioned and wasteful of labour and time, while, owing to lack of capital, a substantial number of them were so ill-equipped with the necessary implements and stock that much of the workers' time, which on a well-equipped factory would have been spent on production, was either frittered away in compulsory idleness or wasted over the production of articles which should have been made in half the time.[2]

Very early in the history of the trade complaints were made that many factories were ill-suited for the economical manufacture of pottery. In 1830, at the time of the Anti-Truck agitation, it was pointed out that some manufactories were so inefficiently conducted that it was impossible for their owners to make them profitable and at the same time to pay ordinary rates of wages to their employees.[3] Writing many years afterwards an old potter said of the pottery factories of the 1840's that many of them were "patchworks of buildings as if a stampede of cottages had been stopped in their march".[4] It was the

[1] *Report of the Proceedings of the Anti Truck Meeting for the Staffordshire Potteries* (1830) (pamphlet).

J. Ward: *History of Borough of Stoke-on-Trent* (1846), 53.

The Third Winter of Unemployment. Report of an Enquiry, 1922 (1922), 289.

The following extract from the rules of the Hollow-ware Pressers Society (1890) is instructive in this connexion: "Members who become employers may be reinstated within three months after they return to the trade."

[2] *U.S.A. Pottery Industry Report*, 1915, op. cit., 58.' 'T. B. Johnson: I firmly believe that in the whole of the Staffordshire district over 60 per cent. of the potteries ought to be scrapped and modern works put up."

[3] *supra*, 51.

[4] Old Potter: *When I was a Child* (1903), 187.

owners of such factories, one imagines, who, during the machinery scare of 1845, were opposed to the use of mechanical methods of manufacture.

At a later period various factory inspectors' reports indirectly testify to the unsuitability of many factories for the economical manufacture of pottery. In reply to the question of the possibility of setting up a system of fans to take away dust in those shops in which certain admittedly dangerous occupations were followed, the representative of the well-known firm of Wedgwood's stated before the Committee of 1893 that on his factory and on all other old factories it would mean either closing down or rebuilding.[1] In this statement of C. Wedgwood there was possibly some exaggeration, which, under the circumstances, was to be expected, but, nevertheless, there would be much truth in the point he made that many factories were unsuitable for the general laying down of mechanical power. Many of the pottery factories had started in a small way and had been added to as business developed, with the result that there were factories which were mere collections of disconnected workshops, grown up without any prearranged plan and totally unsuitable for efficient working.[2]

The geographical position of North Staffordshire had possibly also some influence in preserving the individualism of the master potter, as it helped to preserve other features of the life of the place. That part of North Staffordshire known as the "Potteries" is in the nature of being an industrial island. It consists of a string of six towns running along one of many North Staffordshire valleys. These towns were federated into the county borough (now city) of Stoke-on-Trent in 1909. Although federated, the pottery

[1] *Report on Manufacture of China and Earthenware Potteries Committee of Enquiry*, 1893.
[2] *Profiteering Acts*, 1919–20. *Report on Pottery* (1921), 6.

towns have not lost their separate identity, and there is still an individuality about them which is lacking in the towns and villages which form part of such cities as Birmingham and Manchester.

The city of Stoke-on-Trent gives the effect of one very long street, broken here and there by open market-places, with short crossing and recrossing streets running from the main road, the land on either side rising up in ridges. Along these ridges, and occasionally in the valleys on the other side, lie mines and mining villages forming an irregular dotted ring round the city.[1] Wolverhampton, twenty miles to the south, and Manchester, forty miles to the north, are the nearest towns of any industrial importance to the Potteries. To the east lies the wild hill and moor country of Derbyshire, and to the west the long agricultural stretches of Cheshire and Shropshire. The Potteries is not linked up to other big industrial centres by easy stage of village and town as is the case with the industrial districts of Lancashire and the Midlands.

By the end of the eighteenth century the Potteries had good road and canal communications with the rest of the country, and in 1848 it was linked up with the railway, although it was not until 1874 that the latter service was extended to all the Potteries towns. The main roads and railways of the kingdom skirt by the Potteries, giving a certain isolation to the place—an isolation which was

[1] In this ring, two miles to the west of the town of Stoke, lies the old borough of Newcastle-under-Lyme. Newcastle was never of any industrial importance, its chief function being to serve as a market for the whole area. During the late nineteenth century an industry in contract clothing was established there, and is still carried on, although it has not grown to any great extent. The population of the borough is stationary and small, being but 20,000, which is insignificant when compared with the quarter of a million inhabitants of Stoke-on-Trent.

obviously greater in the nineteenth century when facilities for travel were so much more restricted.

It is easy for anyone to understand the isolation and consequent retention of old-world customs, manners of speech and habits of thought of people in remote parts of rural England, for in thinking of them the imagination is quickly stirred and a romantic glamour created—a truth exploited by novelists—but it is difficult to picture the isolation of an industrial district. To speak of the inhabitants of North Staffordshire as dwellers in an old-world atmosphere may be wrong, but it is probably as true as when the phrase is used in connexion with the people of some of our sleepy old cathedral towns. Even in an industrial age it is not the beautiful alone which lies hidden, the clay-spattered window-pane and the smoking kiln may be as retiring as the thatched cottage and the cobbled street.

If the geographical position of the Potteries helped to preserve the individualism of the manufacturers of that area, it did not affect the actions and ideas of the master potter living in another part of the country. In the case of the latter, however, it must be remembered that he was often the sole master potter of his district, and, in any case, the initiative in trade matters was always left to the manufacturers of North Staffordshire.

The foregoing shows that poor trade organisation and underselling were not specially marked features of the last twenty-five years of the nineteenth century. They had been an integral part of the trade almost from its beginning, but this last quarter was unfortunate in having to meet additional problems and complications. It was a time of great change in methods of manufacture.

If the term "Industrial Revolution" means the substitution on a large scale of manual skill by machinery, then for the potters of North Staffordshire it began in the 'seventies, and the preceding twenty years may be taken as one long introduction to it. Machinery threatened the industry in the 'forties, became established in the out-potteries during the 'fifties and 'sixties, and stormed and conquered the metropolis of the industry in the early 'seventies. From that time onward neither the conservative timidity of the masters nor the opposition of the operatives could prevent machinery from making its conquest complete.

The chairman of the Pottery Manufacturers' Chamber of Commerce, M. D. Hollins, made the following statement in evidence before a Select Committee in 1856: ". . . we are almost entirely dependent upon hand labour, machinery not being used in the production of our goods."[1] In 1860 the Social Science Association reported that: "In pottery there is no machinery invented, or likely to be invented, to supersede the potter, though some may be discovered to facilitate his work."[2] Although the compilers of the Social Science Report may have been ignorant of the matter, M. D. Hollins must have known that at the time he was making his statement machinery was in common use in the potteries of the north. He was thus far justified in his statement that in the Potteries, of which place he was giving evidence, no machinery was used.

The non-use of machinery was not wholly because of the conservative timidity of the masters. As a matter of fact, the North Staffordshire master potters did not admit that conservatism was the reason for its non-use by them at a time when their fellows were using machinery in other districts; they contended that it was due to the

[1] *Report from the Select Committee on Masters and Operatives* (*Equitable Councils of Conciliation*) (1856), 201.

[2] *Trade Societies and Strikes. National Association for the Promotion of Social Science* (1860), 281.

obstinacy of their workmen. In 1850 they complained that not only were the North of England potters using machinery, but that it was also being used on the Continent, and in both cases without interference from the workpeople, while in North Staffordshire, the metropolis of the trade, it was not allowed to be introduced.[1] In 1863, M. Ragout, of one of the largest houses on the Continent, presented F. Wedgwood, of the firm of that name, with a plate-making machine, known afterwards in England as the "jolly". F. Wedgwood showed this machine to his men, who refused to have anything to do with it.[2] This particular machine began to be used in North Staffordshire in the early 'seventies, and a few years later it was in general use throughout the industry.[3]

As the workmen in the 'seventies were just as opposed to machinery as were those of the 'fifties and 'sixties, one can only conclude that before the 'seventies the masters themselves were not over-anxious for it to be introduced. Still, the opposition of the men must not be underestimated, for, as will be shown later, they were capable of allowing a branch of the trade to be wiped out rather than that fresh customs should be forced upon it.[4]

The flat pressers opposed the introduction of machinery into their trade, but by 1876 it was in use in all the large factories.[5] In many instances where it was introduced women were employed for the making of small flat ware, i.e. small plates, etc., the excuse of the masters being that men had refused to operate the machines, but as women

1 *Staffordshire Advertiser*, September 21, 1850.
2 *Pottery Gazette*, December 1880.
3 *Staffordshire Potteries Board of Arbitration. Evidence and Award of the Enquiry before H. T. Hinckes*, 1891. 4 *infra*, 205.
5 G. Bevan: *The Industrial Classes and Industrial Statistics* (1876), 145. *Potteries Board of Arbitration. Evidence given during the Enquiry before J. E. Davis*, 1876–77.

were paid at a considerably less rate than men, this excuse appears insincere.[1]

The hollow-ware pressers were affected differently, but, in the long run, more seriously than the flat pressers. Machinery did not change the essential character of the flat presser's work; the operator still remained a flat presser whether working by machinery or by hand. In the one case he made plates from a mould with the aid of small pitcher tools on a wheel which he propelled himself, while in the other case a mould was used, but the wheel was mechanically driven, and instead of pitcher tools he used one made of iron set to the exact shape of the plate. He employed assistants in both cases.

It is important to note, therefore, that machinery changed, but did not destroy the flat pressers' trade. This was not the case with hollow-ware pressing. Hollow-ware pressers finished completely each article they made and employed no assistants; but hollow-ware made by the aid of machinery was the work of men who employed assistants to do the finishing processes. Machines for the making of hollow-ware were suitable only for round, simple shapes, which meant that the work which paid the hollow-ware presser best was taken from him. Each article leaving the bench for the machine increased the percentage of difficult shapes to be made by hand.[2]

For many years it was impossible to make other than the round and comparatively shallow ware on the jigger, and it appeared as though all other shaped articles were to be left to the hollow-ware presser, and that the movement from hand to machine had stopped, but early in the

[1] *Potteries Board of Arbitration. Evidence given during the Enquiry before J. E. Davis*, 1876–77.

[2] *Potteries Examiner*, September 23, 1871.
Potteries Board of Arbitration. Evidence given during Enquiry before J. E. Davis, 1876–77.

twentieth century two jiggers, one for the making of shallow, oval ware and another for the making of tall, round ware were invented and brought into use. At the same time the process of "casting" ware, which had long been known, but up to this date employed only for the making of fancy articles, such as small vases, scent bottles, etc., became generally used for the making of all kinds of ware.

In casting, liquid clay or slip is poured into a mould, the dry plaster of which absorbs the water from the slip, leaving a coating of clay deposited on the inside. The remaining fluid is then drawn off. When the mould has absorbed further moisture the article can be lifted out. Ordinarily the process of absorption takes a long time, and to facilitate it the manufacturers of the nineteenth century often tried adding washing-soda to the slip. The addition of this substance increased the speed at which excess moisture was drawn from the clay, but, owing to the damaging effect it had upon the moulds, manufacturers were not encouraged to use it. Early in the twentieth century an alkali mixture was discovered which, when added to casting slip, greatly decreased the time which the latter had to remain in the mould without having the drawbacks of soda. This discovery considerably increased the speed at which ware could be cast. Henceforth casting could be used for the production of articles for which it had previously been too slow, and, therefore, too expensive, a process.[1]

[1] *National Council of the Pottery Industry. Faults in Alkaline Slip Casting*. Address by Walter Emery, Esq. (pamphlet, 1925), 3

In 1905 a North Staffordshire manufacturer unsuccessfully tried to obtain patent rights for the use of alkaline casting slips.

". . . the exploitation of alkaline casting slips has been the greatest advance in the methods of manufacturing pottery since the introduction of steel profiles for jollying."

Johnson, founder of group of Johnson pottery factories: "Casting produced a revolution in the trade."—*Pottery Gazette*, September 1928.

These new jigger inventions and the new application of casting doomed the trade of the hollow-ware presser. Oval vegetable dishes, sauce tureens, and all tall, round articles, such as ewers, were given to the jiggerer to make instead of to the hollow-ware presser, while those articles of a shape which could not be jiggered were cast. Like the jiggerer, the caster employed female assistants. There were both male and female casters, the latter working at much lower rates than the former.

The displacement of the hollow-ware presser by the jiggerer and the caster was taking place roughly during the fourteen years preceding the European War. At first the movement was slow, for the new processes were not always successful, and the installation of new methods of manufacture was expensive; but in the latter end of the period the displacement became rapid and, during the war, almost complete.[1]

In addition to the machinery already mentioned, certain important inventions were made in the preparation of clay. The clay filter press was introduced and patented in 1856. This superseded the old method of extracting excess water from the clay slip by means of evaporation, in order to convert it into a plastic and workable state. By the old method the clay slip was run over the surface of a slip kiln, the water being driven off by the heat underneath, while the principle of the clay-filter press is to pump the clay slip into wooden receptacles, lined with strong calico bags, through which the water is forced, leaving the clay behind.

A few years later (in the 'seventies) the mechanical blunger and the pugmill were introduced. The former did

[1] *Commercial Year Book of the North Staffordshire Chamber of Commerce* (1912), 64: ". . . hollow-ware pressing, a process which is gradually being supplanted by . . . casting."

away with "blunging", the mixing of the clay ingredients by hand, and the latter took the place of another laborious process, that of "wedging". Clay direct from the slip kiln or the filter press is not in a state to be worked by the potter without further preparation. Both evaporation and filter pressing give it a cellular and porous texture, making it necessary to drive out all air before it can be used, otherwise it is impossible to obtain a smooth and compact body. Formerly this was done by beating or "wedging" the clay, the process which was superseded by the pugmill.

These inventions had no disturbing influence upon skilled labour, for few men, if any, were displaced by the introduction of either the pugmill or the blunger, both of which considerably reduced the necessity for certain types of unskilled and laborious work.

Changes in other branches of pottery manufacture had taken place during this time, but compared with the changes already described they had affected few people. The mould-makers, a relatively small branch of the trade, were probably favourably affected by the new methods of manufacture, for a greater number of moulds were now required. Changes in fashion and taste, and the introduction of lithographic printing, took away the occupation of male painters and decorators, except at the few firms where ware of a very high quality was made.[1] Of the remaining occupations none was affected by machinery, and one only, that of the ovenmen, was of any numerical importance.

From the brief description given of new machinery and new methods of manufacture, it will be realised that they

[1] *The Official Handbook of the North Staffordshire Chamber of Commerce* (1921), 54: "Lithography is a strictly modern method of decorating pottery."

were not such as to cause a catastrophic displacement of labour. Actually, in the matter of labour saving, there were no discoveries or inventions in the pottery industry at all comparable with those of industries such as the textiles, clothing, etc. In addition, machinery was not suddenly adopted by the whole of the industry, for its adoption was greatly hindered by the practical difficulty of shortage of capital. It is a truism in the trade that external capital could never be induced to enter it. Very little was taken by the pottery manufacturers from that great reservoir of capital which industry was generally able to tap by the passing of the Limited Liability Act. While shortage of capital did not prevent manufacturers from attempting to make technical and other economies, but rather forced them to do so, it prevented the wholesale adoption of any new methods which involved either the laying down of expensive plant or structural alterations.

Another factor which mitigated the hardship which would otherwise have followed labour displacement was the opening up of new branches of pottery production, the chief of which, from this particular point of view, was the manufacture of sanitary ware. During the 'sixties and 'seventies sanitary ware manufacture was in its infancy, and its productions were of a very elementary nature, but new types of ware were introduced in the 'eighties, and from 1890 onwards sanitary earthenware made great headway. The growing standard of sanitation, and the better equipment of dwelling-houses, hotels and other public institutions, all conduced to the prosperity of the trade.

The coming of the telegraph, and, later, the growth of the electrical trade, created another branch of production by the demand for earthenware insulators, switches, etc. Associated with this trade was the manufacture of pottery appliances for the chemical industry, and also for the building trade, i.e. crucibles, door-plates, door-knobs, etc.

During this period the manufacture of glazed tiles developed considerably, owing partly to the same movement of public hygiene which had given an impetus to the sanitary ware industry. The products of the sanitary-ware factory, lavatory basins, baths, pedestal closets, etc., are heavy and bulky articles, practically excluding, by that fact, all women from the trade. The tile, china furniture and electrical appliance trades belonged, in the main, to men, but a high percentage of women were employed.

Owing to the opening out of these new branches and to the steady increase in the general trade technical changes did not at any period before 1914 drive men out of the industry. During the period of the greatest change, 1871–1911, the number of men employed in the Staffordshire pottery factories rose from 17,356 to 26,511.

Such, then, were the conditions which the operative potter had to face: the introduction of machinery and, with it, the influx of low-paid female labour into an industry which, on the employers' side, was suffering from the worst faults of individualism, and which was alleged to be unremunerative. In the following chapter it will be seen how the operative potters met and dealt with these conditions.

CHAPTER XI

HOW THE PROBLEMS WERE MET

Throughout their history the policy of the organised working potters was, on the whole, to favour the regulation of selling prices and the existence of a strong manufacturers' association to enforce such regulation. Normally, they were content to urge the acceptance of their ideas, but at the height of their strength they were able to force them upon the trade. As early as 1825 organised potters were publicly complaining of lack of combination among the masters,[1] and in 1833, as will be recalled, the National Union of Operative Potters prevented the manufacturers from sending goods abroad upon speculation, a practice which often resulted in forced sales and a quick depression in selling prices. Henceforth pottery goods were to be sent out to order only.[2] This action of the Union is

[1] *supra*, 33.

[2] *supra*, 68–9. It had apparently been no unusual thing for goods to be sent to America which had not been ordered, to the ultimate loss of the manufacturer.

Journal of John Wesley, March 29, 1786: "He with whom I used to lodge is no more seen [John Bourne, master potter]. He trusted the Americans with all his substance, and they cheated him out of it all." In reference to this extract from Wesley's diary, the comment of J. Ward, *History of Borough of Stoke-on-Trent* (54), is: "Dr. Franklin . . . (1789) threw the blame on the English merchants who . . . acted imprudently in forcing such quantities of goods on the Americans which had not been ordered by them and were beyond the facilities of their country to consume . . . and the surplus of which was . . . sent to vendors . . . where it was frequently sold at less than prime cost. . . . Spirit of Franklin . . . remind manufacturers . . . of the present day of the little respect they have paid to thy counsel."

Pottery Gazette, October 1911: One of the objects of the 1833 Union "to place a check on the downward course of selling prices by providing that if the masters were determined by destructive

probably the earliest case of a rationalist policy being forced upon an industry from the side of the employees. In 1850 the executive committee of a Potters' Union made the public statement that the great need of the industry was a strong association of manufacturers to keep up the level of selling prices.[1]

This opinion, that the industry needed strong associations to control selling prices, became an article of the journeyman potter's faith, though nothing tangible was done until August 1891, when the unions asked the associated manufacturers to meet them to discuss methods of regulating selling prices. The men wished to propose to the manufacturers that the organised bodies of employers and employees should actively co-operate in checking illegitimate competition and establish, so far as trade conditions would allow, a uniform list of selling prices. The unions were unable to obtain a meeting with the manufacturers' association. In the following year, therefore, they sent letters to that body explaining their proposals for the saving of the trade. Nothing came of these proposals, for the manufacturers declined to move in the matter. The unions had been encouraged to take these steps because the manufacturers' association had complained in its annual reports that it had failed to check underselling through certain firms who had refused to fall into line.[2]

A few years later, as mentioned elsewhere, the men co-operated with the manufacturers in the "New Industrial Alliance", a scheme which failed in the main branch of the industry almost before it came into operation.[3] Not, it will be remembered, because of any hostility on the

competition to depreciate the marketable value of their goods, they should not be allowed to lower the workman's wages to meet the exigency".

[1] *Staffordshire Advertiser*, October 8, 1850.

[2] *Royal Commission on Labour* (1893–94), vol. iii, 401.

[3] *supra*, 184.

part of the men, but because of the active opposition of certain manufacturers. This was the last effort on the part of the men in the period prior to 1914 to establish an understanding with the employers' association, though it does not appear that their views upon the conduct of the trade underwent any great alteration.

The close and undisguised relationship between selling prices and wages in the industry during the nineteenth century makes understandable the anxiety displayed by the men to check unfair competition among the masters. In the beginning of the century a drop in selling prices was followed as a matter of course by the lowering of wages, and although, with the coming of trade unions, wage rates did not respond so rapidly to changes in selling prices, yet the relationship between the amount a manufacturer received from his customers and the wages he paid to his workmen remained a close one. While it was notorious that the firms with low-selling prices were those which paid low wages, and while masters and men alike accepted the fact that for those articles to which custom had given a high selling price a high wage should be paid, and, conversely, that a customary low selling price meant a low wage, the principle that selling prices should regulate wages was not definitely established until the 'eighties.

Before that time the acceptance of the relationship between wages and selling prices was no more than the recognition that, if prices fell faster than the total cost of production, wages were by devious methods reduced, and if wages rose attempts were made to lift prices. That is, according to whether prices or wages were the first to move, so did the manufacturer attempt to recuperate his loss out of either his customer or his employee. The whole history of the negotiations between master potters and their journeymen illustrates this fact. The possibility that the necessary readjustment following a rise in wages or a fall in prices could be made in the processes of production does not appear to have received any serious consideration.

The relationship which experience showed existed between wages and prices crystallised in the semi-legal atmosphere of the arbitration court into the principle that selling prices govern wages. In 1876 the men disputed accepting it as a ruling principle of arbitration, but by the end of a decade it was firmly established, and discussions concerning proposed wage alterations centred round the manufacturers' selling prices and profits.[1]

The change in the manufacturing processes of the industry produced a feeling of pessimism amongst the operatives. Machinery had arrived. The general effects of its arrival were to make hand workers afraid to press for better prices lest they should drive their work to the machines, and the men on the machines were afraid to make any agitation lest they should be ousted by women. In some instances the hollow-ware pressers demanded increased prices for the ware they made, as compensation for the loss of easy shapes which had been taken over by the machines.

On one occasion, in September 1871, when the use of machinery for hollow-ware was new, a master potter of Burslem (Mr. Shaw) introduced the practice of making chambers by machinery at his factory. The hollow-ware pressers in the toilet department being thus left with the worst work demanded an advance on the price of ewers. As the advance asked for was such that had it been granted it would have taken away the profit from machine-made chambers, those articles were given back to the hollow-

[1] *Royal Commission on Labour* (1893–94), vol. iii, 401. *supra*, 156.

ware pressers to make by hand.[1] But this incident took place when machinery for making hollow-ware was in its infancy, and also at a time when trade was very good. Later, when more and more work left the hollow-ware presser for the machine and trade was not so good, it was impossible for hollow-ware pressers to get recompense.

The prices which were at first paid to "jiggerers", i.e. the men who made hollow-ware by machinery, enabled them to obtain exceptionally good wages.[2] Below is given a short list of articles with the prices paid for making them (*a*) to the jiggerer, (*b*) to the hollow-ware presser:

	Size.	(*a*) Per Dozen.	(*b*) Per Dozen.
		s. d.	s. d.
Chambers	Nines	2 6½	3 3
Chambers	Sixes	2 6½	3 6
Round vegetable dishes	6 inches	2 3	2 9
	7 inches	2 6	3 0
	8 inches	2 9	3 3
	9 inches	3 0	3 6
	10 inches	3 3	3 9

These prices deserve very close attention. In the first place it should be noted that they are for articles for which when making the hollow-ware presser got far more than the average wage.[3] In the second place the jiggerer had the advantage of comparatively low-paid attendant labour, whilst the hollow-ware presser had not. The jiggerer

[1] *Potteries Examiner*, September 23, 1871.

[2] *Potteries Board of Arbitration. Evidence given during the Inquiry before J. E. Davis*, 1876–77.

[3] They were the articles for the loss of which the hollow-ware presser had demanded compensation.

employed two or three assistants, and at first, while prices were high, it was customary for one of them to be a man, usually a hollow-ware presser.[1] When jiggerers' prices began to fall it was discovered that it was unnecessary for them to employ men assistants, so they were dismissed and their places taken by women at considerably lower wages.

Had the hollow-ware presser consented to employ assistants he could have worked, without loss to himself, at much lower rates than were actually paid, for if he were earning 6s. a day without an assistant his gross wage with an assistant's help need have been only 8s. a day for his net wage to be the same in both cases, while his output would have been nearly doubled. It will be realised, therefore, that under such circumstances he could have afforded substantial cuts in his piece-rates without having a drop in wages. Nevertheless, knowing that by employing assistants they would have seriously retarded the use of machinery, the hollow-ware pressers steadfastly refused to adopt such a course of action. One master potter made a determined attempt to induce them to employ assistants, but without success. He, W. Turner, in 1884, removed from Victoria Works, Tunstall, to a new factory in Scotia Road, in the same town. At the new works he tried to put into operation a scheme which he had contemplated for some time. By this scheme his hollow-ware pressers would employ female assistants in the same way as did his hollow-ware jiggerers and "jolliers". But his hollow-ware pressers (twelve in number) resisted the scheme. They received a month's notice to leave, whereat they brought the matter to the Hollow-ware Pressers' Union, which upheld their policy. After the men had left,

[1] *Potteries Board of Arbitration. Evidence given during the Inquiry before J. E. Davis*, 1876–77.

W. Turner made a further attempt to put the scheme into operation, but after a few weeks' trial it failed, and no other attempt was made in this direction either by W. Turner or any other master potter.[1] The objection of the men to Turner's scheme was purely that of the introduction of female labour, and had nothing to do with the earning of money, for the wages offered under his scheme were more liberal than those the men were accustomed to receive.[2]

The situation thus created was rather illogical. A jiggerer made a vegetable dish on his machine, and employed a woman to do the finishing processes, i.e. to put on handles, cut off the rough edges and rub it smooth with sponge and water. The hollow-ware presser made a similar vegetable dish, and although the finishing processes required were exactly the same as in the case of the jiggered dish, he would not employ a woman, but insisted upon doing the whole of the work himself. Had the hollow-ware presser taken advantage of the low wages of women to produce his ware at a less price, he would still, in the long run, probably have been unable to compete with the jiggerer in the making of many articles, but the difference in the prices of the two methods of manufacture would have been small, and consequently the incentive to adapt articles to the jigger would have been considerably lessened.

To the flat presser the introduction of machinery meant that in a few years, 1872–6, his trade, so far as the large factories were concerned, had been captured by machinery, and although women apparently had not entered the trade in large numbers, they were potential competitors for his job and, as such, affected his bargaining power. The effect

[1–2] Letter from the Secretary of the Tunstall Branch of the Hollow-ware Pressers' Union, which was the one concerned.

of this upon the mind of the flat presser can well be imagined.

The transition from handcraft to manufacture by machinery was not a steady movement, but occurred in spurts. There were times when it appeared that the change had ceased, but such periods were not long enough to enable the operatives to adjust themselves to the new conditions.[1] The general effect of the transition was that the operatives became pessimistic concerning the future of their trade. This pessimism became considerably weakened during the halts in the march of machinery, but it was there nevertheless all the time, and hindered both the men and their agents in the settling of disputes.

The agents would know better than the operatives how far machinery was taking over work previously done by hand-workers, and also how far women were making articles on machines previously operated by men. Whatever his feelings and inclinations, an agent would thus be compelled to give cautious counsel in most cases where his help was sought. An agent's chief work was, to use the words of one of them, "to intercede for the men with the employers in cases of dispute". Minor disputes between potters and their employers occurred almost daily, and the trade union organiser was called in by the men involved to aid them in a settlement. In the first fourteen months of his appointment an organiser of the Hollow-ware Pressers' Union, Pickin, went on one hundred and thirty deputations for men who were in dispute with their employers.

[1] *Commercial Year Book of the North Staffordshire Chamber of Commerce* (1912), 65: "In connection with this department of the trade (sanitary ware), great developments have taken place in the last few years, inasmuch as the process of 'pressing' the ware—that is to say, pressing the clay into moulds—has been largely superseded by the process of 'casting'. The sanitary ware pressers fought these 'great developments', but failed."

These disputes rarely involved stoppage of work; out of the number just mentioned there were only two cases of stoppage.[1] The majority of these minor disputes were concerned with the settling of the prices to be paid for the making of new shapes or sizes of ware.

Because of his superior knowledge the union agent was often forced to say to the men who had called in his services: "I will try to get the price you want for this article, but you must remember that this same article is being jiggered by a firm in the next town at a much less price than your employer is offering." To the men working on machines he would tell of cases where women were doing some of their work. To the operatives such information and advice appeared to prove the futility of unionism.

There was no conscious attempt on the part of the operatives who were being displaced by either women or machines to resist the new processes by lowering their prices. Their work became more difficult as all easy shapes went to the machine, leaving them the larger and more intricate ware to make, and they were unable to obtain the advance in prices which this change warranted, but prices were not lowered, and except for the general alterations mentioned elsewhere, they remained pretty much the same from the 'seventies up to the period of the war.[2]

The situation which the potters' unions had to meet in the 'seventies, 'eighties and 'nineties does not appear to have been unmanageable, and the pessimistic and fatalistic

[1] *Royal Commission on Labour* (1893–94), vol. iii, 404, 408.

[2] The piece-rate paid to hollow-ware pressers for eight-inch vegetable dishes became the rate for all large vegetable dishes; thus vegetable dishes made by hollow-ware pressers, no matter how large, were paid for on the eight-inch rate.

Pottery Gazette, May 1896: "Sizes greatly increased in recent years . . . curious thing is that increase gone on without protest from operatives . . . power of machinery probably great factor in matter."

attitude with which it was met was not warranted, though it is understandable. Despite the great changes which had taken place in the processes of manufacture the potter still virtually retained a monopoly of his craft, for, unlike the case in many other machine-invaded industries, pottery manufacture continued to require of its male workers a high degree of skill. In spite of the influx of women the number of men employed in the trade tended to increase rather than to diminish. There were complaints of foreign competition and falling profits, but trade, both at home and abroad, continued to expand.

The pathetic helplessness of the potters before the new situation created by the industrial changes is realised by a glance at their schemes and day-dreams during the 'eighties and 'nineties. In the spring of 1881 the Hollow-ware Pressers' Society contemplated starting a pottery factory, and with this end in view it invited B. Slatter, of Manchester, to give its members a lecture on the subject of co-operative factories. After this lecture a decision to start such a factory was reached, and the wish was expressed that the unions of other branches of the trade would co-operate in the scheme.[1]

Although all were agreed that it was desirable for a union-owned factory to be started, the scheme did not materialise. Conditions in 1881, when this scheme was being discussed, were not the same as in 1834, when operative potters owned and managed an earthenware factory. In the earlier period the potters were powerful, successful in their struggles with the masters and filled with optimism for the future, while the proposed scheme of 1881 came after a series of arbitration awards, all of which had gone against the men. It was, moreover, at a time when potters' leaders were stating publicly "that the

[1] *Pottery Gazette*, April 1881.

operatives were too thick on the field, and that a scheme of emigration was necessary to take away surplus labour".[1] The co-operative factory of 1834 was the result of the men's strength and optimism, but the proposal for one in 1881 was the result of weakness and pessimism.

Eleven years later, in 1892, the Brownfield Guild Scheme was inaugurated. During the intervening period the operatives had conducted an unsuccessful strike and an Arbitration Board had been set up and abandoned.

The Brownfield scheme was the outcome of a correspondence between William Owen, Secretary of the National Order of Potters, and Arthur Brownfield, a master potter, which was published in the *Staffordshire Sentinel* immediately after the Hinckes Award.[2] The correspondence was not controversial, and, although some little disagreement existed between them, both the union leader and the manufacturer agreed in stressing the importance of a better understanding between masters and men.

The Brownfield Guild Scheme was one of co-partnership, and was a practical expression of the ideas put forward by Brownfield in this correspondence. Brownfield's factory was valued at £20,000, and debentures were raised to pay out various members of his family having an interest in the firm. A. Brownfield kept his capital in the firm in the form of ordinary shares. A maximum interest of 6 per cent. was placed upon the debentures and 5 per cent. upon ordinary shares. The operatives were allowed to purchase shares in the concern up to the value of £2,000. Those employees wishing to take advantage of this scheme agreed to an arrangement whereby from 5 to 10 per cent.

[1] *Pottery Gazette*, April 1881.
[2] A. Brownfield: *A Potters' Guild* (1892). The first letter is one from Brownfield, May 25, 1891.

was deducted from their weekly wages to pay for their shares. The profits of the concern were divided amongst the workers according to the number of shares held, those holding no shares not participating.[1]

The unions were attracted to the scheme because it offered them the opportunity of getting to know the cost of the production of pottery ware. The lack of such knowledge had handicapped their representatives in discussions with the manufacturers before the different arbitration enquiries. The Hollow-ware Pressers' Union consequently purchased enough shares in the Brownfield Guild to entitle it to a seat on the Board of Directors. These shares, like the investment held by the Brownfields, were subject to a maximum rate of interest. The Hollow-ware Pressers' Union hoped with the knowledge it would thus obtain to do better for the operatives in future arbitration awards.[2]

The Guild Pottery suffered several misfortunes. In March of 1896 it appeared to have turned the tide, and its supporters believed that it was establishing itself as a successful undertaking. At the annual meeting on the 21st of that month a satisfactory balance-sheet and report were submitted to the shareholders. Unfortunately a fire occurred on the following day which did considerable damage to the warehouse.[3] This misfortune, coupled with the expense of a costly lawsuit in which it was then engaged, proved too much for the Guild, and in January 1898 the factory was advertised for sale.[4]

W. Owen, who, through his correspondence with A. Brownfield, had been instrumental in bringing about this scheme, criticised it on the ground that only those work-

[1] *Royal Commission on Labour* (1893–94), vol. iii, 403, 406.
[2] Letters from Pottery Union officials.
[3] *Pottery Gazette*, April 1896.
[4] *Pottery Gazette*, January and February 1898.

men who held shares gained any advantage from it. He had long been an advocate of industrial partnerships, and as far back as 1869 had spoken at the Trade Union Congress to Holyoake's paper entitled "Industrial Partnerships as one means of accomplishing the objects of Trade Unions".[1] The idea of industrial alliance behind the Brownfield Guild was carried farther in 1898, when an attempt was made to apply the "Bedstead Smith" scheme to the earthenware industry. As mentioned elsewhere, this later scheme did not fructify.

These projects of the late nineteenth century have certain characteristics in common with the emigration scheme of 1845, and the requests for strong employers' associations to keep up selling prices which were repeatedly made throughout the century. All of them betray the helplessness of the potter before the real facts of the situation. The emigration scheme of 1845 was a deliberate running away from a phantom enemy. The requests for stronger association amongst the masters, as has been pointed out, is understandable when the close interdependence of prices and wages is considered, but in the form they took they would appear to have been born of an attitude of irresponsibility toward industrial affairs. In asking for a strong association of manufacturers, the potters were, in effect, throwing the onus of responsibility for the evils of their time and trade upon some agent other than themselves, while in the largest branch of the industry less than one-third of their own number was organised.[2]

The project of the co-operative factory in 1881, and the inauguration of the Brownfield Guild, were the side-tracking of energies into the easy day-dream of Utopia, instead

[1] *Birmingham Daily Post*, August 27, 28, 1869.
[2] *Staffordshire Potteries, Board of Arbitration, Evidence and Award of the Inquiry before H. T. Hinckes, Esq., M.P.*, 1891.

of using them for the healthy but arduous and prosaic task of building up trade union organisation. The Industrial Alliance met with the favour of the potters. It promised high wages without struggle with the masters, but the workmen to whom this ingenious scheme was offered were too feebly organised to give any effective help.

This slackness, which took the form of walking round facts instead of facing them, and mistaking imagination for action, possessed potters' unions for three-quarters of a century following the catastrophe of the National Union in 1837. The Arbitration Board encouraged this slackness to some extent. In evidence before the Royal Commission on Labour in 1892 the potters' unions officials admitted that "the men had rested upon the Board's usefulness and had not strengthened their unions".[1]

The attitude of the working potter toward the changes in industrial technique from the 'seventies onward was one of grumbling acceptance. He treated the revolution in his trade as if it were a spell of bad weather, something which, though it caused alarm and perturbation, could not be altered. A further problem, that of the woman worker, which these changes had brought to the front, he treated in almost the same fashion. Up to the end of the nineteenth century the business of organising women was practically left alone, and yet, if the female labour problem was to be solved, that was a necessary preliminary. From 1890 the Printers' and Transferrers' Society had a few hundred women members.[2] The number of women in other potters' societies was insignificant. The

[1] *Royal Commission on Labour* (1893–94), vol. iii, 398.

[2] *4th Report on Trade Unions*, 1889–90 (1891), 278. For the years before 1890 there are no figures available which give a separate female membership. There were female members (*3rd Trade Union Report* (1889), 128): "There are both male and female members, the former being the printers and the latter the transferrers."

largest society, the Amalgamated Society of Hollow-ware Pressers and all Clay Potters, had but forty female members on its books in 1900. This number fell to thirty-six in the following year, and by 1902 the society had no women members.[1]

Two branches of the Women's Trade Union League were formed in North Staffordshire for pottery workers in 1893, which for a few years kept up a membership of two hundred, but in the years immediately before their dissolution in 1903 that number had fallen to thirty and forty respectively.[2]

There was a great addition to women unionists in 1907 owing to the militant activities of the new amalgamated union, but this inrush was of a very temporary nature, and by 1910 the total number of organised women in the pottery trade was less than in 1890.[3] In 1911 the National Amalgamated Society of Male and Female Pottery Workers made special attempts to induce women workers to join its ranks. A woman organiser was appointed, and many factory meetings were held. The result was so successful that in a few years the number of women unionists was quadrupled. The campaign was conducted chiefly amongst the workers in the growing but long-established women's trades, i.e. transferrers and decorators. No very special attempt was made to organise women clay potters, and potters' female attendants were left practically alone. It was nevertheless a creditable piece of work, and it

[1] 13*th Report on Trade Unions*, 1900 (1901).
14*th Report on Trade Unions*, 1901 (1902).
15*th Report on Trade Unions*, 1902–4 (1906).

[2] 10*th Report on Trade Unions*, 1897 (1898).
14*th Report on Trade Unions*, 1901 (1902).
15*th Report on Trade Unions*, 1902–4 (1906).

[3] 16*th Report on Trade Unions*, 1905–7 (1909).
17*th Report on Trade Unions*, 1908–10 (1912–13).

was quite clear by 1914 that henceforth women were to be a power in the Union.[1]

The National Amalgamated Society of Male and Female Pottery Workers had kept the same members' contribution rates as the Amalgamated Hollow-ware Pressers' and Clay Potters' Society, which were 2d. unemployment and 2d. per week no-situation, etc.[2] As it was essential that their contributions should be low, women were accepted to membership on dispute benefit contribution only.

The ill-success of the organised potters during the period 1870–1911 in attracting women workers to their ranks shows in an even poorer light when the rate at which the industry was absorbing female labour is considered. The number of women engaged in pottery manufacture in Staffordshire increased during the years 1871–1911 from 13,923 to 25,851. The rate of increase was steady throughout the period, the figures for the intervening census years being as follows: 15,694 in 1881; 19,160 in 1891; and 21,247 in 1901.

The essence of the female labour problem, the conditions under which women should work at what were once considered to be men's jobs, was not satisfactorily met. In the clay branches the easy way of settlement was taken and women labour was considered to be similar in its nature to that of the male apprentice. That is, the woman cup-maker, handler, flat presser, etc., like the male apprentice, would nominally work on men's piece-rates, but would allow to the master a few coppers in every shilling earned. She was, so far as the trade was concerned, in a permanent state of apprenticeship.

[1] *The Monthly Journal (Pottery Workers' Society)*, September 1911.
B. Drake: *Women in Trade Unions* (N.D.), table i.

[2] *supra*, 173.
Sick and Funeral Benefits had been dropped by the Hollow-ware Pressers' Society before the amalgamation of 1906.

In many instances employers dispensed with the fiction of apprenticeship or allowance and fixed a woman's rate for the operations mentioned distinct from those paid to men. The result was that women's piece-rates in the substituted jobs were in a chaotic state, often being a matter of bargaining between the woman and her employer.

Up to 1914 the substitution of women for men was, compared to what was afterwards the case, only beginning, and it is therefore the more regrettable that something was not then done to settle the female labour problem. In the clay branches there appeared to be a natural demarcation between men's and what could be women's work. Heavy and specially skilled work seemed the prerogative of men. In "casting", which was a comparatively recent development, women were only doing what could aptly be described as "learners'" work. As a body, women casters were as yet learning the trade.

In those clay branches in which machinery was employed the same mutual demarcation obtained. Only that work which required but little strength and skill, cup, saucer, small plate making, etc., was taken over by women. Moreover, up to 1914, neither in casting, which was new, nor in jollying, which was forty years old, had the women taken over all the light and lesser skilled work. It hardly seemed necessary to make a collective agreement as to what should be men's and what women's work.

The cotton trade's solution of practically the same problem, and the one which Mr. and Mrs. Sidney Webb had been trying from 1891 to force upon the attention of trade unions—the logical application of the standard rate—was one which the potters do not appear to have entertained. For this lack of a considered policy in reference to female labour the whole body of potters must take the blame; their excuse is the unsettling conditions of their time. Little blame can be attached to the harassed trade union official, or to that staunch handful of working potters who in good years and bad had stuck to their trade organisation. The energy of the union was expended in fighting for the day only and in making the best bargains it could for workers, the bulk of whom, both men and women, were non-unionists.

The disparity of the wages paid to workers in the same trade of approximately the same skill had long been a feature of the industry, but it was aggravated by the state of craft confusion into which the trade was thrown through technical changes. In 1836 the Potters' Union tried to lessen these disparities by demanding that both the best and the worst paid work should be distributed equally amongst all the workmen in the branch concerned, and it also attempted, by a series of small strikes, to bring a standard list of piecework prices into the industry.[1]

Attempts were made in later years to enforce standard piece-rates, notably in the early days of the new union of 1845,[2] but these attempts were to some extent nullified by the apparent impossibility of obtaining standard conditions of work. From 1880 onward—that is, from the time the Arbitration Board ceased to be an effective instrument until the time of the new Amalgamated Union of 1906—little concerted action was taken to deal with the problem. Potters at individual firms whose piece-rates for certain lines of work were exceptionally low occasionally attempted to remedy matters by direct negotiation with their employer, and in such cases the trade union gave assistance.

The problem was a complicated one. Some firms paid higher rates than others for the same class of work. In some factories conditions of work were such that the

[1] *supra*, 80. [2] *supra*, 112–14.

operative was able to achieve a higher output than the normal, and, finally, for some classes of work the piece-rates were such that the workman could get high wages with ease, whilst in other equally skilled work he could not, even with the greatest exertion, earn other than very low wages.

A few figures relating to the largest branch of male pieceworkers in the industry at that time will serve to show the extent to which wages varied. For 1876 G. P. Bevan (*Industrial Classes and Industrial Statistics*) gives hollow-ware pressers' wages as varying from 24s. to 42s. for a full week's work, and his figures "suppose competent workpeople, constant work, steady habits and a manufactory of respectable position in the trade".[1] The Earnings and Hours Enquiry of 1906 gives full-time weekly wages of hollow-ware pressers as varying from under 20s. to over 45s., with 30s. as the median wage, 25s. the lower quartile and 36s. the upper quartile. In other branches wages also show a considerable variation.

Technical changes in the industry helped to cheapen production without benefiting either profits or wages, the consumer being almost the entire gainer. Competition continued to keep profits down, and from 1872 until 1900 the only general change in wages was the 8⅓ per cent. reduction of 1879.[2]

On February 11, 1900, the potters of North Staffordshire gave notice that they would require an advance in wages and other changes in existing conditions. In certain respects the time was propitious for the making of these demands. During 1899 trade, especially in the latter part of the year, had been exceptionally good. Of it the *Pottery Gazette* said: "The most prosperous year of the last decade."

[1] G. P. Bevan: *The Industrial Classes and Industrial Statistics* (1876), 150.
[2] *supra*, 158.

The hollow-ware and flat pressers asked for an immediate advance of 5 per cent. and a further advance of like amount in the following year. The ovenmen asked to be advanced from 4s. 7d. to 5s. per day. The printers and transferrers wanted a return of a penny in the shilling taken off their wages by the award of 1879, and a rearrangement or levelling-up of counts, i.e. the number of articles of various kinds that constitute a nominal dozen.

When the period of notice expired, the printers and transferrers and ovenmen, to the number of between 3,000 and 4,000, ceased work. The pressers, however, gave a further notice of four weeks to terminate their engagements. During the interval a number of firms wholly or partially ceased work, whilst others came to temporary arrangements with the operatives whereby work could be continued. Within a little over a week after April 21st, when the pressers joined in the strike, 20,000 operatives were involved. A conference was held on May 26th between the manufacturers and the representatives of the workers, at which the manufacturers offered an advance of 8½ per cent. to the ovenmen and 5 per cent. to the other branches, to date from the following October 1st. The question of "counts" was to be dealt with by conciliation committees. These terms were placed before the men and accepted two days later.[1]

For some years after 1900 no demands were made for further wage advances. The industry was changing, devious methods to reduce wages were practised, working potters grumbled about both wages and conditions, but no action was taken by the unions until the end of 1907, when the National Amalgamated Society balloted its members upon the advisability of giving notice for a 15 per cent.

[1] *Report on Strikes and Lock-outs*, 1900 (1901).
Pottery Gazette, March, April, May and June 1900.

rise in wages. Apart from the fact that they considered potters' wages to be so low that an advance was urgently needed, the executive of the union gave as further justification for the step they had taken that two or three years previously the manufacturers had risen their selling prices.[1]

The dispute which followed the demands of the operatives culminated in the formation of a Conciliation Board. During the few years immediately before the war every section of the potters received increases in wages as follows:

1908 Ovenmen, advance of 5 per cent., awarded under Conciliation Board.[2]

1911 Flat and Hollow-ware Pressers, advance of 5 per cent. Rockingham and Jet Potters, advance of 8 to 9 per cent., arbitration award under E. Moon, K.C. (Chairman of late Conciliation Board).[3]

1912 Ovenmen, Transferrers and Printers, advance of 5 per cent., negotiation between employers and trade unions.[4]

One only of these advances was secured under the Board, although it started negotiations for those of 1911.

In the china trade no general advances in wages were given or demanded during this period, but in August 1911 the National Amalgamated Society of Male and Female Pottery Workers drew up a scale of minimum piece-rates, to which it asked the manufacturers to comply as early

[1] *Pottery Gazette*, January 1908.

[2] Board of Conciliation and Reference for the Staffordshire Earthenware Manufacturers and Operatives.
Award, September 1908.

[3] *Pottery Gazette*, September 1911.

[4] *Pottery Gazette*, March, April, June 1912.

as possible. Enquiries which the union officials had made in the china industry showed that the rates paid to operatives for the making of similar articles varied a great deal from factory to factory.[1]

The presentation of the list was followed by protracted negotiations, which terminated favourably to the operatives.[2]

It is illustrative of the bad organisation of the trade at this period that promises of wage increases made by the manufacturers were not infrequently unfulfilled. In 1912, six weeks prior to March 25th, the customary period for giving notice of a desired wage change, the hollow-ware and flat pressers from several factories sent in claims for the 5 per cent. wage advance awarded them in July 1911 but which they had not yet received.[3] Two years later, February 1914, the same thing happened again, but this time the printers and transferrers from various factories, in addition to hollow-ware and flat pressers, sent in claims for the payment of the 1911 awards.[4]

[1] *Pottery Gazette*, September 1911.
[2] *Pottery Gazette*, November, December 1911.
[3] *Pottery Gazette*, March 1912.
[4] *Pottery Gazette*, March 1914.

CHAPTER XII

TO-DAY

Unlike most other industries the manufacture of pottery was not to any great extent dislocated by the European War. There was some unemployment in the industry at its beginning, but before long there was an actual scarcity of labour. Both masters and operatives took advantage of wartime conditions to strengthen their organisations, and the coming of peace saw each in a very powerful position.[1]

The various sections of pottery manufacture had individual employers' associations, and in the New Year of 1919 a further step toward unity was taken by the employers when the British Pottery Manufacturers' Federation was formed. This was a federation of associations, and its objects were to watch and to promote the interests of the manufacturers as a whole, and to be the channel through which manufacturers would consult with operatives and government officials.[2] The manufacturers' associations, though at no time taking in the whole of the trading interest, were yet sufficiently powerful to control the trade. The Profiteering Committee on Pottery said of them that, although there was no evidence that they had raised prices without reasonable excuse, yet they were strong enough to make it advisable that the Government should take steps to safeguard the public interest.

The operative potters were equally successful in their efforts to build up powerful organisations. In the last few months of the war the membership of the largest of the potters' unions rose to the unprecedented figure of 28,000,

[1] *Profiteering Acts*, 1919–20. *Report on Pottery* (1921), 4.

[2] *Profiteering Acts*, 1919–20. *Report on Pottery* (1921), 5. *Pottery Gazette*, August 1919.

and by May 1919 this had risen to 33,000.[1] In August of that year the divers potters' unions amalgamated. This resulted in a union, "The National Society of Pottery Workers", with a membership of 40,000.[2]

The high membership number of the new amalgamated union reflected the enthusiasm for trade union solidarity with which the potters, in common with workers in other industries, were at that time possessed. Members of the pottery industry to whom the idea of trade unionism had been repugnant in the past now dropped their prejudices and became organised. At the end of 1917 a Potters' Clerks' Guild was formed which allied itself to the Stoke-on-Trent branch of the National Union of Clerks.[3] In less than a year afterwards pottery managers and officials formed an association for themselves,[4] and in March 1920 the modellers followed suit and formed the "Association of Pottery Modellers".[5]

It is pleasing to note that the flourishing growth of association amongst the operative classes was not frowned upon by the manufacturers, but was often actually encouraged by them. Many manufacturers permitted union officials to enter their works in order to canvass the operatives.

The amicable spirit which existed between pottery manufacturers during the war and post-war boom expressed itself most vividly in the formation of the Pottery Joint Industrial Council in January 1918. This was the first new scheme of industrial relationships to be promulgated or discussed in the pottery trade since the time of the experiment of the New Industrial Alliance in 1899. An Arbitration Board was established, but arbitration and conciliation were old ideas containing no element

[1] *Pottery Gazette*, November 1918, June 1919.
[2] *Pottery Gazette*, September 1919. [3] *Pottery Gazette*, January 1918.
[4] *Pottery Gazette*, December 1918. [5] *Pottery Gazette*, April 1920.

of freshness. During the whole of that period the imaginative inventiveness of the potters was not brought to bear upon anything other than narrow trade matters, but the establishment of the National Council for the Pottery Industry proved that this faculty was not dead.

The origin of the Council is to be found in the conference of labour leaders and employers of various industries, together with E. H. C. Wethered and Professor H. Clay, convened by A. Rowntree in February 1917, to discuss the necessity for industrial reconstruction. The conference issued a report recommending that industry be organised on a national basis, the unit to be the trade as a whole and not the individual business.

As a practical expression of the conference Messrs. Rowntree, Clay and Wethered decided to make an experiment with the pottery industry along the lines recommended. From the point of view of the task which they had in hand that particular industry had much in its favour. It was highly localised, a good feeling existed between employer and employed and, most important of all, a great interest in problems of reconstruction had been aroused throughout the Potteries area by the Tutorial Class Movement.[1]

Largely through the instrumentality of the gentlemen before mentioned, conferences were arranged in April 1917 between representatives of both employers and operatives in the pottery industry. A joint conference was held in May 1917, a month before the interim report of the Whitley Committee was circulated, at which it was decided that it was to the interest of the industry as a whole to form a joint council. In the opinion of the conference it was essential to both employers and employed that their

[1] *Report on the Establishment and Progress of Joint Industrial Councils* (1923), 29.
National Council of the Pottery Industry. Annual Report (1918–19), 3.

organisations should be made more effective, and in this work a joint council would be of great assistance.

Following this conference the project of a joint council was submitted to the various employers' and employees' associations concerned. By July 1917 the trade had finally decided to form a joint council, but it was some months before a scheme could be drafted that was acceptable to all the associations concerned. On January 11, 1918, the the Joint Industrial Council for the Pottery Industry—the pioneer experiment along the lines of the Whitley Report—held its first meeting. At the meeting a member of the Manufacturers' Association was elected chairman, and an official of the National Union of Pottery Workers, vice-chairman. Under its constitution the membership of the Council was to consist of an equal number of representatives of employers and operatives, the total number in no case to exceed sixty.

The employers' representatives were to be appointed by the manufacturers' associations and the operative representatives by the trade unions. The Council had the power to co-opt honorary members, having the right to attend meetings, serve on commissions, etc., but not to vote. Works committees were set up, but owing to the localisation of the industry it was not deemed necessary to set up district councils. The Council aimed to unite "all sections of the industry in a great co-operative effort to increase and improve both the technical and industrial efficiency of the industry for the betterment and welfare of all concerned". The objects of the Council were designed with this end in view.

From its inception the Council was active in carrying out its programme. With the view of getting all operative potters organised in a trade union, posters were displayed on factories advising all workers to join the National Society of Pottery Workers. The Council also requested manufacturers to grant facilities to trade union officials to enter factories at meal-times for propaganda purposes, or at such other times as were convenient. This request was fairly generally granted, with the provision that there was to be no undue interference with the carrying on of the operatives' work.

While not intending to supersede the existing methods of collective bargaining, the Council had power to intervene in those disputes between employer and employed where the existing machinery proved inadequate. Upon two occasions only, 1920 and 1924, when by its mediation it prevented threatened stoppages of work, have its services in this connexion been required.[1]

The health of the worker has received special consideration. Unhealthy processes have been investigated with the object of discovering how danger to the operative could be lessened or removed. As a result many practical recommendations have been made to secure the provision of workshops, materials and implements, which, whilst efficient, are more satisfactory from the point of view of the health of the worker than those in ordinary use. Pamphlets containing hints upon the preservation of health have been circulated from time to time amongst the operatives, leaflets have been sent to manufacturers for distribution to managers and foremen, drawing attention to the need of the study of health conditions in the factory, and posters have been displayed in factories showing how the taking of simple precautions materially improves the health and comfort of all engaged in the industry.

The Council is also actively concerned with welfare work and the provision of increased educational facilities for juvenile workers. In this connexion two reports issued

[1] *Report on the Establishment and Progress of Joint Industrial Councils* (1923), 102.

with reference to the Education Act of 1918 have attracted attention outside the pottery industry.[1]

Through the channels of the Council, manufacturers and others interested are made acquainted with the types of ware sold by England's competitors in the foreign markets, and it has made representation to the Government urging that the scope of the British Empire Marketing Board be enlarged so as to enable it to advertise British manufactured goods in the Empire on the same lines as the Board now advertises Empire goods in this country.

Statistics of profits, wages, etc., are periodically furnished to the Council, and a census has been taken of workers in the industry.

It has been impossible to do more than mention in passing many of the activities of the Council. It would require much more space than can be given here to do them full justice, but enough has been said to indicate the lines along which the work of the Council runs.

Success in the building of the National Council did not mean any slackening on the part of trade union workers in their endeavours further to strengthen their position, or in their attempts to improve the operatives' conditions through trade union channels. The Council was not used as an easy substitute for trade union activity.

Most of the battles of the trade unions were fought over the matter of wages, although working hours, trade customs and health conditions received a fair amount of attention. Wage advances in the pottery industry during the war were steady and not, as in some industries, phenomenally rapid. The first general rise in wages took place in 1915,

[1] *National Council of the Pottery Industry. First Report of Enquiries into and Recommendations made in connection Education Act,* 1918, *July* 1919, *having special regard to appropriate Education for Juvenile Pottery Workers, July* 1919. *Second Report, July* 1920.

when the manufacturers agreed to pay a war bonus of 7½ per cent. Subsequent advances raised wages 108 per cent. above the pre-war rates of 1914,[1] but this upward trend in the general rates of wages was reversed when the post-war boom in pottery production came to an end.

From the war period until the end of 1920 the industry enjoyed remarkably good trade, but in February of 1921 the signs of a depression began to appear. Certain firms went on short-time, but as yet there was little unemployment and trade reports were far from alarming. In March the Operatives' Union had but 900 members either unemployed or partly unemployed out of a total membership of 40,000.[2] Two months later the whole industry was brought to a sudden standstill by the dispute in the coal trade. The effects of this upon the industry were disastrous. Having little accommodation for coal many factories had immediately to close down, and almost all were compelled seriously to curtail production within a few days of the declaration of the strike. The Potters' Union was soon in financial difficulties. For some time its members were paid full unemployment benefit, which was later reduced to half, but even at half-rates the drain upon the union was exceptionally heavy. It was enabled to carry on by a loan of £10,000 from the Burslem Co-operative Society.

Altogether this strike cost the Potters' Union no less than £60,000.[3] The position of the manufacturers was also gravely effected by the stoppage. Not only was the loss they sustained during the weeks of the stoppage serious, but orders were discouraged by the state of unsettlement into which the trade was thrown.[4] Immediately after the

[1] *Pottery Gazette*, November 1918.
Pottery Gazette, October 1921. [2] *Pottery Gazette*, April 1921.
[3] *Pottery Gazette*, June and December, 1921.
[4] *Pottery Gazette*, May 1921.

resumption of work the manufacturers expressed their intention of reducing wages in view of the trade outlook. This intention was executed in October, when the operatives were served with 28 days' notice of a reduction of 20 per cent. in net earnings. With funds gone and the burden of a heavy debt upon it the National Potters' Union was in no position to resist the claims of the manufacturers. The fact that the U.S.A. potters had not long before accepted a reduction of 19½ per cent. strengthened the position of the manufacturers considerably. They suggested reforming the old Conciliation Board and placing the matter before it, but the operatives refused to agree to this. While perfectly willing to have the case put before the Ministry of Labour, they would not agree to the appointment of an umpire under the rules of the old Conciliation Board. After some discussion the idea of arbitration was dropped and the operatives agreed to a reduction of 20 per cent., half to come off in the following December 1921 and the remaining half in February 1922.[1]

The fact that the manufacturers were prepared to submit their case to arbitration would suggest that they were convinced of the equity of their demands, and that they were not taking advantage of the weak state of the Operatives' Union, though one can understand the latter view being both held and expressed. Twenty per cent. was the full amount that could be taken from the operatives' wages at that time without violating the customs of the trade. Before this reduction, potters' wages had been made up of base rate, 66⅔ per cent. incorporated bonus and 25 per cent. floating bonus. Any alteration in the base rate or in the incorporated bonus could be made only on March 25th after six weeks' notice of the desired alteration had been given. The floating bonus was determinable

[1] *Pottery Gazette*, December 1921.

at any time, and it was this floating bonus of 25 per cent., the equivalent of 20 per cent. net earnings, which was taken from the potters' wages. At the time of the reduction the manufacturers agreed not to make any attempt further to alter wages at the normal settling time, March 25th. As the floating bonus was now gone this meant in effect that wages were safe from interference until March 25, 1923.

Despite the drop in selling prices which followed wage reductions, trade continued to be in a depressed condition, and six weeks prior to March 25, 1923, the manufacturers gave notice of a further 20 per cent. reduction in wages. The operatives put in a counter claim for 8⅓ per cent. rise, which would bring the existing bonus up to 75 per cent. over base rates, the equivalent of the cost of living index figures at that time. Negotiations between the two parties moved with difficulty and the operatives finally gave notice to cease work. However, on April 19th, a few days before the expiration of notice, a reduction of 10 per cent. on gross wages was agreed upon.[1]

To neither party did this settlement bring the assurance that wages had reached a stable level. To the operatives the large reductions experienced in the past eighteen months appeared excessive, unwarranted by either the circumstances of the trade or in relation to the cost of living. From the manufacturers' point of view trade conditions were bad, the highly remunerative years were slipping away and the strains and stresses of moderate trade had to be faced.

On February 12, 1924, notices for alterations in wages were again sent by both manufacturers and operatives. The former asked for a further all-round reduction of 10 per cent., while the latter wanted the existing 50 per cent. incorporated bonus raised to 66⅔ per cent. Negotiations proceeded between the two parties, but they could arrive at no settlement,

[1] *Pottery Gazette*, May 1923.

and it was eventually decided to lay the questions at issue before the National Council of the Pottery Industry.

The Council met in April and appointed a special Committee to deal with the dispute. This Committee was composed of six operatives, six manufacturer members and three honorary members of the Council; the three honorary members, E. H. C. Wethered, the Chairman, A. Rowntree and Professor H. Clay having final powers of decision in the event of disagreement. Power was given to the Committee to institute enquiries into average selling prices, earnings, costs and aggregate profits in the industry as a whole, and to employ, if required, independent accountants for this purpose.

Particulars of information resulting from the enquiry were to be for the use of the Committee only, and not for publication. Four meetings were held during April and the first week in May, and the claims of both the manufacturers and the operatives were discussed. In view of the difficulties a settlement would involve without adequate information of the industry, it was decided to appoint an accountant to conduct an independent investigation and report to the Committee as to the comparative average selling prices, earnings of the operatives and aggregate profits in the industry as a whole. The accountant was to report to the honorary members as to the aggregate profits of the various sections of the industry.

These instructions to the accountant involved an exhaustive and prolonged investigation into the industry, and it was not until July that he was able to present his report to the Committee. During this month the Committee met several times to discuss the claims of the two parties to the dispute in the light of the information contained in the report. The Committee published its award and a report of its proceedings on July 18th. Owing to the terms of reference it was impossible to give detailed particulars of conditions, but certain valuable observations were made in general terms upon the industry in the report. It pointed out that "a comparison with other industries shows that in the Pottery Industry wage rates of some classes of workers are exceptionally low, while, on the other hand, the rates and earnings of other classes of workers compare favourably with those of workers in other occupations". The same difference was exhibited in profits. Certain sections of pottery production showed a comparatively high profit, while others were carrying on with a very small margin. Furthermore, in the main, the lower rates of wages were being paid in those sections of the industry in which there were the greatest number of firms making little or no profit, while the higher rates were given in the sections which were doing well.

To have based the award exclusively on a comparison with other industries would have meant lifting up wages in those sections which were least able to bear it, and an award based upon the profitableness of the industry would have given advances to already highly paid operatives without touching the low wages. Neither of these considerations was regarded by the honorary members of the Committee as the sole determining factor in coming to a decision. They did not minimise the importance of these considerations and they were undoubtedly influenced by them, but their award was chiefly guided by another factor which arose out of the accountant's report. This was that the facts of the industry showed that the reduction of wages in the previous year had not been altogether warranted, and therefore the honorary members decided that some portion of that reduction should be restored to the operatives. A general advance was made as follows: 2½ per cent. to operatives in general earthenware, fine china, jet and rockingham, and 5 per cent. to operatives in sanitary earthenware, fireclay and tiles. In addition, certain workers excepted from the above awards were granted advances ranging from 5 to 7½ per cent.[1]

From the foregoing it would appear that the post-war organisation of the potters had done little to improve the position of the operatives. Here they were, with a strong national union, which embraced potters from every branch of the trade, and with a Joint Industrial Council, getting on a general award in their favour far less bonus on base rates than was commensurate with the increased cost of living, as registered in the Government Cost of Living Index Numbers.

If the improvements in the pottery workers' wages had consisted only in general rises, then it would be true to say that the union had not achieved very much for its members, but this was not the case. In many instances base rates had been rising, not merely for low-paid workers, such as warehouse women, whose pre-war wage of 9s. per week was risen to base rate of 16s., but of relatively well-paid workers, too, such as ovenmen, whose pre-war wage of 5s. 9d. had risen to base rate of 7s. per day. In the case of pieceworkers the establishment of minimum rates of pay and the abolition of the custom of "good from oven" and of the system of stoppages meant that many of them had substantial rises in wages. So much so that in March 1923 the manufacturers alleged that 125 per cent. more nearly represented the advances in wages which operatives had received since 1914 than did the 66⅔ per cent. which they were getting over base rates.

The principle of a minimum wage had been established in many branches of the china trade in 1911—the flat pressers in general earthenware in 1911, and the printers

[1] *Staffordshire Sentinel*, July 18, 1924.

and transferrers in 1912,[1] but it was not until April 1920 that this was extended to the pottery trade as a whole. Stoppages from wages for lighting, sweeping of workshops, preparation of materials, etc., had, to a great extent, been commuted before the war period, and those which survived were abolished in October 1919.[2] A few months previously a much-needed reform in the method of wage payment to potters' attendants had been introduced.[3] Henceforth attendants were to receive their wages direct from the offices of the factory and not, as previously, from the potters by whom they were employed. The securing of direct payment from the manufacturer's office was an attempt to check the evils existing in relation to the remuneration of attendants.[4] This agreement, which protected the attendant from the cupidity of the working potter, also contained among other clauses those which abolished the custom of "good from oven" and fixed a working week of forty-seven hours' duration.

The abolition of the custom of "good from oven" touched the imagination of the potters. For a century "good from oven" had been a fruitful source of discord and unrest in the industry, and, consequently, its termination was received with more elation on the part of the potters than its mere financial gain warranted. It was a symbol of better conditions. A Bastille in the trade had been taken, and the past definitely cleaved from the present. What it meant historically to the potters was shown at the first quarterly meeting of their union following its abolition, when the members proposed the inauguration of a scheme of endowment for the North Staffordshire

[1] *Pottery Gazette*, March and September 1911; March 1912.

[2] *Pottery Gazette*, January 1920. [3] *Pottery Gazette*, May 1919.

[4] *Pottery Gazette*, May 1919: ". . . some of our own members employing juveniles and not paying a decent wage."—S. Clowes, Secretary, National Society for Pottery Workers, at meeting, March 25, 1919.

Hospital as a permanent memorial of the abolition of "good from oven".[1]

In the establishment of a forty-seven-hour week the great difficulty lay with the workmen rather than with their employers. Even with new methods of manufacture many pieceworkers were still independent of machinery, and of those who were not many had certain necessary operations to perform which did not require the running of a machine. This fact tended to make the men's hours of working very erratic, and being accustomed to coming and going practically as they chose, they did not relish the idea of being tied down to set hours, even to their own advantage. Thus, although the forty-seven-hour week reduced the length of the working day for all workers, it did not receive that strict observance given to hours agreements in the textiles and similar industries.[2]

With regard to the improvement of health conditions for the workers in post-war years the organised potters did much effective work through the machinery of the Industrial Council. Of the two diseases to which pottery workers are peculiarly liable, lead-poisoning and silicosis, the former had been scheduled as a compensatory disease in the late nineteenth century, and had come under the special governmental regulations laid down in those occupations in which it was contracted.

Until recent years silicosis was not a scheduled disease for compensation. In 1907 the Departmental Committee on Compensation for Industrial Diseases reported silicosis as a special trade disease among workers in various industries, including potters engaged in certain processes. It considered that there were practical difficulties in the

[1] *Pottery Gazette*, June 1919.
[2] *Pottery Gazette*, May and October 1919.
Labour Gazette, January 1929.

way of scheduling the disease under the Workmen's Compensation Act of 1906, and recommended that it should be dealt with in special trade schemes. Nothing further was done, however, until the Workmen's Compensation (Silicosis) Act of 1918 was passed, which made silicosis in certain specified industries a compensatory disease, but pottery workers were not included under the Act.[1]

The National Society of Pottery Workers immediately commenced an active campaign for their inclusion. Representations were made to the Home Office, politicians were acquainted with the facts of the disease and a leaflet giving the case for the potters was distributed at the Trade Union Congress in September 1922,[2] whereupon the General Council of the Trade Union Congress took up the matter on their behalf. They were informed that the Home Office had power to bring the pottery industry under the provisions of the Act, but that a medical enquiry was first necessary to ascertain facts of incidence of the disease in the industry. The Home Secretary approached the National Pottery Council, asking it to undertake the medical enquiry, but the Council replied that it could not see its way clear to do so. Under these circumstances the Home Office took upon itself the responsibility, and in 1925 a medical enquiry was instituted.

As a result of the enquiry an order was issued by the Home Office in 1928 providing a compensation scheme for silicosis in the pottery industry. The scheme came into force on February 1, 1929, and applied to all operatives employed in certain processes on and after January 1, 1929. It perhaps falls short of expectation in that it applies only to total disablement and death.[3]

[1] Home Office: *Report of the Departmental Committee on Compensation for Silicosis, Dealing with the Pottery Industry* (1928), 5.

[2] *Pottery Gazette*, May 1922, September 1923.

[3] Home Office: *Report of the Departmental Committee on Compensation for Silicosis, Dealing with the Pottery Industry* (1928), 9.

Upon the present position of the industry and of the place of the organised worker in it one hesitates to speak with certainty. The English pottery trade is sharing in the general depression, and various conditions which now prevail may no longer do so when industrial prosperity returns. There are, however, certain features in the present position which appear to be of more than a transient nature. Because of the changes in manufacturing processes some of the skilled branches of the trade are definitely doomed and have no hope of revival, while others have lost their handicraft character owing to the introduction of mechanical appliances.

It is extremely unlikely that any change in fashion or taste will bring back the older methods of working, for the designer of pottery is no more restricted under the new than he was under the old processes of manufacture, so that no matter in which direction the public fancy may lean there is no hope of recovery for the decayed trades.

Changes in manufacture, coupled with the tendency of increased division of labour in all departments where it is considered to be practicable, has led to a diminution in the amount of skill demanded of an operative by his employment. One result of this has been a greater freedom from one to another of the related trades of the industry—a movement which was accelerated by the labour-shortage conditions of the war period. This, so far as the men are concerned, has on the whole been a good thing. The jobs in new have been taken over by workers from the old occupations, and the skill required in pottery production is still sufficiently high as to give potters a virtual monopoly of the industry.

This greater freedom of movement within the industry will make it very difficult in the future to re-establish single craft unions. It is probably more than coincidence that the lowering of craft barriers was accompanied by the coming together of all potters into one union.

On the side of the employers a similar tendency is at work. With the operatives craft sentiment is giving way to industrial economic unity; with the employers individualism is falling before federal action. Businesses are combining, and the present tendency appears to be toward further combination. In the report upon conditions in Stoke-on-Trent in *The Third Winter of Unemployment* (p. 292) the writer gives as his opinion that "Probably there will always be small businesses doing special work in the Potteries, but there are signs that they will not long survive extensively.[1] There are syndicates and rumours of syndicates. What appears to be a group of little concerns is found on investigation to be a single business."

The safeguarding of the English porcelain manufacture is illustrative of the downfall of individualism in the pottery industry.[2] The application for safeguarding was brought by the British Pottery Manufacturers' Federation on behalf of a constituent body, the English China Manufacturers' Association. In the main, the applicants were concerned with low-priced English chinaware; the manufacturers of high-grade porcelain were not seriously affected by foreign competition and consequently did not ask for protection.

The application did not receive the official support of

[1] *Pottery Gazette*, June 1, 1929: "During recent years the number of derelict potteries has materially increased."

[2] From April 19, 1927—for five years—a duty of 28s. per cwt. upon imported foreign translucent or vitrified table ware. The applicants for Safeguarding asked for an *ad valorem* duty of 33 per cent. upon those articles which came within the scope of the application, but the Board of Trade Committee of Enquiry, which dealt with the matter, decided that a duty on weight rather than on value would more nearly meet the needs of the case. An *ad valorem* duty would press very hardly on the import trade of high-grade expensive porcelain, such as that of the Royal Copenhagen Porcelain Factory, against which it was not regarded that protection was required.

the Council of Stoke-on-Trent, in which city the whole of the cheap china trade is centred, nor of the National Society of Potters.[1] This latter body took up a neutral position, its members being divided in their views. It represented workers in all sections of the trade, and if the contention of the opponents of safeguarding, that the biggest competitor of English bone china was not foreign felspar porcelain but English earthenware, had been established, it would have no interest in a safeguarding measure. To the National Society of Potters it mattered little whether a worker made an earthenware or a china cup. Concerning this point the majority report of the Committee which considered the application for Safeguarding, stated that they were not able to accept the suggestion that replacement of china by earthenware fully accounted for the decrease in the volume of china produced. In this they were supported by the English earthenware manufacturers.[2]

Almost at the same time as the china trade came under the Safeguarding Act the British Pottery Industry made successful application under the General Merchandise Marks Act to have all foreign pottery marked with the country of its origin.[3]

[1] *Pottery Gazette*, September 1925.

[2] *Times Trade and Enquiry Supplement*, January 8, 1927.
Board of Trade Safeguarding of Industries. Report of the Committee on Tableware of Translucent Pottery (1927), 13. At the beginning of 1929 the British Pottery Manufacturers' Association lodged an application with the Board of Trade for a safeguarding duty to be imposed on earthenware, but, owing to the fact that a general election was near, it was decided to go no further in the matter as there would not be time to get a measure through before Parliament dissolved.—*Pottery Gazette*, March and April, 1929.

[3] *Board of Trade Merchandise Marks Act*, 1926. *Report of the Standing Committee respecting Pottery* (1928). The application of the Merchandise Marks Act to pottery ware was approved July 13, 1928, and operated from January 13, 1929.

The important point to remember about these trade applications is not so much the seeking of legislative protection as the readiness displayed by the pottery manufacturers to adopt federal action in order to secure their ends.

If one must venture on a generalisation respecting the organisation of operative potters, it is that the present tendency in the industry towards the adoption of efficiency methods in administration, planning and operation will continue, and this, more than anything else, will determine the lines of the future activities and policies of the trade unions concerned. Discipline in the industry will grow and may bring spiritual loss, but it will certainly bring financial gain. The days "when half the time of a pottery worker was spent . . . running about for tools" and, "as long as people were seen to be carrying ware about, or running up and down steps, . . . were adjudged to be working", are going.[1] Days, hours, and even minutes, will come to have value to both operative and employer.

Not one of the problems the organised potter has to face is peculiar to his trade. The difficulties arising from the use of machinery, the introduction of scientific management, the settling of women labour rates, are all found and met in other industries. The present unfortunate position of having large numbers of men registered at the Employment Exchanges as "unemployed potters", who are unlikely ever again to be absorbed into the industry, is the result of the abnormal rapidity with which changes in methods of working were made during the war period owing to labour shortage, and is unlikely to be repeated. One may hope and expect for the future that the supply of labour will more nearly adjust itself to the demand.

At the moment the English pottery industry is in a state of transition. The changes indicated earlier are not

[1] *Pottery Gazette*, June 1929.

complete, nor is the process of change a steady tide without counter-currents. The immediate trade depression, whilst operating in the main as a spur to further efficiency, is also an inducement to procure business in ways that are not desirable from the point of view of the industry as a whole. Despite strong associations covering every section of the trade, and agreements fixing minimum selling prices, it can still be said that "price-cutting to-day is one of the pottery trade's biggest menaces".[1] Many manufacturers have reorganised their plant and layout to fit modern requirements, but others are carrying on under conditions which are not suitable to economic production.

The Safeguarding Committee, while reporting in favour of the English manufacturers, admitted that certain small firms were unable from lack of capital to maintain their works on the most modern lines, and consequently were not in a satisfactory competitive position. The Statistical Committee of the Pottery National Council reported in July of this year (1929) that it hoped to induce the industry to achieve economies by the limitation of the sizes of various specified articles. This aim is laudable, but very unambitious when compared with the aim of the Committee at the beginning of its investigations. Then it hoped that shapes and decorations could be standardised, but in the report mentioned above it had to confess that such an object was neither feasible nor politic.

The expressed policy of the organised potters is on the side of regulation and efficiency.[2] It is in a well-managed industry, by whomsoever owned or controlled, that the Potters' Union will be best able to fulfil its purpose, which is the maintenance and improvement of the conditions of the working lives of its members.

[1] A pottery manufacturer quoted in *Pottery Gazette*, January 1929.

[2] Address by A. Hollins, M.P., General Secretary National Pottery Workers' Society.—*Pottery Gazette*, January 1929.

APPENDIX A

WAGES IN NORTH STAFFORDSHIRE POTTERY INDUSTRY

It is an extremely difficult task to draw up a really satisfactory table of wages for the Pottery Industry. Wages in many of its branches varied so considerably between worker and worker and between factory and factory that in many instances it is almost impossible to discover the normal wage.

The sources from which the following table of wages is drawn are given below together with the author's comments, which may help the reader to judge for himself their value in the purpose for which they have been used.

A potter's wage in 1825 is given as 25s. for a full week. The only evidence for this figure is given in a letter in the *Pottery Mercury*, June 22, 1825, which stated that some workmen were getting from 28s. to 30s. a week, but that others were getting only from 16s. to 18s. a week, with the inference that the majority of workers were earning wages between these extremes. This evidence is not perhaps very reliable, but in no subsequent issue of the *Pottery Mercury* were they either denied or commented upon.

The wages of 1815 may be constructed from the demands made by the potters in 1825, when they tried to obtain the piece-rates of 1815, so that a moderate workman could earn 5s. a day (*Pottery Mercury*, June 22, 1825; *Staffordshire Mercury*, October 30, 1830).

The published statement of the Chamber of Commerce (*Staffordshire Advertiser*, October 15, 1836) gives potters' wages for 1833 as from 17s. to 21s. a week, and for 1836 as from 21s. to 28s. a week. These figures appear to be reliable. There is plenty of good evidence of wage reductions between 1825 and 1833, and equally good evidence of wage increases between 1833–6 (*Pottery Mercury*, August 17, 1825; *Staffordshire Advertiser*, October 15, 1836).

Returns of wages for 1841 are given by S. Scriven to the *Children's Employment (Trades and Manufacturers) Commission* (1843), part i, c. 3. The wages he gives for pieceworkers are for full time, but, nevertheless, appear too high: Throwers, £2; Turners, £1 12s.; Platemakers, £1 18s.; Pressers, £1 10s.

For timeworkers he gives: Ovenmen, 18s.; Sliphousemen, 18s.; Warehousemen, £1 4s. It is probable that his piece-rate earnings are those of picked men.

In 1850 the Flat Pressers' Union gave the average wage of flat pressers as 4s. a day (*Staffordshire Advertiser*, October 13, 1850). This figure probably errs on the low side as the Union at that time was making out a case for an increase of wages.

The Trade Article in the *Staffordshire Advertiser*, November 20, 1852, reported the potters' "wages are much higher than some years ago".

Evidence of wages was given before the Select Committee on Masters and Operatives in 1856 (*Report from the Select Committee on Masters and Operatives: Equitable Councils of Conciliation* (1856), 202, 217). The evidence of W. Maitland, the witness for the workmen, was that potters' wages were 20s. a week. This average was arrived at as the result of an enquiry by the operatives held a few years previously. The evidence of M. D. Hollins, manufacturer, before the same Committee, was that many workmen received 30s. a week, but that the average wage was 25s. or 26s. a week. W. Maitland considered these figures true of porcelain factories, but not for the main industry of general earthenware.

The Report on Trade Societies and Strikes: National Association for the Promotion of Social Science (1860), 281, states that piece-rates would make wages about 30s. a week if trade were brisk, but owing to fluctuations in trade the average wage was much lower. It states the case of a potter whose wage during the preceding seven years had not, owing to slackness of work, averaged 18s. a week.

For the period 1855–83 the most reliable wage figures are those of *Labour Statistics: Returns of Wages: H.M. Stationery Office* (1887), 231. The pottery wage statistics given in these returns were supplied in the first instance by various Chambers of Commerce and private firms. There is thus the likelihood that the more reputable manufactories are unduly represented, in which case the wage averages given would err on the high side.

The wage particulars given by G. P. Bevan, *The Industrial Classes and Industrial Statistics*, 1876, suffer from the disadvantage that they "suppose throughout competent workpeople, constant work, steady habits and a manufactory of respectable position in the trade".

	1825, per Week.	1833, per Week.	1836, per Week.	1841, per Week.	1855, per Day.	1866, per Day.	1877, per Week.	1883, per Day.	1908, per Week.	March, 1924, per Week. (a)	(b)
MEN											
Piece Workers—	s. d.	s. d.	s. d.	s. d.	s. d.	s. d.	s. d.	s. d.	s. d.	s. d.	s. d.
Throwers	25 0	17 0–21 0	21 0–28 0	40 0	6 0	6 6	33 0–42 0	7 0	27 10	76 2	99 6
Turners	25 0	17 0–21 0	21 0–28 0	32 0	4 6	4 6	26 0–32 0	5 6	26 10	58 9	71 8
Handlers	25 0	17 0–21 0	21 0–28 0	—	4 0	4 0	27 0–29 6	5 0	28 2	52 4	63 2
Hollow-ware pressers	25 0	17 0–21 0	21 0–28 0	30 0	4 0	4 6	28 0	5 0	24 9	48 5	58 5
Flat pressers	25 0	17 0–21 0	21 0–28 0	—	4 0	4 6	28 0	4 6	28 9	55 5	70 5
Printers	—	17 0–21 0	21 0–28 0	—	4 6	4 6	24 0	4 6	24 3	51 0	61 10
Mould-makers	—	17 0–21 0	21 0–28 0	30 0	4 6	4 6	26 0–30 0	6 6	38 0	68 0	81 6
Jiggerers	—	—	—	—	—	—	—	7 0	35 1	67 9	83 4
Casters	—	—	—	—	—	—	—	—	—	61 7	66 2

Time Workers—											
Warehousemen	—	—	—	24 0	4 6	4 6	26 0	4 6	—	45 0	—
Ovenmen*	—	—	—	18 0	3 0	4 6	26 6	4 7	30 0	56 4	73 1
Sliphousemen†	—	—	—	18 0	3 6	4 6	24 0– 30 0	4 6	—	52 0	67 4
WOMEN											
Time Workers											
Throwers' attendants	—	7 0– 9 0	9 0 12 0	9 0	—	1 8	12 9	2 0	—	24 0	—
Turners' attendants	—	7 0– 9 0	9 0 12 0	10 0	—	1 6	—	1 10	—	24 0	—
Jiggerers' attendants	—	—	—	—	—	—	—	1 4	11 0	24 0	—
Warehousewomen	—	7 0– 9 0	9 0– 12 0	9 0	1 2	1 2‡	6 0§– 9 0	—	9 0	24 0	—
Piece Workers—											
Handlers	—	—	—	—	—	—	12 0	3 0	14 7	23 3	29 10
Flat pressers	—	—	—	—	—	—	—	3 0	16 11‖	37 10	47 9
Casters	—	—	—	—	—	—	—	—	—	29 7	36 5
Transferrers	—	7 0– 9 0	9 0– 12 0	10 0	—	1 6	10 0	2 0	10 10	25 2	31 2

* Ovenmen: Sometimes paid a bonus on all ware beyond a certain specified quantity placed in the oven.
† Sliphousemen: Since the introduction of the filter press (invented 1856) many of them piecework.
‡ This for 1860. § This for 1874. ‖ Saucer Makers.

The wage statistics submitted before the various Arbitration Boards are interesting as showing the wide range of wages, but are of little use for the purpose of giving a normal wage. The list submitted by the employers before the Arbitration Board of 1908, which gave averages of wages from thirty representative factories, is an exception. It was not seriously disputed by the workmen. All concerned knew that if the Chairman of the Board were suspicious of the accuracy of the figures submitted he could have them verified by an independent accountant.

The U.S.A. Pottery Industry Report on the Cost of Production in U.S.A., England, Germany, Austria (1915), gives rates of wages in North Staffordshire for 1914, but they are the rates which were paid by good firms, for the establishments which permitted investigation into their private accounts were those of the foremost potters of England.

The table of comparative earnings 1914–20, given in the *Report on Pottery: Profiteering Acts*, 1919–20, suffers from the same defect, for it was "compiled and received from a modern well-equipped, scientifically managed Pottery Works".

The National Council of the Pottery Industry Enquiry of 1924 was conducted by an independent firm of accountants, which had unrestricted access to the books of the manufacturers.

1825	*Pottery Mercury*, June 22, 1825.
1833–36	*Staffordshire Advertiser*, October 15, 1836.
1841	*Children's Employment* (*Trades and Manufactures*) (1843), part i, c. 3.
1855–83	*Labour Statistics: Returns of Wages H.M. Stationery Office* (1887), 231.
1908	*Wages Arbitration, September* 1908 (for women attendants); *National Society of Pottery Workers' Handbook of Agreements*, 1926 (for warehouse-women); *Profiteering Acts*, 1919–20. *Report on Pottery* (1921).
1924	*National Council of the Pottery Industry Enquiry*, 1924.

1825	Rate for full week: 10½-hour day.
1833–36	Rate for full week of 54 hours.

1841 Rate for full week of 63 hours. These rates were taken "during an extraordinary depression of the trade". Thus pieceworkers' wages are made to appear higher than they really were. Working two days a week a pieceworker earns far more than a third of a full week's wages.

1855–83 Average rates of wages paid: general earthenware rates: wages in porcelain industry slightly higher.

1908 Average of wages paid: general earthenware rates: proportion of time worked to full time: 72·03 per cent. (For ovenmen, warehousewomen and women attendants the rates are for a full week.)[1]

1924 Column (*a*) average of wages paid; column (*b*) what would have been paid had a full week of 47 hours been worked. (For warehousemen, warehousewomen and women attendants the wages are minimum rates for a full week.)[1]

(NOTE.—Minimum rate for warehousemen of 25 years of age and over, having control of books and orders, 56s. 3d. per week.)

Hours: For the nineteenth century, except in the case of timeworkers and pieceworkers using machinery, not much reliance can be placed upon the item "number of working hours a week". See also pp. 40–2,235.

PRESENT WAGE AGREEMENTS

Present wages are those of 1924 plus wage award of July 1924:

Minimum wage of warehousewomen and potters' attendants increased to 25s. per week.

Male workers in general earthenware in the following occupations, 5½ per cent. increase: handlers, saucer-makers, cup- and bowl-makers, hollow-ware pressers and casters.

All other workers in general earthenware, 2½ per cent. advance.

See also pp. 217–8.

[1] Wage figures for 1924 given by permission of Mr. S. H. Dodd, British Pottery Manufacturers Federation; Mr. F. H. Hand, National Council of the Pottery Industry; Mr. A. Hollins, M.P., National Society of Pottery Workers.

APPENDIX AA

(*Reprinted from "Staffordshire Sentinel", July 18, 1924*)[1]

POTTERY OPERATIVES' WAGES

CORRECTED TEXT OF THE REPORT AND AWARD

Appendix 5

WAGES ENQUIRY, 1924

A Note on Systematisation of Wages

(By PROFESSOR HENRY CLAY)

1. OBSTACLES TO SATISFACTORY SETTLEMENT.

Three obstacles to a prompt and friendly settlement of wages have presented themselves in this as in previous negotiations: the difficulty of saying what wages actually are being paid, the difficulty of finding how much wages have advanced or been reduced since any earlier settlement and the difficulty of dealing with the main claims in a way that does not leave over for adjustment a mass of minor differences that will keep the parties busy negotiating for another six months.

These obstacles exist, and make wage negotiations much more difficult than in other industries, because the majority of workers are not covered by standard time-rates or common piece-lists. Owing to this lack of rates common to all the workers of any particular class or grade in the industry, there is no assurance of uniform payment for uniform effort and skill. Rates and earnings for the same or similar work vary from factory to factory, and even in the same factory vary in a way that cannot be explained by differences in the skill or exertion of the workers. The variations may be slight, but in so far as they lack a rational justification they are bound to create discontent and the suspicion of exploitation.

These variations are so numerous and difficult to deal with that every year, in addition to claims for a general advance or reduction, there are a large number of individual and departmental notices. The net result is a vast waste of time in

[1] By permission of Prof. H. Clay.

negotiations and great irritation on both sides, and the danger of a stoppage repeated annually.

2. Recent Improvements.

Great advances have been made in the direction of simplifying and standardising wages in recent years by agreeing on common minimum price-lists for certain goods in whole sections (e.g. China Section), minimum time-rates for women time-workers (e.g. Warehousewomen) and by departmental settlements. But the necessity the present Committee found itself under of calling in an accountant to conduct an exhaustive investigation to get figures of earnings and advances that could be accepted by both sides shows how much remains to be done.

3. Special Difficulties of the Pottery Industry.

The difficulty of adjusting rates and piece prices so that they shall yield approximately uniform remuneration for uniform skill and effort is exceptionally great. Conditions, methods of work, varieties of product, vary enormously from factory to factory and section to section. Processes change, and new types of product are constantly being brought out.

4. A Comparison with other Industries.

In some industries there is not enough repetition to make piecework practicable, and the relatively simple system of standard district time-rates is adopted; in pottery, piecework for the majority of workers is probably necessary, and the general adoption of timework unlikely. Where all the work is repetition work as in textiles, piece-lists common to the whole industry are sometimes adopted. This is probably the most satisfactory way of proportioning pay to work, but common district lists are possible only where conditions are fairly uniform, and experience has made it possible to make allowance in the list for every possible variation in method, product and condition. The pottery industry will probably in time tend to adopt more and more this method of detailed common lists; but at present conditions vary so much from factory to factory that any piece-lists that allowed for everything would be unmanageably complicated. On the other hand, lists that do not make allowance for every variation in conditions will tend to be either so low that the workers in an old fashioned factory cannot earn a living wage on them, or so high that the employer in a modern, well-equipped factory gets no advantage from his expenditure.

Probably the closest parallel to pottery is found in those industries which do not seek to fix piece-lists for the whole industry or adopt the system of timework, but leave each factory to fit its own piece-lists for each class of product, with the proviso that the piece price, whatever it may be, must be sufficient to enable an ordinary worker at the ordinary speed to earn a given number of pence per hour. Thus, there is fixed for each class of worker a certain figure, say 1s. 6d. per hour; an individual operative working piecework may earn more or less than this figure, but the piece-rate is adequate if, when tested, it is found to yield to an ordinary worker 1s. 6d. on the average for every hour he works. If in any adjustment this base figure is changed, say raised to 1s. 10½d., then all piecework prices will have to be changed in the same proportion. In this case increased 25 per cent. The adjustments made in the 1923 settlement in the Electrical Fittings Trade were apparently based on this principle, since they were to be made "on the basis that with the percentage addition an average worker shall be able to earn no less wages per week than the weekly wage of a day wage operative of the same age".

5. Method of Simplifying Pottery Wages.

If this principle commends itself to the Committee, I should suggest that a small Committee be appointed with the following reference:

(*a*) To group the different classes of pieceworkers into a number of grades.

(*b*) To suggest for each grade a minimum rate of so many pence per hour, which an ordinary worker in that grade should be able to earn by ordinary diligence. The basis for these rates should be the ascertained earnings per hour of the workers in each grade, revealed by the Independent Accountant's Report, and should be such that it would not involve raising the wages of more than, say, 20 per cent. of the workers in the grade.

If an agreement on such a Committee's report can be reached, it will be necessary to set up some organisation which can decide whether any particular piece-rate is too low in the circumstances of the case to enable an ordinary worker to earn his appropriate wage, or so high that the Employer may reasonably claim to have it reduced. The best form such an organisation might take is that of an Independent Chairman appointed for a long term sitting with two assessors representing Employers and Operatives in the section of the trade affected, and hearing cases only where the Employer and Workman affected, or Union and Employers' Association, had been unable to agree.

NOTE.—In this memorandum I have been concerned only with the FORM of wages and methods of simplifying the present confusion, not with raising or lowering wages. The question of advances and reductions and also the question of minimum weekly rates for timeworkers I have assumed will be settled by the Special Committee for whom this memorandum is prepared.

(*Signed*) HENRY CLAY

5th July, 1924

Appendix B

The chief materials in the manufacture of pottery are:

China clay (kaolin or Cornish clay), obtained from Cornwall and Devonshire, the main constituent of china, and used in earthenware also.

Ball clay (or blue clay), from Dorsetshire and Devonshire, the foundation for earthenware.

Flint (calcined and ground), chiefly used in earthenware.

China stone (Cornish stone, petuntse or pegmatite), a fluxing material used in china and smaller quantities in earthenware.

Felspar, largely used as a fluxing material, and the chief constituent of Parian or statuary porcelain.

Bone (calcined and ground), an important material in the making of china.

A greater variety of materials enters into the constitution of glazes, some of them being white lead, borax, lime, flint, china stone, felspar and china clay.

Each of the clay bodies is ground separately and when sufficiently fine is allowed to run into a series of vats for storage. From these the body mixture runs off accurately measured quantities into the mixing tank, where it is thoroughly mixed either by machinery or hand.

The body is now in a liquid or slip state, and it is free from the excess of water so as to convert it into a plastic, workable state. Originally this was done by running it over the surface of slip kilns, the water being driven off by means of the heat of the flues underneath. Now, however, the clay press is generally used, the principle being to pump the slip into spaces lined with strong calico cloths or bags, through which the water is forced, leaving the clay behind. On being removed from the press the clay is wedged by hand, or worked in the pugmill to a uniform density and consistency that leave it ready for the manipulation of the potter.

Throwing.—The thrower receives from his assistant a ball of clay, which he throws upon the head of the wheel before him and presses it with both hands; the rotary movement causes the clay to rise. He inserts his thumb into the mass, moulding and fashioning the outside with the other hand. The vessels made by the thrower, after leaving his hands, are allowed to dry for a time and then finished on the lathe, much after the manner that the woodworker uses that machine. If the pieces he has been engaged upon require handles they are then added by the handler. The handles have been formed by pressing clay between plaster moulds, and they are attached to the vessels by means of a little slip or liquid clay. Then, after the necessary drying, they are ready for the first firing in a biscuit oven.

FLAT PRESSING.—On the disc or head of the jigger (a form of wheel) is placed a plaster mould which produces the upper part of the plate or saucer. The workman, having beaten out a lump of clay in the form of a thin bat, throws it on to the mould. While the mould is revolving he applies to the clay a profile, which gives the shape of the back part of the plate or saucer. A piece having thus been made, the mould is carried away to dry, and when the plaster has absorbed sufficient moisture from the clay the article is easily removable.

HOLLOW-WARE PRESSING.—The operative is provided with a mould, generally in several pieces, and into this he presses by hand thin bits of clay, which thus assume the desired shape. When the clay has given up to the plaster mould sufficient of its moisture, the mould is taken to pieces and the article of clay is removed. With hollow-ware pressing articles varied in shape can be made.

CASTING.—This process is entirely dependent on the absorbent nature of the plaster mould, which may be of endless variety as regards shape. For casting, slip and not clay is used, and into the mould, which may consist of several parts secured together, is poured sufficient slip to fill it. The plaster absorbs sufficient water from the slip, and when the caster decides that sufficient absorption has proceeded, he empties out the surplus slip. Inside the mould a thin coating of clay has been left, and when comparatively dry the mould is taken to pieces and the clay article is removed.

FIRING.—The ware having reached the stage of being fashioned in dried clay, the process of firing has to be entered upon. Saggars are used for the protection of the ware during firing. The saggars are boxes made from fire clay and contain a number of pieces. In the oven, a cylindrical chamber fitted with flues and an outlet at the top for the smoke, the saggars are piled one on top of the other into tall columns, and in this form the ware is subjected to its first fire.

PRINTING.—When the ware has been taken from the biscuit oven and cleaned it is ready for printing. Originally only flat copper plates were used for printing, but now it is done by means of machines with engraved rollers. When the design has been printed on to paper it is cut up into sections and carefully applied to the ware by the transferrer. The paper is washed off and the colour, being mixed with oil, remains adhering to the ware. Having been subjected to a mild kiln fire, which burns out the oil from the colour, the ware is passed to the dipper, who immerses it in the glaze. After that it is ready for the glost oven. This is similar to the biscuit oven, but the handling and placing of the ware is different. The effect of the glost fire is to melt the glaze.

DECORATING.—(Except in the most expensive ware women only are employed in the decorating processes described below.) If decoration other than printing, or additional decoration to the printed ware, is required, it is done over the glaze, after the ware has left the glost oven, with colours or gold. After decorating, additional firing or firings are necessary. For this purpose a kiln, somewhat similar to the one for printed ware, is used. There are several methods of over-glaze decoration.

GILDING.—A solution of gold is mixed with oil. The action of the fire in the kiln drives off the oil and leaves a film of gold on the ware. Gilding is mainly used for the edges of cups, plates, etc. For gilding of edges a horizontal solid wooden wheel is used. The gilder places the article upon the centre of the wheel, which she is slowly revolving with her left hand, whilst with her right she holds a fully charged brush of gold against the edge.

ENAMELLING.—Filling in a printed outline with enamel paints. An enamel is a paint mixed with glass which, on being heated, fuses into the glaze of the ware.

BANDING AND LINING.—Painting bands and lines on ware. This work is similar to gilding, except that colour is used instead of gold.

LITHOGRAPHING.—The placing of lithographic prints upon ware by means of paper transfers. The making of lithographic prints is not, as in the case of blue prints, done in the pottery factory. Some prints come from abroad, but in the main they are made at lithograph establishments in the Potteries.

AEROGRAPHING.—Colour is mixed with water or thin oil, placed in a suitable vessel and blown into a spray, the blast for which is kept under control by a stopcock. It is the same idea as in scent-spraying. Aerographing is specially useful if a shaded ground or a graduation of colour is required.

OTHER PROCESSES AND OCCUPATIONS

FLAT DISH AND BAKING DISH MAKING.—As in flat pressing, the mould is carried on a revolving head or jigger, and the clay is shaped by pressing a tool against it. As these dishes are oval, the jigger does not revolve truely, but with each revolution moves backwards and forwards to allow the tool, which is pressing upon the clay in the mould, to remain stationary. (Men only employed in this occupation.)

CUP AND BOWL MAKING.—
HOLLOWWARE JIGGERING.—
WASHHAND BASIN MAKING.—
} As in flat pressing, except that the mould forms the *outside* of the article being made. Many washhand basins are made, however, on the same principle as flat pressing, i.e. the mould forming the inside. As a rule men are employed in these processes, but in the making of such articles as cups and small bowls women are often engaged.

These are the more important occupations. There are many others.

Appendix C

Letters to Robert Owen, [1]
Co-operative Union,
Holyoake House,
Manchester.

To the Editor of the *Crisis*,
Staffordshire Potteries. 24 *Sept.*, 1833.

A great point has been gained in this district by union. The people have at last discovered the great secret that they are the real producers of wealth, the most of the masters have had the good sense to meet the working dupes halfway and there is little doubt but that the two parties will adjust amicably their differences a deputation from the masters and one from the men are now meeting daily, the points decided so far are as follows: 1st. Hours of working not before 6 in the Morning and not after 6 in the Evening. 2nd. No one to receive less than 5/– a day for his labour. The Union are now (which shows the people have more regard for the masters than they for them) making a tariff of prices—they also prohibit the sending any of the manufactures abroad on speculation, this produce must be limited to actual orders. The masters were at first highly indignant at this dictation from the mob. . . . There is no section of the country where the march of intellect is making more rapid strides than this and I beg you will make public this first solid proof of the disposition and ability of the people to look after their own interests.

R. G.

. . . There is a great hue and cry against you, all the religious world so called are opposed to you. This is very natural and I fear it will do us much more mischief than any other subject. . . . The principal objection to establishing your system here, is, it being a trade that requires a large outlay of capital, before there are any returns. If it was commenced and the masters made a regular stand against it, what would be the consequences? You will please turn your attention to this—in other trades you get an almost immediate return. . . .

Tho. P. Simpson.

20th. Oct., 3

[1] Published by permission of the Co-operative Union.

STOKE. *Nov. 12th.*, 1833.

DEAR SIR,

. . . The first meeting of our Grand Lodge after you left I found it out who had been at work against us. The Methodists and the Overlookers, the one with all their sectarian bigotry, the other with all the little cunning they possess. . . . I am happy to say both are overcome as to their intent viz. the commencement of a Substantial Cooperative Society in the Potteries. The Seed you sowed when you were here has taken a deep root. . . . We have been compelled in order to keep the Bigots with us to Separate it from the union and from you also. . . . I judged it prudent to let the fire you lighted go out but kept at work with single individuals, where in a shop of a dozen or more they were opposed to it—by thus bringing the leading man over it has brought the whole shop, that shop part of the manufactory . . . they others so that the under current is working. Surely and faster than I could have anticipated my reasons are many warehousemen . . . had actually withheld their subscriptions from the Union until they were perfectly satisfied the Union had nothing to do with it . . . now for our work we have had for nearly a month two manufactories and partly another large Manufactory out—What Madness you will say with me— Still it is the best policy for the present—how I will show—we cannot enter into anything like a discussion as to Manufacturing for our-selves I am forbidden by my obligations to tell you why—t'is so is all I can say, more on this after I have told you how the Masters are going on. They last Monday but one sent for a deputation from our Lodge to the Swan Inn much compliments!! You can do anything you please. I & Fudge. They would be glad if we would consent to the foundation of a Council consisting of seven Masters and six of our Lodge to meet at stated periods in order to discuss little differences which might arise betwixt the two parties and which they thought would often prevent that, we had been so often compelled to resort to—a strike! We agreed to it and framed ours directly—Your humble servant is one—that being the last thing of importance we settled with them. I will tell you how they are acting (as they think without our knowledge), they have actually doubled the price of their ware which has struck the dealers with consternation I will not say of everything but of most things. this . . . is the paltry expedient they have had recourse to, in order to convince us that the extravagant demands (as they called them) which we made upon them at the time of the formation of the List has led to a deprivation of Trade. . . .

HENRY L. PRATT.

STOKE. *November 13th.*, 1833.

DR SIR,

Having just returned from the Meeting which has been a most anxious and crowded one, at the Sea Lion, I inform you how we have arranged matters. The committee have shown a deal of Tact in framing the resolutions they have passed unanimously and the feeling of pleasure everyone expressed exceeded even most Sanguine expectations. I was surprised to find so many that went decidedly opposed to it come forward to put down their names—there should be a Meeting in every Separate district to explain the Matter and then a general one of the whole to choose officers, pay Monies, and commence immediately. The first Meeting at Burslem 14th, Tunstall 15th., Stoke 19th., Lane Delph 20th., Lane End 21st., the General Meeting to be on Tuesday—20th. (I had the pleasure of putting down my name first of all and had the further gratification of adding to the amount of 46 names out of one meeting—you will say a good start. I must now beg the favour of a line in the way of advice.

D., Sir Your Most

HENRY L. PRATT.

P.S. Your Letter has quite put them in spirit.

DEAR SIR,

T. Simpson and the rest of us are as you thought much impressed at what you have all but accomplished in that link of human misery. . . . You my Dear Sir have it now in your power to work out our complete emancipation. I have with Lancaster, Simpson, Taylor and others been the whole district through, and have done far better than our most Sanguine expectations led us to believe. If we shall not have five hundred by the General Meeting we shall not have far off that number and the rapidity with which they are flocking to our standard

warrants me in saying in a very little time we shall number one thousand out of two assemblys at Lane Delph and Lane End we got upwards of one hundred and ten names to enter on the subscription list, and sold at one meeting 70 copies of resolutions, we cannot, in short, be going on better, *but* we must have you—your advice, your practical experience, the materials are truly to hand but the design is wanting our exertions have completely d. . . . a small party of moneyd men who though in the Union were for putting their money together and starting a manufactory for their exclusive l . . ? it, we have had too much of this to tolerate it for a moment, I think in last I did not tell you Stacy has had Several dealers applying to him in case the Union would Manufacture they would give ready money for all goods we would [supply] their neighbourhood with. . . . in this position we stand and we do beg of you most humbly and earnestly if you possibly can you will favour us with your attendance on Tuesday evening next at the. . . .
HENRY L. PRATT.

STOKE. *November 22nd.*, 1833.

HANLEY POTTERIES,
STAFFORDSHIRE,
June 14th., 1834.

ESTEEMED SIR,

A communication from you at this moment recommending the propriety of Consolidation at this time to our most excellent Friend Mr. Simpson would have a most beneficial tendency towards bringing over that very well organised and consequently influential body the operative Potters whose numbers are 8000, . . . our worthy friend Simpson is deservedly a very influential man in the Union, and it appears to me he rests much on your opinion as to superiority of Potters Union and the great objects well directed it was capable of accomplishing, but Sir this you will recollect was prior to institution of Consolidation. The cause of amelioration is much indebted to Mr. Simpson who has most kindly rendered Booth, Mac Grath and myself every information and accommodation possible, to morrow we are to meet several leading officers of the Potters Union at Mr. Simpson's and I have much confidence of success. We only arrived in the Potteries last

Evening 11 o'clock, we feel we have been very successful in our Mission, but waiting or would give particulars.

Yours devotedly, N. R. Wood.

P.S. Mr. S. informs me on his inspection of the accounts of Potters since the 12th. of August last they have expended the enormous sum of £6223. 2. 11 in futile strikes, which if it was not experience would be decided waste to them, but the popular feeling now arising is employing themselves and it appears they are just now about commencing to work at a very large establishment of their own. Mr. and Mrs. Simpson desire their sincere regards to you and Mr. S. was much in favour of Consolidating as also a many friends when they were told you were its advocate and Grand Master of Auxiliary Lodges, . . . The fact of cost of Potters Strikes is not for publication only among confidentials since above Mr. S. offers to get a number of Tradesmen who are True men such as himself for auxiliary Lodges, please advise me as to that point.

Appendix D

The Times. August 22, 1835.

Committal of 30 workmen to prison. On Friday last, some important cases of dispute between masters and workmen in the pottery business, at Lane End, were heard at Leek, before the Rev. J. Sneyd and Captain Powys, two magistrates for the county. The first charge preferred was that of Messrs. Chetham and Robinson against 18 of their workmen for leaving their work, when twelve of them were convicted. The men were urged by the magistrates to come to terms with their employers, and an agreement seemed to be nearly completed, when the men refused to pay the costs, in consequence of which the convictions will be acted on. The next charge was brought by Mr. Hawley against 28 of his men; and Mr. Hawley being sworn, stated that the defendants were all hired to serve till next Martinmas, at prices agreed upon, and had left his employ without just cause. Fifteen of these men, it appeared, had been committed for three months for leaving Mr. Hawley's employ in April last, and the charge against them was that they had not returned to their work at the expiration of their imprisonment. All the defendants refused to return to their work, and were sentenced to three months' imprisonment. Disputes, it appears, have for some time existed in the potting trade respecting wages, and these charges originated out of them. When the above cases had been disposed of, four other journeymen potters were charged with the offence of "intimidation". The evidence against them was that of Mr. Goodwin, Messrs. Knight & Elkin, and Mr. John Mayer, who stated that they advanced their prices in consequence of the defendants, who acted as "plenipotentiaries for the men". It was urged by counsel on their behalf, that they had not made use of a single threat, or committed any act of intimidation; but Mr. Sneyd said it mattered little whether the language was mild or otherwise, when the intent was so apparent. Two of the defendants were sentenced to be imprisoned for two months; one, one month; and one 14 days. Notice of appeal was given in all cases, and recognizances entered into to appeal at the Sessions. *Wolverhampton Chronicle*.

Staffordshire Advertiser. November 16th, 1833.

Mr. Owen. This projector, after twenty years of unsuccessful exertion to establish his favourite system, first in the Old World and then in the New, has at last discovered a fulcrum on which to place that co-operative lever which has to raise the world, to fill the purses of the master manufacturers with great rapidity, and to shower down abundance upon their workmen. This instrument is none other than the Trades' Union, and the Short Time Committee. By the organisation of these societies our manufacturing establishments are to equal that at New Lanark, where, as Mr. Owen states, from 200,000£ to 300,000£ was realised in a few years, and the workpeople are to earn their three to four pounds a week each by six hours labour in the day!

The worthy projector has been so obliging as to show us his scheme as formed for the operatives in the Staffordshire Potteries, but we see nothing new in it, except the term "Trades' Unions"; and we strongly suspect that the fate of all Mr. Owen's other schemes to render men rich and happy awaits the one now promulgated. *Leeds Mercury*.

Appendix E

The Case of the Manufacturers of China and Earthenware in the Staffordshire Potteries with some Account of the late Turn-Out, its Origin, Proceedings and Termination, 1836–37, published by authority of the Chamber of Commerce, Hanley (pamphlet).

. . . It is now two years since the workmen, (formed for some time previously into a Union), engaged in serious disputes with several of the Manufacturers . . . a friendly meeting, which was arranged to be held between a few of the masters, a few of the Independent Workmen, and a few of the Unionist workmen; but with a distinct pledge that no member of the Board of Management was to be amongst the number. At this meeting the differences were to be discussed before two . . . magistrates, not acting officially, but as gentlemen. . . . The meeting was fixed to be held at Betley on the 30th. of December, but an unexpected circumstance occurred on the day preceding to swell the numbers of the party who were to attend. On the 29th of December, while the Chamber of Commerce were assembled, a note was presented to the meeting, signed by seven persons representing themselves to be delegates from Bristol, Sheffield, Birmingham, Worcester, Glasgow, Manchester and Huddersfield, and stating that they and many other delegates from various parts of the Empire had assembled at Hanley, to investigate the position of the working potters in Staffordshire, and offered themselves to the notice of the Chamber; adding that, if something was not speedily done, "National means" would be taken in aid of the workmen. The person who presented this note having stated that the writers of it were then in attendance, the Chamber admitted them to an interview, and informed them of the intended meeting at Betley on the morrow, and invited them to attend it. It appeared afterwards that they understood the permission to have extended to all the other delegates assembled at Hanley as well as themselves and so on the following morning about 40 of these strangers proceeded to Betley. By the hour appointed, a deputation of 8 manufacturers, and 6 of the Independent Workmen, and the same number of Union workmen with many others of these classes were also met in the presence of George Tollet and Francis Twemlow, Esquires.

Appendix

IMPORTANT MEETING OF DELEGATES

IN THE POTTERIES IN BEHALF OF THE STAFFORDSHIRE POTTERS, ON DECEMBER 28TH, 29TH AND 30TH, 1836

In consequence of the disputes which have recently arisen between the Operative Potters in the Staffordshire Potteries and their employers, business in that populous district has been generally suspended, and nearly 20,000 persons thrown out of employment.

The Operatives in consequence requested the aid and assistance of their fellow-workmen throughout the kingdom, and their appeal was handsomely responded to; but for the purpose of strengthening their claims, they determined upon laying their case more fully before the public; and they therefore requested that Delegates might be sent from all the populous districts in the country, by whom the merits and demerits of the disputes might be fully investigated.

Upwards of forty Delegates assembled in consequence, and the following is—

A Report of their Proceedings

At a Meeting of Delegates and Operatives, held at the Saracen's Head Inn, in Hanley, in the Staffordshire Potteries, on Wednesday, the 28th day of December, 1836, Mr. Kirk, delegate from Sheffield, in the Chair, and Mr. Light, a delegate from Bristol, Vice-Chairman.

Mr. Prideaux, from Bristol, stated that the object of the delegates was to obtain the fullest information possible relative to the causes of the disputes between the Operatives and their employers, in order that on their return to their respective constituencies, they might be enabled to give a full, fair, and just account of the real merits of the case. He therefore begged leave to move—

"That some of the officers of the Operative Potters' Society would give them the information required."

The motion having been seconded by Mr. Robert Buchanan, of Huddersfield—

Mr. MARK LANCASTER, on the part of the Board of Management, rose and spoke as follows:

"I willingly answer to the call for information, and I will detail minutely the nature and cause of the disputes unfortunately existing between the men and their masters. It has been a system here for the masters to hire their men upon agreements in which there was no mutuality; no certainty; no reciprocity. In nineteen cases out of twenty whilst the agreements have fastly bound the men to serve the masters for twelve months, there was no obligation on the part of the master to find the men even a day's employment. In numberless instances when cases were investigated before the magistrates, it was decided that although they afforded to the employers every protection, they left to the law no power to serve the men; and whilst the master could play the tyrant, the men were left as slaves. We have had an immense number of cases before the various County Magistrates, but the result was almost invariably against us. About eighteen months ago a manufacturer near Lane End refused for upwards of three months to find sufficient work for his men, and they could obtain no relief, whilst the same master, if his men had neglected their work for comparatively only a few hours, he might take advantage of the agreement and send them to the treadmill. A circumstance which makes our situation still more hard is, that the masters not only refuse to find work, but they also refuse to allow the men to get temporary employment elsewhere. In this instance the master refused to find employment for the men, whilst at the same period he was actually purchasing from other manufacturers that ware, which he would not allow his own men to make, though they were literally starving all the time. The master was taken before the magistrates assembled at Leek—the case was fully made out on the part of the men—the injustice shown clearly as noonday sun, until the master produced the agreement when it appeared that there was no obligation on the part of the master to find them employment, and although JUSTICE was with them, the LAW could afford them no protection. Such was the magistrates' conviction of the injustice of the case that one of them emphatically exclaimed, 'If men are such fools as to sign agreements such as these, I for one neither can nor will assist them.' The same opinion has been repeatedly expressed by other magistrates in the county before whom similar cases have been investigated; and although the prejudices (if I may use the term) of the magistrates were formerly strong against us, these cases I think I am justified in saying have turned them as strongly in our favour. I will mention another instance which recently occurred, to prove still further the injustice of the system against which we complain. An apprenticed printer had been summoned by his master for neglect of work and he was ordered upon the hearing of the case either to return to his work or go to prison. He went again in his master's employ; but after the lapse of a short time his master refused to find him either sufficient work or wages. The apprentice applied to a magistrate for a summons against his master and was told by the magistrates, 'If your master does not find you work we will assist you.' The case was heard; and although the apprentice had the benefit of professional assistance, yet when the indenture was produced, it turned out to be like the agreements for hiring—all on one side. No redress could be had—there was no stipulation on the part of the master to find employment, and the case was necessarily dismissed. This is not an isolated case, for from one end of the Potteries to the other, the forms of agreement for hiring have been in substance nearly the same. For these reasons we thought it our duty to prepare fresh forms of hiring, and we accordingly prepared one which we intended should establish a fair and reciprocal bargain between master and man. Under the old forms we had found that the law was of no assistance to us, they gave to the masters *every* chance—to us *none*. I will read to you one of their forms (here the old form was read). Thus you see the workmen agree to serve the master for twelve months, and there is a stipulation on the part of the master that he will pay certain wages for the work done, but there is not a syllable binding the master to find that work. If therefore the master starved his men, they had no redress—if the man offended his master, the usual expression was, 'I'll fix you'; and shortly afterwards the poor fellow found his words but too true. It was under these circumstances that we prepared the form of agreement which I have read to you, and we offered it to the masters at the usual hiring time. It has been customary for the masters to hire one, two or three months before Martinmas, and about that time our agreements were prepared and presented to them, when they told us that they were not prepared to give us a specific answer then—they shuffled the question and put us off for a month. The custom of 'WORKING GOOD out of the oven' became a subject of discussion, and the men thought that this was a fair opportunity for trying the question. Mr. Adams consented to make the experiment, and his men are now employed on our agreement. In the meantime the masters prepared their agreement, which whilst it retained all the objectionable clauses of the old agreement, contained a fresh clause which they termed 'A suspension clause', still more unjust than before. But this agreement turned out to be such a deformed, ricketty bantling, that they were ashamed of their own offspring. They then produced a second agreement (this was read). Now this agreement was somewhat improved in appearance, but it was precisely the same in reality as its predecessor. We took the opinion of counsel on the subject without either note or comment to bias his judgment; and he stated 'that the new agreement like the old one, was bad for want of certainty—want of mutuality—and want of sufficient consideration'. Shortly afterwards the masters took the opinion of another barrister, who stated 'that he thought that they might give the requisite degree of certainty to it by limiting the master's power to suspend work at their manufactory to a definite period—viz. six weeks.' But let them qualify it how they may, the agreement is most unjust; under the old agreement we had no redress for injury—but under the new form, the man is actually required to sign a clause expressly acknowledging the master's right to starve him to death! Disappointment was the natural consequence of this tyranny, and the men at fourteen manufactories stopped on one day. It was too evident that a struggle must ensue, and as the masters refused to hire except on their own terms, turn-outs took place. Under the old agreements we had no redress for injuries sustained, and under the new agreements we were required to submit to all the old abuses, and, in addition, sign a warrant for our own starvation!!"

Mr. PRIDEAUX wished to know whether there was any necessity for the suspension clause?

Mr. Lancaster: "Not the least. There has been no suspension clause for upwards of thirty years, and if it is necessary now, it was before. The object of that clause is to destroy our society—they say it is necessary to check turn-outs, and they have no other aim.

"This is the first ground of dispute between us; the second is what is termed 'Good out of oven'.

"The first process in making pots, is to mix up the clay with water and bring it to about the consistency of thick cream; it is then placed on flat kilns, and the water being driven off by heat, it is brought to something like putty. In making tureens, jugs and other articles of that description, the person employed forms them in moulds to the proper shape, and having done that, the whole of his duty is discharged—they are then carried into the drying room, afterwards into the kiln, placed in cases, and fired. After this they are taken into the warehouse and prepared for finishing. Now if, in any of these subsequent stages, any part of the ware is injured, the man who formed it receives not a farthing of wages, although he has no control whatever over the persons through whose hands it passed after it left his care."

Mr. Prideaux asked whether supposing ware was injured by a too hasty alteration of temperature, the workman lost his wages; also, whether if bad or improper materials were used, the same would be the case.

Mr. Lancaster: "Certainly, the cooling of ovens too suddenly causes ware to crack; the use of improper materials will do the same; or if ware is over fired or improperly placed in the saggar or in the oven, it will be injured; and in all these cases the wages are stopped, although afterwards in many cases, much of the ware is finished and sold for best.

" 'Working good out of oven' causes more crime and drunkenness than any other circumstance. Sometimes ovens are not set in regularly, and the ware in consequence cannot come out regularly, and men therefore not only lose a week's wages, but often two or three weeks, and the man is sent home to his family without a farthing. At this moment men have work done prior to last Martinmas, which is not paid for yet! Ware, too, is frequently missing, and although the man is quite confident that he has made a certain quantity, he is told it cannot be found, and deductions are made from his wages in consequence. The necessary result is disappointment and vexation, and if there is a public house where he can get drink on trust, he will seldom face a starving wife and family until he has screwed his courage up with a drop of comfort. As a proof that the system is not necessary, we have now fourteen manufactories at work on our plan, and there is no complaint, except for occasional bad work.

"These are the two principal grounds of dispute between our masters and ourselves, and I leave you to say whether we have not justice on our side. If I have not made myself sufficiently understood, or if any more information is required, I shall be happy to answer any question which any delegate may wish to ask."

Mr. PRIDEAUX asked whether those fourteen manufactories who had hired on the new agreements had any allowance for breakage, etc.

Mr. LANCASTER: "Yes, we have offered and allowed a percentage. The other manufacturers refuse to accept an allowance, or to agree with us on any terms except 'good from oven'."

Mr. STORKE (Sheffield), asked, supposing a master to have a private pique against a man, could he not, under the old system, injure him in various ways?

Mr. LANCASTER: "If a master feels inclined he can compel a man to work for any length of time without wages by not allowing his work to be fired."

Mr. HOLMES (Sheffield): "Is not a workman sometimes forbidden to go into the place where his work is deposited, whilst others are allowed to go or perhaps work in the place—and then if any injury be sustained, does the workman suffer?

Mr. LANCASTER: "The men are so in some instances prohibited. Now suppose work not to have been counted, but merely deposited in the place appropriated for that purpose, printers or others may go into the room, and without detection may take a portion of it away. When it comes to be counted, a part of the man's work cannot be found and he loses his wages; but this is not a general case."

Mr. BUCHANAN (Huddersfield): "What defence do the masters set up for a custom which appears so unjust?"

Mr. LANCASTER: "'Ancient usages', which they say are necessary for the trade—and so they may be necessary for one part of it, viz. necessary for the master's pocket—but highly injurious to ours."

Mr. HOLMES: "I understand you have made a calculation as to the comparative advantages and disadvantages to the masters by adopting the new or pursuing the old plan, and that the masters would be gainers by the new arrangement? If so they must be influenced by a most abominable and tyrannical principle—can you explain it?

Mr. LANCASTER: "To an honest manufacturerer two and a half per cent. would cover his losses, but to a bad one, ten per cent. would not be equal to the gains of the present system."

Mr. PRIDEAUX asked whether men might not patch up a piece of ware so as to hide any defects until they had been tried by fire?

Mr. LANCASTER: "A man might deceive an inexperienced eye, but not so as to hide it if properly looked over by one understanding the trade."

Mr. HOLMES: "A man informed me that he had ere now completed work for which he ought to have received thirty-two shillings, but to his surprise he found there was no wages for him—that he inquired the cause and could obtain no answer—that he went to the master to complain, when the latter replied, 'I'll give you four shillings, but mind I do give it you,' although he had done work for which his wages amounted to thirty-two shillings."

Mr. CHARLES STANLEY: "When a man is working 'good out of the oven' if a mould is not made as it ought to be, or if bad or improper materials are used the ware is sure to be injured and the workman loses his wages, although he had nothing whatever to do in the formation of the mould or the mixing of the ingredients. I recollect, particularly on one occasion, when there were great complaints about bad ware, the men could get but little wages, and general dissatisfaction prevailed. I went with my master to see the ware, and it struck me that the fault was in the mould and that it might easily be remedied. I tried the experiment with complete success, and there were no complaints afterwards, although the workmen suffered the loss so occasioned."

Mr. OWEN: "I remember my master once receiving a particular order, and he directed me to print a quantity of plates of a peculiar shape. I told my master I had looked over the stock and could find no plates of the kind required, and he immediately went to the seconds ware and found the quantity. Now the seconds ware is that which has been thrown out by the master as imperfect, and for which the workmen receive no wages. I printed them; the whole order was executed, and the ware sold as best."

Mr. Richards: "There is not a potter from one end of the district to the other, who is not acquainted with the bad effects of working 'good out of the oven'. I well know an instance, where one person had three weeks work on the bank unpaid for, and when he asked for wages, he was told that the ware had not been fired. 'But', said the poor fellow, 'I have a child dead in the house and I want money to bury it.' The master's reply was, 'What's that to me?'

"My own son made in one week twelve dozen of cover dishes, for which of course he expected wages; but his master told him that the claim was dishonest for he had only made six dozen. Words ensued between them and the imputation on his character drove him from the trade.

"The masters support their claim to the system of 'good out of oven' on the plea of 'ancient usage' and that it has existed 'time immemorial'. Now time immemorial means in a legal and constitutional sense, any period not subsequent to the reign of Richard the Third; but potters' time immemorial means a period of forty years only, for I well know that the custom has not existed longer than that time.

"In a conversation I had with Mr. John Ridgway a short time ago I asked what loss would the masters sustain by abolishing the custom of good from oven and substituting good from hand. He replied 'Not two per cent., it is not the loss we look at, but the system is so convenient on other grounds.'

"I think it is important that the system of hiring in the Potteries should be entirely and radically altered—it is too defective to be well patched up; but potters must have the aid of other parties before they can achieve for themselves that to which they have an indisputable and unalienable right. I am aware that trade unions have in some few instances succeeded single-handed in obtaining the objects for which they have contended, but in a far greater number of instances they have failed. It is only by a general union that any real and substantial good can be acquired. This is a contest of money against labour—money which makes one man arrogant, the other a slave—a contest in which money is endeavouring to lessen the price of labour. It is a contest, then, in which the operatives generally are deeply interested, and in which all ought to be generally united. I recommend to the delegates to use every exertion in their respective districts to form a general union; when so formed men may obtain their own, and prevent those catastrophes which the masters now pretend to fear."

Mr. PRIDEAUX: "I think we should not be doing our duty to those who sent us, if we do not make at least an attempt to appeal to the Chamber of Commerce. Our object is to obtain all the information we can, and not to be satisfied in trying a cause with the evidence of one side only. I would not enter into the details of their trade—they might impose upon us by sophistry and falsehood, or bewilder us by technicalities but I would keep to abstract principles. I would endeavour to show that hiring by the year, and paying by the piece is an anomaly, and that their system of making one man answerable for the faults of another, is unjust. By making an overture to them, we shall ascertain whether or not they will assent to your agreement—if not, what they will do—if they won't consent—they must submit. It is all nonsense for them to say they won't treat with you, or those who represent you in a body, for so long as you are united, by treating with you individually, they treat with you all.

Mr. BUCHANAN: "I am afraid all attempts on our part to obtain an interview will be useless. I am informed they have refused the mediation of the magistrates, and the clergyman and therefore I entertain but faint hopes that they will accept of ours. For this reason I am afraid that our attempt to mediate will go for nothing, and while it wastes our time will be productive of no good—their pride will not allow them to be just."

Mr. PRIDEAUX: "Let us try them. If they give us a proud frown of contempt, let us meet it with one still prouder—their looks will not alter either my face or my heart."

Mr. THOMAS CARTLIDGE (Congleton): "We are delegated to come here to use our best endeavours to reconcile all parties, and I think that in the spirit in which we are come, we ought to leave no stone unturned to effect our object. I would therefore recommend a deputation, for if it does no good, it can do no harm. If they will listen to our statements, all well; if not, well still; for should the masters treat us with contempt, that fact will raise a spirit among the people which will ultimately put down their insolence. Let us go before the masters, and if scornfully rejected, we can raise throughout this empire an opposition before which the power of money itself would quail."

Mr. KELSEY (Newcastle): "I think a great responsibility rests on the delegates—we must use every exertion to accomplish the conciliatory object we have in view. Let us try the masters again—if they treat us with contempt, what does it matter—thus much it will benefit you—we can say when we go to our respective districts, we have done our duty, we have tried all means, and the masters have refused to see us. On their side let the onus lie."

Mr. SIMPSON (Manchester): "I remember a very severe struggle between the plasterers and their masters, the former sought for an interview which the latter refused; shortly afterwards the masters altered their minds, accepted a deputation, and the men succeeded."

Mr. LEWIS (Birmingham): "I rise for the purpose of moving a resolution, which I will take the liberty of reading to the meeting:

> " 'That a deputation of seven be appointed to confer with the Chamber of Commerce.'
>
> " 'That the following persons form the deputation chosen by the delegates, viz.:
>
> " 'Mr. J. Kirk, of Sheffield; Mr. G. W. Prideaux, of Bristol; Mr. R. Buchanan, of Huddersfield; Mr. J. Simpson, of Manchester; Mr. J. Wood, of Worcester; Mr. W. Lewis, of Birmingham; and Mr. T. Kelt, of Glasgow.' "

Mr. CARTLIDGE (Congleton): "You all expect support from the different districts from whence we come—can you have a better claim to that support than by getting all the information in your power? What you do, do kindly, and justly, but at the same time promptly. I am an old veteran, and I expect that 'sharp shooting' and 'hard fighting' must be resorted to. Let us then be prepared, for if the masters gain this victory, bastilles and workhouses will in future be the workman's home. Let us get information if we can, and if they treat us with disdain, what then—RETURN IT."

Mr. WOOD (Worcester): "It appears to me very questionable whether there is not a great deal of ignorance displayed in the masters' agreement. If I am correctly informed, it is as untenable in law as it is unjustifiable in equity—an outrage upon both.

"There is no difference between potting and any other business—one branch is not more dependent on another than in many other trades—take for instance the gun trade—there are ten different branches, all dependent on each other, and it is precisely the same in the potting trade; and there is no more reason why there should not be perfect mutuality in the agreements here as well as elsewhere. In the extensive and well-conducted manufactories of Worcester there are no hirings (in fact hiring is a system of slavery) still there is no shifting about from one master to another—each party is friendly with each other, because each party is dependent on each other, therefore they respect each other. Look again at the glove trade, in which 30 or 40,000 hands are employed. None are hired, and still they continue in their old situations. Why then should masters here say that such a system is impracticable—for what honest purpose can they tell us that the constitution would be overthrown, and that dreadful convulsions would result if they were to enter into honest and mutual agreements with their workmen? Why should they attempt to cram such trash down our throats—we do not wish to insult them—I trust our sole object is to do good to the whole human race."

The resolution was then seconded by Mr. Shires and passed unanimously.

It was then agreed that the deputation appointed to meet the Chamber of Commerce should proceed to Newcastle for that purpose the next morning at ten o'clock, and that this meeting should be adjourned until the hour of two in the afternoon on the same day.

SARACEN'S HEAD, THURSDAY, DECEMBER 29, 1836

The adjourned meeting was held pursuant to appointment, and Mr. Kirk again took the chair supported as before.

Mr. Holmes: "I beg leave to request that the deputation to the Chamber of Commerce will favour us with a report of their proceedings."

Mr. Prideaux commenced by reading a copy of a letter which had been addressed by the deputation to the Chamber of Commerce requesting an interview; and he then stated that whatever doubt might have existed in the minds of the delegates and others during the progress of yesterday's proceedings, "I", said Mr. Prideaux, "am glad to say that the result of to-day's interview ought to disperse them. The deputation was received in a gentlemanlike manner, and I rejoice in it, not because it has the least effect upon myself individually, but because I thought it was an omen of good to the potters. In the first place we presented to the secretary the letter of which I have just read you a copy, and we were told that the Chamber was ready to meet us. Some gentlemen entered into explanation with us, and stated 'that their object was to disseminate truth and that therefore they were glad that we had stepped in'. We replied, 'all we wish for, is to hear your statement, as well as the statements of the workmen.' It was finally agreed that a meeting should take place to-morrow at Betley before the magistrates, at which six manufacturers as individuals divested of their characters as members of the Chamber of Commerce; six members of the Union in their individual capacities; and six workmen, not members of the Union, should be present. That the whole of the delegates should be in attendance also, and that with the magistrates they should institute a kind of friendly court for the purpose of discussing the questions at issue. Such is the report I have to give of our interview, and I now earnestly and solemnly request that every delegate will be at his post to-morrow morning. The door for pacification appears to be open, and every honest exertion must be made on our part to bring this struggle to an end without sacrificing the just rights of the potters or compromising our own principles."

The meeting was then adjourned to the same place on the following day at four o'clock.

In the meantime a private meeting was held at the Sea Lion for the purpose of making the necessary arrangements for the meeting on the following day at Betley.

BETLEY, 30TH DECEMBER, 1836

The proceedings of the magistrates and masters at this meeting having been published it is unnecessary to give a detailed account of them here. We trust it will be sufficient to say that the delegates unanimously authorised us to state that in their opinion both themselves and the Operative Potters Society were unfairly dealt with by the masters, and that any further attempt to obtain a fair hearing before such a tribunal would be the height of absurdity.

SARACEN'S HEAD, HANLEY, FRIDAY (Eleven o'clock), DECEMBER 30TH, 1836

At a meeting held this evening pursuant to adjournment, Mr. Kirk in the Chair:

Mr. Davenport asked for a report of the proceedings in the early part of the day at Betley.

Mr. PRIDEAUX rose and said: "I scarcely know how to begin, for I dare not trust myself to describe the shuffling, evasive conduct of the masters, or the want of discrimination on the part of the magistrates. We met by appointment to discuss the subject of the disputes between the masters and men on principle; we were not partisans on either side; we wanted to know whether the men were right in their demands upon their masters, or whether the masters were justified in endeavouring to enforce the agreement which they appeared determined to compel their workmen to sign. But in the first onset the masters violated that appointment, first by requiring the expulsion of Mr. Lancaster because he was too good a tactician for them, and secondly for treating Mr. Mousley in the same way because he was too well acquainted with those facts which, if proved, would have condemned their case and established yours. All I heard there convinces me that you are right—they are wrong. After what they heard from the workmen they durst not attack you on principle—no, the whole of their speeches were invectives against men. They admitted that under their system both parties may do wrong, and inflict injuries on each other. What is the fair inference from that admission?—Why, that the system is bad—good causes do not produce bad effects. Fear made them step from the threshold of justice and they packed the meeting—they knew where to cast their eyes for their own men whom they had smuggled into the room, and whenever an appeal was made to the junta they answered like a key to a lock. You ask for principles, not for additional wages—they durst not meet you in argument, but they shuffled from the question, and poured out on you a torrent of abuse;—you ask only for your rights—take nothing less. The delegates have come to unanimous determination to support you. Go on, improve your own condition—make yourselves acquainted with your own rights—happiness springs from knowledge—knowledge from happiness. Do not be deceived by specious promises, for you may depend upon it they have no wish to serve you unless they can better serve themselves—their want of temper is a proof. They are on the wane—you are on the ascent—proceed and we will assist you—what good we can do shall follow us."

Mr. BUCHANAN: "I have taken a number of notes of the proceedings, which I will read to you." (After Mr. B. had read them he proceeded.) "The meeting was not fair—it was packed, and the room half filled by a set of creatures in a compact body to whom alone they appealed and to whom they spoke. Besides the cases which I have read over to you in my notes, there were many others supporting Mr. Lancaster's statement of Wednesday evening, but nothing to alter it. I have heard nothing to raise a doubt in my mind, but everything on the contrary. The Ridgways and others never dared to attempt an answer to the men, but always shuffled off from the principle. However, if they durst not venture upon argument they were abundantly lavish of their assertions—for instance they told us that the body of the masters were in favour of the men—do you believe that?—that the present situation of the Potteries was entirely the fault of the men, and not of the manufacturers; do you believe that? that the masters are all kind and good—Heaven forgive him—That your union is the cause of the present disputes;—Aye, there's the rub. This is the real bugbear; but keep it up—keep together for the protection of your rights—'tis true they are afraid of your union—it was established for good purposes, and therefore inimical to their scheme—be firm and we will support you—their object was to prejudice us, but they have not succeeded—our conviction in your favour is still stronger than before, and we are determined to agitate the question in our respective constituencies, and to assist you with pecuniary aid—do not allow yourselves to be bought and sold like slaves—you must not allow yourselves to be shuffled or canted out of your just rights—stick steadfastly to your own forms of hiring and do away with 'good from oven'—it robs you and enriches them. By what argument can human ingenuity support such a system?—I might as well say if a weaver makes a bad web the man who spins the yarn ought not to be paid for his labour; or if a tailor makes a coat badly the draper ought not to be paid for his cloth.—Monstrous. But they say it must be supported because it is an ancient usage. This argument is resorted to only by the advocates of oppression. But supposing the argument to be borne out, to what would it amount?—Why that a pair of worn-out old shoes are better than new ones on account of ancient usage—or an old coat, out at the elbows, better than a new one—or a toothless old woman of ninety, a better wife and companion for a young man than a lady of twenty-five because the old one is better acquainted with the usages of ancient times. But out with such trash, and I firmly hope the masters may see no grounds for their present fears, but on the contrary will say, 'We have seen the evil of our ways and will sin no more'. I now address myself to the delegates, and beg leave to move the following resolution:

> "Resolved: 'That although this meeting of Delegates have attended upon the Chamber of Commerce, and upon the meeting appointed by Manufacturers and the various workmen (potters) their conviction of the justice of the position of the Staffordshire Potters is by no means shaken but more confirmed, and that this meeting pledges itself by every means in its power to raise funds to support them until the principles they contend for are obtained.'

"This resolution requires but little comment—I consider the arguments brought forward by the men perfectly satisfactory—those by the masters shuffling and evasive. Delegates, agitate your respective constituencies, obtain funds, for no battle of this nature can be won without—we must meet Mammon with gold. I trust every delegate will pledge himself to support the potters, and put their pledges into effect."

Mr. PRIDEAUX seconded a resolution, and stated that as pledges were fashionable, I, said he, will pledge myself to furnish every farthing I can raise. I will call meetings of all the different trades at Bristol, Taunton, in fact throughout the whole West of England. The cause is a holy one, and we are bound in honour and honesty to support it.

Mr. CARLIER urged the necessity of applying to every town in the kingdom, and by every honest means raise support.

Mr. REANEY (Sheffield): "I pledge myself on behalf of the inhabitants of Sheffield to use every exertion to assist you so long as we can raise a farthing. Our subscriptions have been tolerably liberal already, when we only partially understood your case—now we will double or treble that amount."

Mr. KELT (Glasgow): "At a meeting called at Glasgow for taking this subject into consideration, we had a most numerous attendance, and we unanimously agreed to support the Operative Potters of Staffordshire. Delegates were sent to Edinburgh, Aberdeen, and other principal towns in Scotland, in all which places they are prepared to support you."

Mr. AYRE (Manchester) pledged himself on behalf of the various trades there.

Mr. DAVENPORT (Wolverhampton), after detailing the particulars of a strike at Wolverhampton, said that the operatives considered it needful to call a public meeting on the subject of the potters' turnout, but we would not adopt that step until we had obtained the fullest information on the matter. It was for this purpose we were delegated to come among you. I own myself pleased with all that I have seen and heard on the subject, and particularly with the sobriety, order and decorum with which your proceedings are conducted. I will go home and call a public meeting without a day's delay, and I have no doubt that manufacturers and tradesmen will join us in such an honest cause.

Mr. KELSEY pledged himself on behalf of Newcastle.

Mr. BUCHANAN pledged himself on behalf of Huddersfield and the adjacent parts.

Mr. SHIRES of Newcastle pledged himself to aid his colleagues, and promised to visit Macclesfield, Congleton, etc., with the same view.

Mr. DISNEY pledged himself in a similar way for Bristol, etc.

Mr. WOOD (Worcester) said the main reason which enables the masters to play the tyrant is the want of organisation among the workmen generally; and some principle must be adopted to establish a general understanding—why not subscribe 1d. each week for a general fund?

Mr. ELIBY (Derby) pledged himself to use every exertion.

Mr. LEWIS (Birmingham), after detailing particulars of various disputes between masters and their men, said, "we wanted information, as to the cause of the potters' strike. A public meeting will be called for Monday next, for the purpose of giving the information we have collected, and plans to be adopted for raising funds."

Mr. DRUMMOND (Manchester) on account of the bricklayers, pledged himself that every exertion should be made.

Mr. HARPER (Ashton-under-Lyme) same.

Mr. DUTTON (St. Helens) same.

Mr. DISNEY (wood sawyer, Bristol) said energetically, "My trade is good, and whatever deficiencies may be caused by the depression of one trade, may be made up by the contributions of others. If I have not the talents to address you as some other delegates have done, I have still the heart to feel for your distress, and the determination to assist you."

Mr. LANCASTER: "I am sure our delegates ought to be very proud of the respectable company with which they have mixed to-day.—They were quite above us, for Mr. Mousley and myself were placed on the 'suspension list'. The masters durst not admit us—they were afraid of our evidence—they knew we could tell too much about the treadmill—the inequalities and injustice of their agreements. We were rejected because of our information respecting their conduct.—Mark the injustice of their proceedings; the moment we had left the room the character and proceedings of the Board of Management was most scandalously assailed. What bravery, to attack an enemy whom they had previously disabled. I stated that Mr. Mousley appeared there as a reporter; the reply was 'there are reporters enough'. But the cause did not suffer in consequence of our absence; if we had been there, or even if angels had been there, it would all have been of no use. No stronger proof could be afforded of the rascality of some of those who appeared to-day as speakers against us, than the fact that they were members of our Board or Society so long as it would admit them; and they only became open enemies when it would not allow them to remain. Mr. Ridgway knows that what he has said to-day in advocating the course of the Chamber was nonsense; he talked about the American trade, I know well that orders are frequently received by masters which they know they cannot execute in the given time, but they accept them for the purpose of getting money as early as possible, transactions of this nature are of everyday's occurrence. With respect to the month's notice, it is in truth a protection for masters as well as men. With regard to 'good from hand', we show that the good-out-of-oven system is injurious to us—the masters say that under it robberies are committed upon them—then why not alter the system—such an alteration would produce heaven on earth instead of the hell we live in now. They need not tell us it is for our good—if they could get us to work for half-price would they stand out then? If we give up the point of 'good-out-of-oven' we disgrace ourselves and bequeath misery to our offspring—the evils of the system have been too well depicted before to need repetition now. No persons can conscientiously advocate the system—if one trade ought to do it no others have a right to be free from it—one or the other must be wrong. The present system is the fruitful parent of drunkenness. When a man goes home week after week without the wages for which he has honestly worked, and finds that for a wife and family he has no food, he will resort to the cup; and if he can find a house where he can obtain liquor on trust he will endeavour to drown sensibility by intoxication. Our causes of complaint are summed up in a few words:

"First—Good from oven.

"Second—Neither mutuality nor certainty in our agreements.

"Third—No protection for the men.

"All these facts prove that an alteration in the system is required—the spread of intelligence induces men to demand it, and the co-operation of our worthy delegates will enable us to obtain it in spite of every difficulty."

The following resolutions were passed unanimously:

Proposed by Mr. Davenport, seconded by Mr. Holmes:

> "That this meeting do approve of the conduct of the Operatives of Staffordshire, and are satisfied that the object they are desirous to obtain is both just and reasonable, and that they are deserving of the best support of every friend of justice and humanity throughout the kingdom, till their

grievances are satisfactorily redressed; and the delegates now present do earnestly pledge themselves to use every exertion in their power in their respective districts and connection till the desired end is obtained."

Proposed by Mr. Prideaux and seconded by Mr. Buchanan:

"That this meeting, after the full and lucid statement of the officers of the Operative Potters Society, of Staffordshire, offered for its consideration, is unanimously of opinion that the system which the Chamber of Commerce insist shall be the one of hiring would be an usurpation of their just rights as men, and that it demands of every person interested in the extension of human happiness, and consequently the extinction of human misery, to use their cordial and energetic support and co-operation to place them upon a more equal footing."

Proposed by Mr. W. Lewis of Birmingham—seconded by Mr. N. Lynch of Newcastle:

"That this meeting being convinced of the justice of the Staffordshire Potters claims, and the probability of the present disputes remaining unsettled, are hereby determined to apply to the highest constitutional authorities not only for redress of present grievances but for the means of preventing the cause of them in future."

Proposed by Mr. R. Buchanan of Huddersfield—seconded by Mr. W. Shires of Newcastle:

"That as Fergus O'Conor, Esq. has taken a very active part in behalf of the Staffordshire Potters in several large manufacturing towns in the empire, this meeting resolve by written communication, most respectfully to request him to use his best endeavours in their behalf in all the large towns he may visit in the kingdom."

Thanks being voted by the Delegates to the principal officers of the Potters Society, and by the Potters to the Delegates, and the thanks of the whole being given to the Chairman, the meeting broke up, as it had commenced, in the utmost order.

Printed by W. MOORE, *Hanley*, 1837.

BEVAN, G. P. Industrial Classes and Industrial Statistics, 1876.
COOPER, T. The Life of Thomas Cooper written by himself, 4 edit., 1873.
CROMPTON, H. Industrial Conciliation, 1876.
DAVIS, W. J. Trade Union Congress History, 1910.
EVANS, W. Art and History of Pottery Business, 1846.
FALKNER, F. The Wood Family of Burslem, 1912.
FAULKNER, H. U. Chartism and the Churches, 1916.
JONES, L. Life and Labours of Robert Owen, 3rd ed., 1900.
KENDALL, H. B. Primitive Methodism, 1905.
METEYARD, E. Life of Wedgwood, 1865.
OWEN, H. The Staffordshire Potter, 1901.
"OLD POTTER". (Introduction by Spence Watson.) When I was a Child, 1903.
PAYNE, W. Stafford Gaol and its Associations, 1887.
SHAW, S. History of Staffordshire Potteries, 1829.
WARD, J. History of Borough of Stoke-on-Trent, 1846.
WEBB. History of Trade Unionism, 1920 ed.
WEDGWOOD, J. Letters of Wedgwood to Bentley, 1762–1780 (1903)

PAMPHLETS AND OTHER PUBLICATIONS

BROWNFIELD, A. The Lockout. A Potters' Guild: proposal by A. B., Hanley, 1892.
ANON. The case of the manufacturers of China and Earthenware in the Staffordshire Potteries with some account of the Late Turn Out, its Origin, Proceedings and Termination, 1836–37, pub. by authority of Chamber of Commerce.
MAYER, J. Art of Pottery, Liverpool, 1871.
BOYLE, J. An Account of Strikes in the Potteries in 1834–36. Journal of Statistical Society, London, vol. i, 1839.
Trades Societies and Strikes. Report of National Association for Promotion of Social Science, 1860.
Trade Union Congress Reports.
U.S.A. Bureau of Foreign and Domestic Commerce. The Pottery Industry. Report on the Cost of Production in U.S.A., England, Germany, Austria; Washington, 1915. U.S.A. Bureau of Foreign and Domestic Commerce. Miscellaneous Series No. 21.

Newspapers (Weekly)

	Library
The Beehive, 1869–76	British Museum
The Crisis, 1832–34	Birmingham
The Northern Star, 1838–52	British Museum
The Potteries Examiner, 1871–80	British Museum
The Potteries Examiner, 1843–45	Hanley
The Pottery Mercury, 1824–30	William Salt Collection, Stafford
The Staffordshire Advertiser, 1830 to date	Hanley
The Staffordshire Mercury, January 2, 1830, to March 1, 1834, continued as North Staffordshire Mercury, March 8, 1834, to April 12, 1845. Continued as Staffordshire Mercury, April 1845 to May 1848	British Museum
The Staffordshire Potteries Telegraph, October 2 to December 31, 1852	British Museum
The Voice of the People, January to September 1831	British Museum
The Pottery Gazette (monthly), 1880 to date.	

Newspapers (Daily)

The Birmingham Post.
The Times.
The Staffordshire Sentinel.

Parliamentary Reports and Papers

Report of the Select Committee on the State of Children employed in the Manufactories of the United Kingdom, 1816.

Children's Employment (Trades and Manufactures) Commission, 1843.

Report from Select Committee on Masters and Operatives (Equitable Councils of Conciliation), 1856.

Report from the Select Committee on Masters and Operatives, 1860.

Reports of Commissioners on Employment of Children in

Trades and Manufactures not already regulated by Law, 1863.
Report from the Select Committee on Master and Servant, 1866.
Report of the Royal Commission appointed to enquire into the Organisation and Rules of Trade Unions: 10th Report, 1868; 11th Report, 1869.
Report of Commissioners appointed to enquire into the working of the Factory and Workshops Acts, 1867.
Reports of the Royal Commission on Labour, 1892.
Report on Manufacture of China and Earthenware: Potteries Committee of Enquiry, 1893.
Earnings and Hours Enquiry, 1906.
Report of Department Committee on Truck Acts, 1908.
Report on Rules of Voluntary Conciliation and Arbitration Boards, 1910.
Reports on Trade Unions (from the 3rd (1889) to 17th), (1912–13).
Reports on Strikes and Lock Outs (annual) (from 1889 report to 1913 report).
Profiteering Acts, 1919-20. Report on Pottery, 1921.
Report on the Establishment and Progress of Joint Industrial Councils, 1923.
Board of Trade Safeguarding of Industries Report of Committee on Table Ware of Translucent Pottery, 1927.
Home Office Report of the Departmental Committee on Compensation for Silicosis, 1928.
Board of Trade Merchandise Marks Act, 1926. Report of the Standing Committee respecting Pottery, 1928.

NATIONAL COUNCIL OF POTTERY INDUSTRY PUBLICATIONS

First Annual Report, 1918–19.
First Report of Enquiries into and recommendations made in connection Education Act, 1918 (1919), second Report (1920).
Faults in Alkaline Slip Casting: Address by Walter Emery, Esq., 1925.

INDEX

Adams, Messrs., 89, 267
Aikens, Rev. R. E., 121
Allowance System, 106–12, 137
Annual Hiring, 12, 44–6, 50, 89, 98, 142, 146–9, 168, 261, Appendix E; *Suspension clause*, 90, 91
Apprentices, 106–10, 108 n. 1, 109 n.1, 166–7
Arbitration, *Boards of*, 14, 39, 83–5, 114, 126, 129, 139–42, 144–6, 150–5, 157–68, 176, 203, 213, 217, 223; *Clause*, 142, 144–6, 149
Astbury, Robert, 21
Ayre, Mr., 279

Baker, Robert, 39
Bedstead Smith Scheme, *see* Birmingham Alliance
Beehive, 157
Bennett, Arnold, 11, 125
Bevan, G. Phillips, 49, 218
Birmingham Alliance, 184–5, 201–2, 213, 223
Booth, Enoch, 21
Boyle, John, 95
Brassey, Thomas, 39, 159
British Pottery Manufacturers' Federation, 14, 222, 238
Brownfield, Arthur, 210–11
Brownfield Guild Scheme, 210–12
Buchanan, Robert, 265, 269, 272, 273, 277, 279, 282
Burslem Co-operative Society, 228
Buxton, Jesse, 59 n. 2

Carlier, Mr., 279
Cartlidge, Thomas, 272–3
Casting, 195, 195 n. 1, 216
Chamber of Commerce, 32, 50, 82, 88, 90–4, 96, 102, 139, 142, 145, 168, 181, 183, 183 n. 3, 192
Chartists, 15, 118–19, 133; *Riots*, 120–2, 135–6
Chetham, Messrs., 87, 261
China Potters, 178, 220–1, 233; *Unions*, 55–6, 178
Clay, Professor H., 224, 231
Conciliation, 91–2, 219–20, 223, 229; *Committee of*, 14, 114, 164–5 (*see also* Arbitration)
Conferences, Employers and Employed, 94–7, 100, 142, 219
Conference of Trades, 170
Cooper, Thomas, 119–21
Co-operative Production, 31, 31 n.4, 32 n. 4, 74, 76–7, 209–10, 212, 257, 259
Crate Makers, 134–5; *Unions*, 173, 175

Daniel, Ralph, 21
Danyell, Thomas, 20
Davenport, Mr. (of Wolverhampton), 276, 279, 281
Davenport, Henry T. (later changed name to Hinckes, *which see*), 154
Davis, James E., 155
Decorating, 19, 24 (*see also* Enamelling, Printers, Gilders, Lithographing, and Appendix B)
Dippers, *Unions*, 177
Disney, Mr., 279–80
Disputes (*see* Strikes and Lockouts)
Doherty, John, 54
Drummond, Mr., 280
Dutton, Mr., 280

Electrical appliances, 198–9
Eliby, Mr., 280
Emigration, 114–15, 117–18, 212
Enamelling, 22
English China Manufacturers' Association, 238
Engravers, *Union*, 178
Evans, William, 113–14, 119, 131, 133, 141

Factories, *Ill Equipment of*, 188–9, 241
Female Labour Problem, 15, 33, 37–8, 43, 213, 215–16
Forrester, Mr., 121
Foster, Thomas, 54

General Merchandise Marks Act, 239 239 n. 3
Gilders, *Union*, 178
Glasse, Robert, 59 n. 2, 104
Glazing, 19, 21–2, 24 (*see also* Dippers)
Good from Hand (*see* Good from Oven)
Good from Oven, 12, 44, 46, 50, 60, 89, 91, 98, 101 n.1, 143–4, 146, 152, 152 n. 3, 154, 166–7, 233–5, Appendix E
Goodwin, Messrs., 88, 261
Grand National Consolidated Trades Union, 78
Granville, Lord, 121

Handlers, 27, 29, 48–9, 156, 159; *Unions*, 177
Harper, Mr., 280
Hatherton, Lord, 158–9
Hawley, Mr., 87–8, 261
Health, 49, 50, 226 (*see* Silicosis and Lead-poisoning)
Heath, Messrs., 146
Hinckes, Henry T., 162
Hodgkins, Jonathan, 54
Hollins, Michael Daintry, 147, 147 n.2, 150–51, 168, 192
Holmes, Mr., 269–70, 275, 281
Holyoake, George J., 212
Hours, 40–3, 235
Humphries, Edward, 132, 135

James, Frank, 162
Jet and Rockingham Potters, 220; *Unions*, 177
Jiggerers, 204–6

Kelsey, Mr., 273, 279
Kelt, Mr., 273, 279
Kilnmen, 156; *Union*, 177
Kirk, Mr., 264, 273, 274, 276
Knight & Elkin, Messrs., 88, 261

Lancaster, Mark, 59 n. 2, 82, 132 132 n. 2, 258, 265, 268–70, 276–7, 280
Lead-poisoning, 235
Leeds Mercury, 75
Lewis, Mr. W., 273, 280, 282
Light, Mr., 264
Lithographing, 197, 197 n. 1
Lockouts, *see* Strikes and Lockouts
Lynch, Mr. N., 282

Machinery, *effect of*, 156, 176, 192, 198, 203–8; *non-use of*, 25–6, 192, 235; *opposition to*, 115–18, 125, 130, 172, 192–3, 205–6; *Blunger*, 196–7; *Clay filter press*, 196; *Cup-making*, 117; *Jigger*, 194–6; *Printing*, 115–17, 197; *Pugmill*, 196–7; *Plate-making*, 115, 193–4

Maitland, William, 168
Manufacturers' Association, 184, 225
Mason, Charles J., 115
Mason, Mr. (of Wetley Abbey), 83
Mawdesley, James, 162
Mayer, John, 88, 261
McKinley Tariff, 179, 182
Merchandise Marks, 239 n. 3
Methodists, 72 n. 4, 72–4, 123–5, 124 n. 4
Middleton, Richard, 20
Miers, Mr., 59 n. 2
Miners, *organisation*, 57 (*see also* Strikes and Lockouts)
Minton & Co., Messrs., 147, 154, 160
Modellers' Pottery, *Association of*, 223
Moon, Ernest, 220
Mouldmakers, 20–1, 197; *Unions*, 177
Mousley, Mr., 276, 280
Mundella, Anthony J., 147 n. 1, 151

National Amalgamated Society of Male and Female Pottery Workers, 14, 177–8, 214–15, 219–20
National Association for the Employment of Labour, 125, 127–9, 13 133–4, 136
National Association for the Protection of Labour, 52–9
National Association of United Trades for the Protection of Labour, 125, 127, 135, 138, 140–1, 147
National Conference of Trades, 113–14, 126, 128
National Council of the Pottery Industry, 14, 223–7, 231, 233, 235–6, 241
National Order of Potters, 13, 177
National Society of Pottery Workers, 11, 13–14, 223, 236, 239
National Union of Clerks, 223
National Union of Operative Potters, 13, 56, 64–6, 70, 81, 99, 102–3, 106, 112–13, 132, 200, 213
New Industrial Alliance (*see* Birmingham Alliance)
New Moral World, 104
New Trades Combination Movement (*see* Birmingham Alliance)

O'Conner, Feargus, 118–19, 282
Out-Potteries, 60, 64, 68, 109, 113, 135, 171–2, 177–8
Ovenmen, 29, 31, 156, 197, 219–20, 233; *Unions*, 169, 177–8
Owen, Robert, 59, 70–9, 70 n. 4, 79 n. 1, 87, 104, 134, 262; *Letters to*, 256–60
Owen, William, 151, 160, 210–11
Owen, Mr. (potters' printer), 270
Owenism, 15, 70, 72–4, 105, 134

Packers, 31; *Unions*, 177–8
Painters, 29, 197; *Union*, 56; *Painters and Gilders' Union*, 134, 134 n. 4, 135, 234
Parker, Mr., 121
Philanthropic Hercules, The, 33 n.
Pickin, Thomas, 207
Piece Rates, 29, 30, 33, 64, 204–5, *Union lists*, 15, 61–3, 67–70, 80–1, 84–5, 217, 220–1 (*see* Sizes of ware)
Plot, Robert, 18, 20

Poor Relief, 51, 101 n.
Porcelain, 23
Potteries, The, 189–91
Potteries Examiner, 151
Potters' Clerks' Guild, 223
Potters' Emigration Society, 114, 118–19, 133, 135–6, 138
Potters' Examiner, 115
Pottery Gazette, 39, 218
Powys, Captain, 87, 121–2, 261
Pratt, Henry L., 59 n. 2, 74, 258–9
Pressers (Flat), 29, 48, 145, 156, 158–9, 193, 206, 219–21, 233; *Unions*, 169–70, 173–4
Pressers (Hollow-ware), 29, 48, 145, 155–6, 194, 203–6, 219–21; *Unions*, 169, 171–4, 176–8, 205, 207, 209, 211, 214
Pressers (Sanitary), 207 n. 1; *Unions*, 177
Prideaux, Mr. G. W., 264, 267–70, 272–3, 275–6, 278, 282
Printers, 23, 31, 155–6, 158, 219–21, 233; *Unions*, 116, 169, 173–5, 178, 213

Ragout, M., 193
Rathbone, John, 59 n. 2
Reaney, Mr., 279
Redgrave, J. Alexander, 35
Richards (journeyman potter), 59 n. 2, 271
Richards, John, 132
Ridgway, John, 115, 271, 277, 280
Robinson, Messrs., 87, 261
Rose, Mr., 121
Rowntree, Arnold S., 224, 231

Safeguarding, 238, 238 n. 2, 239, 239 n. 2, 241
Saggar-makers, 156; *Unions*, 177
Sanitary ware, 198–9
Scriven, Samuel, 39
Selling prices, 33, 69, 155–7, 179, 200–3, 230; *Agreement*, 28, 67–8, 80, 89, 181–2, 184
Shaw, Mr., 203
Sheffield delegates, 118 n. 2
Sheffield Trades, 103, 113, 118, 133
Shires, Mr. W., 274, 279, 282, 289
Silicosis, 235–6
Simpson, Mr. J., 273
Simpson, Thomas P., 59 n. 2, 72, 78, 256, 258–60
Sizes of Ware, 29–30, 32, 32 n. 1, 33, 181, 208 n. 2
Slatter, Mr. B., 209
Slipmakers, 27, 29
Smith, Mr. E. J., 185
Sneyd, Rev. J., 87–8, 261

Stacey, William, 59 n. 2, 77–8, 259
Staffordshire Sentinel, 210
Stanley, Charles, 270
Strikes and Lockouts, 29–31, 69, 81, 83–6, 89–99, 102–3, 114, 138, 149, 154, 158, 160–1, 163–4, 219; *Miners'*, 119 n. 4, 119–20, 122, 228, Appendix E
Stoppages, 12, 35–6, 233–4
Storke, Mr., 269
Suart, Benjamin, 162
Summonses of Workpeople, *intimidation*, 88, 261; *Breaking Contract*, 46 n. 1, 87–8, 148 n. 1, 174, 261

Third Winter of Unemployment, 238
Throwers, 27, 29, 48–9, 159; *Unions*, 177–8
Tiles, 199
Tollet, George, 96, 263
Trade Union Congress, 170, 212, 236
Transferrers, 158, 174–5, 178, 213–14, 219–21, 234 (*see* Printers)
Twemlow, Francis, 96, 263
Truck, 29–30, 33, 50–5, 60
Turner, William, 205–6
Turners, 27, 29, 48–9, 156, 159; *Unions*, 55–6, 171, 177
Tutorial Class Movement, 16, 224

Underselling, 12, 33, 51, 63–4, 180–4, 191, 200 n. 2, 241
United Branches of Operative Potters' Society, 111–12, 114, 122, 125, 129–31, 133, 136, 138, 141
United Kingdom Alliance of Organised Trades, 170

Vale, The Rev. Dr., 121
Voice of the People, 39, 57

Wages, 28, 40–2, 113–14, 123, 137–8, 154–5, 158, 162, 164, 185, 202–5, 217–19, 227–34, Appendix A
Warehousemen, 27, 73
Warehousewomen, 223
Wedgwood, Cecil, 189
Wedgwood, Francis, 193
Wedgwood, Josiah, 22–3, 27–8, 39
Wedgwood, Josiah (son of above), 28, 38–9
Wedgwood, Messrs., 160
West, John, 131–2
Wethered, Ernest H. C., 224, 231
Whitley, Right Hon. J. H., 14
Women's Trade Union League, 214
Wolsey, Sir Charles, Bart., 92 n. 4
Wood, Mr. J., 273–4, 279
Wood, Mr. N. R., 260
Workers' Educational Association, 16

For Product Safety Concerns and Information please contact our EU representative GPSR@taylorandfrancis.com Taylor & Francis Verlag GmbH, Kaufingerstraße 24, 80331 München, Germany